Sportsproview

www.sportsproview.com

From 'The Fall, Death and Rise of Cork City FC'

Part Three: Seasons 2010–14 and Beyond

Autobiography of an Irish Footballer

THE CROSS ROADS

Rise of the Rebel Army and Crisis at the FAI

by Neal Horgan

Published by Sportsproview

© Copyright 2019 Neal Horgan

Print edition

ISBN 978-0-9930622-9-2

Cover art by Barry Masterson

To my beautiful wife, Caroline.

And in memory of Sean Ryan (Riverview and Glasheen), James O'Sullivan (Bishopstown and Wilton United), John Gildea (Sandymount and St Finbarrs), Cathal Murphy (Bandon and Cork City FC) and Rob Savage (Saleen and Cork City FC).

Neal Horgan is a practising solicitor and a frequent contributor to the *Irish Examiner*'s sports pages. Neal spent 15 seasons playing as a conservative full-back for Cork City FC in the League of Ireland and loved (almost!) every minute of it. His debut book, *Death of a Football Club?* was published in 2014 and was followed by *Second City*. This is his third book.

Also by Neal Horgan:
Death of a Football Club? Season 2008
Second City, Season 2009
Both published by Sportsproview

Contents

Preface

How important is Irish domestic football to the future of Irish national football? Will the League of Ireland remain as a rusty product in a fragile state? Will professional Irish football clubs continue to walk a tightrope just to survive? Will a new-look FAI – or a whole new entity – finally take the bull by the horns and make the required investment into the league so that it can progress?

This book, along with its predecessors, *Death of a Football Club?* and *Second City*, contains my first-hand accounts in respect of Cork City FC's relationship with the professional game.

Readers of my previous books will note that the diary entries in this one are less regular. This is because my football career had by this point moved from full-time professional to a part-time role. As I became increasingly involved in my full-time role as a practising solicitor, working in or about Cork City's historic business thoroughfare (the South Mall), I naturally became more removed from the club – albeit I was still, and will always be, heavily invested in its well-being and future.

The Cross Roads describes the rise of Cork City FC during seasons 2010–14, as well as the unfolding crisis at the FAI.

Neal Horgan, August 2019

Neal Horgan

Introduction – The Rise of the Rebel Army and the Fall of the Ancien Régime

The spirit of rebellion was stirring amongst the Irish football community long before the fall of the ancien régime. But while that spirit was growing, it always seemed to remain on the periphery of things, with the Football Association of Ireland (FAI) showing an impressive ability to sweep 'negative' news under the carpet. The image of the Aviva Stadium, with its modern, outward-looking and ambitious design, was the image that best reflected the way in which the FAI wanted to be portrayed. For a long time, journalistic endeavours to question the level of FAI debt attached to the stadium, and the impact of that debt on other strands of Irish football such as the League of Ireland (LOI), were easily swept aside on the promise that any monies owing on the stadium would be paid off by 2020.

We know now that this will not come to pass. That promise has proven to be as much of a fallacy as the image that the FAI were portraying. At the time of writing (August 2019) the FAI have conceded that the stadium debt will not be paid off before 2030. Worse still, on 17th July 2019 Sports Ireland CEO John Treacy raised concerns in respect of the continued existence of the FAI itself:

> *'I would hope that FIFA or UEFA would bail them out. ... It's not in anyone's interest that a national body would go under.'*

Despite the growing undercurrent of discontent among stakeholders within the game, knowledge of the true and sorry state of Irish football had failed to reach the general public until quite recently. In fact, it wasn't until a series of revelations about the FAI surfaced following a failed application for an injunction by John Delaney against *The Sunday Times* on the 16th March 2019 that the general public began to learn of the culture of misgovernance and inappropriate behaviour that had existed within the FAI. The image of the Aviva, of the national team qualifying for the Euros under Trapattoni or Martin O'Neill, had prevailed up until that point. The FAI were still cosily sitting in positions of power, focused on the national team while treating the League of Ireland and its problems as an afterthought which had very little to do with them.

> *'While not a universal view, it has become, for some, a conveniently held position ... that issues affecting a club's operation or viability are the responsibility of the FAI.'*

In my view the above quote from the Conroy Report (2015) best encapsulates the approach of the ancien régime towards the League of Ireland. This report into the LOI was praised by the FAI (who had commissioned it) but seemed to point the finger squarely at the league's clubs for any problems the clubs were encountering. I feel that the above quote sends the message, *How dare anyone think that the FAI could be responsible for the health of LOI clubs?* In fact, if there was such a thing as a convenient position, it was held by the FAI; they were apparently happy enough to be part of the good-news stories about the LOI, while stepping aside and pointing the finger at others when it came to the recurring bad-news stories emanating from our national league.

Irish football people have known for a long time that we're fortunate to have former St Patrick's Athletic and national team manager Brian Kerr fighting the cause for the game here; and happily, when the moment arose, he didn't fail to make the point.

Brian Kerr blasts FAI as funding row rumbles on
... While the vexed issue of the FAI's €5,000-per-club in strategic planning funding brought matters to a head, it seems a catalogue of others had been festering in the background.

"The frustration levels across the league are remarkable," thundered Kerr.

"I speak to managers every day.

"The frustration levels within the supporters around the facilities, the lack of facilities for women and the pitches are there. The dressing rooms are desperate.

"All around the country there are ferociously bad facilities and there is nothing being done about it for years and years.

"Talking about strategic planning now for five years' time is a load of bunkum.

"The €100,000 for all the clubs is a pittance in terms of the money the FAI are getting in.

"Where is the leadership in the FAI in relation to the league?"

That the leader of the organisation governing football, chief executive John Delaney, branded the league a "difficult child" last year served only to deepen scepticism amongst the fraternity.

Kerr credits the "genius" of manager Stephen Kenny and his players for Dundalk's success in Europe, rather than any dividend from the FAI's attempts to create an environment for professionalism.

It was therefore inevitable he would react when Gavin claimed the association introduced "an atmosphere to allow the likes of Shamrock Rovers get into the group stages of the Europa League (in 2011)".

Kerr interjected: "You created that atmosphere? The clubs and the manager created the atmosphere, with respect." ...

(John Fallon, <u>*Irish Examiner*</u>, 10th August 2016)

Today, the FAI can no longer take that convenient position of associating itself with the achievements of LOI clubs while disassociating itself from LOI problems. This owes a lot to the FAI's weakening position as well as the rising strength of the spirit of rebellion. Social media has also played a part in allowing fans to have their voice and encouraging the spread of information and ideas about domestic football. But there were always good writers in Irish football media who, like Kerr, have given honest views about the corridors of power in the FAI – even in the face of the threat of legal action by an overprotective association and board.

I became aware of the potential difficulties involved in writing on Irish football when I was finalising these books. At the launch of my previous book, *Second City*, I made a speech to the assembled guests that made reference to 'sharks lurking in the waters of the ocean that is Irish football'. I pointed out that, 'I have to be careful,' just like the daily Irish football writers at the time, 'not to stray too far into the dark waters.' The threat of injunctions and defamation proceedings was real. A quick search on the Irish court services website (www.courts.ie) would reveal numerous High Court proceedings issued by John Delaney over the last 10 years against newspapers and media platforms in Ireland, including against state broadcaster RTÉ, and against the holding companies behind the *Irish Independent*, the *Irish Examiner* and SportsJOE.ie.

It is somewhat revealing to look back now at all the efforts made to suppress criticism and debate of the FAI's management of Irish soccer over the past 10 years or so. My uncle, former Cork City chairman Brian Lennox, has often described to me how the FAI attempted to stifle his articles in Cork City match programmes that were critical of the FAI. The banning of media questions from FAI AGMs from 2012 onwards was another measure clearly designed to mute debate around their activities. The 2015 Conroy Report again, in my opinion, espoused a view in respect of the LOI that was consistent with the ancien régime's wish to silence any discontent or criticism:

> *'Yet the League suffers from a certain negativity that
> dominates. While some of this is undoubtedly cultural,
> a concerted effort by all parties within the game must
> be made to engage more positively around the brand.
> As a start, the game needs everyone from within to
> avoid being negative in public.'*

It is perhaps apt (or ironic), then, that it was a further effort
to suppress negative information – a failed injunction – that
brought about the demise of the ancien régime. That *The
Sunday Times* supported their writer Mark Tighe to go head-
to-head with John Delaney in the High Court may be deemed
as a vital turning point for the health and prosperity of the
game here.

The successful resistance to that injunction opened the
floodgates for revelations about the internal workings of the
FAI, which in turn have been followed by a more meaningful
and accurate public discussion of the state of Irish football.
The FAI are no longer able to swan into government
committee meetings and take the praise for everything good in
the game while dismissing the negative aspects as issues
outside of their control.

The stakeholders of soccer in this country therefore owe the
press – and the Irish footballing journalists in particular – a
debt of gratitude. The articles of dissent and discord (some of
which are reproduced in this book) continued despite legal
threats, and ultimately cracked the oppressive regime. The
subtitle of this book, in referring to the 'Rebel Army', is
primarily the doffing of my cap to the supporters of Cork City
FC for having the balls to take over the running of my club in
its time of greatest need. However, the subtitle also has a
second meaning, in recognition of our football writers who
rebelled against the FAI's suppression and attempts at
silencing criticism. Those writers, from their different media

outlets, were the 'Rebel Army' that finally brought down the ancien régime.

The issue of government oversight in relation to soccer in Ireland has also raised its head. Even allowing for the necessity of the FAI to be independent (as required by UEFA and FIFA) the question still arises as to whether our politicians or Sport Ireland were found wanting in previously accepting the FAI's views without much examination. At what point in the future would an Oireachtas committee or Sport Ireland have started asking real questions if John Delaney had been successful in his application for an injunction against *The Sunday Times*? It's very possible that, just as they had done before, they would have left the inner workings of the FAI alone and accepted without much inquiry the FAI's views on the LOI.

(Note: the following are selected extracts from a 2009 joint committee debate on the League of Ireland. The extracts are not intended as a summary of the discussion. A full account can be found at
https://www.oireachtas.ie/en/debates/debate/joint_committee_on_arts_sport_tourism_community_rural_and_gaeltacht_affairs/2009-12-16/2/)

[Oireachtas] Joint Committee on Arts, Sport, Tourism, Community, Rural and Gaeltacht Affairs debate –
Wednesday, 16th December 2009
League of Ireland: Discussion with Football Association of Ireland

Chairman [Deputy Tom Kitt in the Chair]: *'I welcome the delegates from the Football Association of Ireland, FAI: Mr. John Delaney, chief executive; Mr. Eamon Naughton, chairman of the national league executive committee; Mr. Fran Gavin, director of the League of Ireland; Mr. Padraig Smith, internal compliance officer; Mr. Richard Fahy, director* *of club licensing; and Mr. Noel Mooney, head of league marketing and promotion. ...'*

John Delaney: *'I thank the joint committee for its recent support. We were before the committee five or six weeks ago talking about the funding of sport. The correspondence of the committee with various Ministers and the Taoiseach has resulted in the retention of the Ministry and a reduction of only 4% in the funding of the Irish Sports Council. On behalf of everybody involved in sport, I thank the committee for its help in this regard. I also thank it for its correspondence with the president of FIFA. The cross-party support we received, including from this committee, was great in terms of expressing our disappointment at the result of the game between Ireland and France. Not only were those in football disappointed, everybody else was also. ...*

'At the end of the 2004 season, League of Ireland clubs were in serious difficulty and the future of League of Ireland football was hanging in the balance. The FAI and the clubs invited Genesis Consulting Ltd. to conduct a review. The ensuing white paper called for radical action, the most significant proposal being a merger between the league clubs and the FAI to facilitate a stricter regulatory environment in which clubs would operate. ...

'Notwithstanding the progress made, there is no underestimating the damage that is done each time a club is a party to legal proceedings involving Revenue or any other creditor. Club mismanagement of finances, as exemplified by high profile cases such as this season's disappointing incidents in Cork City FC, undermines the integrity of the competitions, weakens the credibility of the regulatory processes and reflects poorly on the sport overall. Each participant club must appreciate the impact of mismanagement where it fails to meet its obligations not only on its own club's stakeholders but also on the overall image of the League of Ireland. ...

'It was common practice here, and indeed still is across Europe, for directors, benefactors and investors to put money into clubs in the form of soft interest-free loans with recourse to cover losses. This practice is not allowed under the FAI's financial regulations. ...

'The improvement in the financial management practices in clubs must be acknowledged. A number of clubs have completely overhauled their financial controls and reporting has improved. This is to be welcomed. There are clear examples, such as Shamrock Rovers, Sporting Fingal and UCD, to name just a few. In recognition of the FAI's work in this area, UEFA has invited the FAI's internal compliance officer, Padraig Smith, who is with me, to join its club licensing working group as it looks to improve the effectiveness of financial regulations and controls across European and domestic competitions. Indeed, UEFA's CEO at the time, David Taylor, is on public record as commending the FAI's work on good governance, especially in the area of financial regulations and commending its success in running licensing across each of the national league divisions. This work is held up as a benchmark for other member associations, as currently Ireland is among only 20 of the 53 members which license all their national league clubs. It is up to the national association whether to adjust the licence for teams that will play in Europe or in premier divisions. We license all our clubs. ...'

Later in the discussion, in response to questions raised, John Delaney further comments as follows:

'I cannot talk about what will happen tomorrow but the owner of Cork City FC has been charged with bringing the game into disrepute and he must attend a disciplinary hearing. The actions of that owner over the past 12 months have brought the game into disrepute and given an image of League of Ireland *football that is unfair to the other clubs which have behaved well.*

'One of the problems has been player salaries. One player in the League of Ireland was on €4,000 per week up to recently, which is unsustainable. One club had eight or nine players on over €100,000 a year, which is also unsustainable. Full-time football is sustainable in this country but with a proper wage structure rather than the crazy figures I have just outlined. Five clubs work on a full-time basis. It is affordable but only when the correct wages are paid. ...

'I was secretary of Waterford United football club and used go around on Fridays, raising money to pay the wages and always tell this story as an example. When Waterford was drawn against Dynamo Tbilisi in 1980, after winning the FAI senior cup in that year, there were no subsidies of any kind from UEFA. The club had to go door to door in Waterford to raise £20,000, the cost of going to play Dynamo Tbilisi. It raised £8,000 but nobody ever asked where the extra £12,000 came from. My dad wrote a personal cheque to ensure the team could get to Europe. These are things one does not forget. I was part of it too, writing my own cheques at times to ensure that wages were paid in Waterford United, because that was the culture.

'However, having moved to the position I hold now and understanding the problem, I know one has to understand it to resolve it and reach a solution. ...

'We cannot have people running clubs who are not fit to run them or who run them in a cavalier way that ultimately affects the community. ...'

Some of the responses made by Deputies and Senators during the course of the meeting are worthy of note and a selection of them are reproduced here in no particular order:

Deputy John O'Mahony: *'I thank Mr. Delaney and his colleagues for giving us a picture of what it was like and what* *it is like now. I commiserate with them on their recent result. I know the deep sense of unfairness they felt, but I congratulate them on the performance. It lifted the country and although I know the witnesses are not into moral victories maybe the success that will eventually come will be all the sweeter as a result of having to move on and overcome the deep sense of unfairness that we all felt on that night.*

'As somebody involved in sport but looking in at this from the outside, I congratulate the FAI on the improvement in facilities at Tallaght, Cork and so on. ...'

Deputy Michael Kennedy: *'I welcome Mr. Delaney and the delegation and congratulate them on all of their work and all of the fantastic volunteers the FAI has throughout the country. As a Fingal man, it was a great pleasure for me to be at Tallaght Stadium a few weeks ago to see Sporting Fingal bring the cup back and to win promotion to the premier division. I hope we get a good draw for the European competitions — Paris might not be too bad. It was a great day and the entire basis on which Sporting Fingal came about is the way forward. ...'*

Senator Paul Bradford: *'I welcome Mr. Delaney and his colleagues. ... At the invitation of Senator Cummins from Waterford, Mr. Delaney attended a meeting of the Fine Gael parliamentary party some years ago. He provided an interesting outline of his plan for development work with local authorities. It was one of the best presentations I saw before a political party. I did not pursue the detail of the presentation afterwards but I presume most of it has come to pass. That is very helpful. I note what Mr. Delaney said in his presentation about the benchmark for the senior game in respect of administration and financial management. Much progress has been made in that regard. I congratulate the FAI. Mr. Delaney also pointed out that the FAI has achieved what it set out at the beginning of 2007. Well done on that.*

'If we want to take our heads from the sand, what concerns me is that League of Ireland soccer is failing to capture public attention in terms of support. When I was a child fan in the 1970s, alongside tens of thousands of soccer fans, the soccer club one followed on a Sunday – Cork Hibernians – was as important as the team one followed on a Saturday – Tottenham Hotspur in my case. I agree with Deputy Ring's prediction for British soccer. We lost the battle in respect of loyalty to a club. Cork Hibernians tragically disappeared, as did Cork Celtic. This was replicated across the country. ...

'I hope we can find a new approach, ideas and marketing. I appreciate the money, time and effort spent and the opportunities that have come as a result of the success of the international team but the sum of all those efforts still means that League of Ireland clubs are failing. ... I wish the delegation well; its members are extremely professional and work very hard. We support them but we have to get people back.'

~~~~

This discussion occurred on the day before Cork City FC's holding company were subject of an application to be wound up in the High Court. John Delaney's salary for the following year (2010) was reported to be €431,687 per annum.

I feel that the above responses are fairly reflective of politicians' attitudes at the time. A little distracted, understandably, by the recent national team result against France and the Thierry Henry handball; but while they were showing a clear concern in relation to LOI affairs (with Senator Bradford in particular showing a good understanding of Irish and Cork football), it's evident that they trusted that the FAI and John Delaney were doing as much as they could for the game in Ireland and for the League of Ireland.

Hindsight, of course, is 20/20 – but given the live and regular issues that were occurring at League of Ireland level, and in particular at my club, I feel that the congratulations and commiserations given to the FAI top brass at this discussion show how people accepted that 'Aviva Stadium' image of the FAI without too much thought or insight.

The above responses also reveal the extent to which politicians (and perhaps also the general public) in 2009 equated the performance of the FAI with that of the men's national team. Deputy O'Mahony provided the clearest example of this:

> *'I thank Mr. Delaney and his colleagues for giving us a picture of what it was like and what it is like now. I commiserate with them on their recent result. I know the deep sense of unfairness they felt, but I congratulate them on the performance.'*

Reading this, one might think that John Delaney was playing alongside Richard Dunne at centre-back.

In any event, recent revelations about the FAI have broken any trust they may have enjoyed, and there's a marked difference between the atmosphere in the Oireachtas discussion back in 2009 and the tense exchanges in the Oireachtas meeting with the FAI 10 years later (which I'll come to later in this book). Another consequence of the breakdown in trust in the FAI is that since 16th March 2019 the performance of the men's national team has not been the main measure by which politicians and the general public have assessed the FAI. This is a good thing. However, it is not necessarily a permanent change. It might only take qualification for a future European Championships or World Cup to move the focus away from the required holistic critique of the FAI and from the need for real change.

In the afterword to *Second City*, entitled 'The Need for Change', I wrote the following:

If the FAI were ambitious for our league and gave the attainment of domestic professional football the priority it deserves, then we could still see real progress for our domestic leagues and for soccer in this country over the next 10 to 15 years. But this type of progress firstly needs a realisation that major transformative changes are needed, which implies an understanding that all is not OK with the League of Ireland today. Unfortunately, instead of a plan for the major structural changes that are required, we seem only to have a plan to keep negativity away from the media and away from the League, and to reduce the number of teams from 12 to 10. If we continue going down the road we are on, fighting amongst ourselves, then there is a danger that we may at some stage need the government to step in and sort out the growing mess. I'm hoping this never happens, but only time will tell.

My fears back in 2016 that the government might have to step in appear to have proven well founded, given Sport Ireland's decision of 9th April 2019 to suspend funding to the FAI. However, the suspension of funding did not occur due to any concern from the government or Sport Ireland in relation to the FAI's continuing neglect of the LOI. Sport Ireland did not intervene because they felt major transformative changes were needed in Irish domestic football. No: Sport Ireland only got involved because of concerns relating to corporate governance at FAI board level, after alarming details emerged – following that failed injunction application made by John Delaney a few weeks previously – relating to Delaney's personal (and interest-free) loan to the FAI in 2016 (more on that later also). As such, once the corporate governance issues are sorted it's possible that Sport Ireland will be satisfied and we could return to normal: the LOI as an afterthought.

Since the publication of *Second City*, and despite some progress by the clubs themselves, things have not really changed on the ground in the LOI. As I write, the players at Limerick FC are on strike for non-payment of wages, and there are alarming rumours in relation to the financial situation of other clubs in the LOI. John Caulfield, the hero of Cork City FC and a man who must have spent as much time as an active participant in this league as anyone, will attest to the continued vulnerability and mere survival of clubs like Cork City FC later in this book. He speaks of the FAI's lack of interest and the game face of those involved in junior football with regard to a professional game here.

The wolf is still at the door of LOI clubs. The stepping down of John Delaney as CEO of the FAI does not necessarily mean the LOI will be treated any better by his successor(s).

So why rebuild a club, or restructure or even remove the governing association, if in the end the LOI remains in such a fragile state? Prioritising the LOI and the move towards developing a full-time professional league on the island of Ireland are in my opinion crucial at this moment in time. The plans of Niall Quinn and his backers to transform Irish football have been attacked as lacking detail, but they do at least prioritise the LOI. Businessman Kieran Lucid's proposal to form an 'all-island' league have found favour, with the detail of his plans being praised. For what it's worth, I believe an all-island league could dramatically change the game both here and in the North for the better. I also believe that parallel plans for the further progression of our women's national league must form part of any proposals for the future of the game here.

If, as I fear, we do go back to seeing the men's national team's results as the main measure of the FAI's performance and of the health of Irish football, then we'll be accepting that we're not really ever meant to have full-time clubs or fully functioning professional leagues in Ireland like they have in the rest of Europe. We might all get back on the merry-go-round and be happy qualifying the senior team for the ever-enlarging European Championships every now and again, perhaps hosting a game or two. That's a depressing thought and one that is not worthy of the great sporting people of this country.

Neal Horgan

Chapter One – Season 2010

I'd walked away at the end of 2009 – with 10 seasons at Cork
City under my belt – and into retirement at the relatively
young age of 29. I'd been having knee problems, but the real
reason I was keen to get my P45 was the need for security.
There was also a great deal of relief in getting away from the
daily carnage that was going on at the club at the time. Now I
could get on with other things, and start my planned career in
the legal industry. It felt good and wise to get away from it all.
Unfortunately, the club couldn't walk away from its problems.

Cork City wound up at High Court
*Cork City Football Club have failed in their eleventh hour bid
at the High Court to save the Leeside club from going out of
business.*

*The club sought a stay on an order winding up the club,
however, Ms Justice Mary Laffoy said she could see no reason
to grant a stay of execution and said her decision to grant a
winding up order stood.*

*Cork City are now considering their position with a trip to
the Supreme Court the only viable option available to the
club's owners.*

*City owner Tom Coughlan said he was deeply disappointed
with the court's decision.*

*He told reporters outside the court that he was seeking
legal advice and was not giving up just yet.*

*Coughlan said he would welcome the financial support of
anybody who wanted to save Cork City.*

(RTÉ, www.rte.ie, 23rd February 2010)

Quintas criticise Coughlan as FAI pull plug on Cork's Premier Division status
*Cork City fans today woke up to the miserable – but not
unexpected – news that the city will be without a top-flight*

club next season following the late-night decision by the FAI's licensing committee to deny the club a Premier Division licence for the 2010 season.

And today fans' group FORAS were immediately at work to see if they could salvage soccer at any level for Cork next season by competing in Division One, after they were formally granted a First Division licence by the FAI.

It was a long and traumatic day for Cork fans yesterday, one which began at 11am with yet another appearance in court before Justice Mary Laffoy and which ended at 9.38pm last night, when an FAI statement confirmed that the licensing committee had made the only decision possible: to kick the entity that is known as Cork City out of the Premier Division, and in effect end the life of the club as it's known.

That could lead to a rebirth of soccer in the city as FORAS are aware of the great work done by the 400 Club in rescuing Shamrock Rovers and transforming them from the basket case of Irish football into the most stable club in the country. ...

But the entity known as Cork City, which was owned by Tom Coughlan with a team managed by Roddy Collins, is now effectively dead. And the players who had been at the club under Collins, such as former Cork heroes George O'Callaghan and Greg O'Halloran, are now in limbo as the club they were attached to until recently is now dead, so any contracts they had are effectively null and void. ...

There is a lot of work ahead of FORAS in a short space of time and today they were still assessing the damage.

"Our initial frustration and anger was directed at the FAI but looking at it now, the FAI had no real choice," FORAS spokesman John O'Sullivan said today, after yesterday's court drama which saw the takeover bid involving FORAS collapse due to the club's inability to meet their debts in time for the FAI's deadline.

"We have to respect the clubs that did things the right way," he said. "The deal that was on the table 10 days ago was the same deal that was on the table yesterday. We finally

*got the audited accounts at 5.50 last night, which wasn't
enough time to do the work to get a licence in time."*

*A statement from Quintas, who were working with FORAS
to take over the club, confirmed that the deal was dead in the
water.*

*"Quintas Group can confirm that the FAI Licensing
Committee has rejected Cork City FC's bid for a premier
league licence," said the statement.*

*The decision of the licensing committee means that the deal
to buy Cork City FC from Tom Coughlan will now not go
ahead and the club will be wound up by the High Court. ...*

*"This is a sad day for us, the FAI and Cork City, as we are
now left without top-flight soccer in the country's second city,"
said the statement.*

(Aidan Fitzmaurice, *The Herald*, 23rd February 2010)

I had a lot to learn in my role as a trainee solicitor and I
tried to concentrate on that. The hustle and bustle of my new
office life on the South Mall in Cork had me running through
various offices and streets around the city doing a range of
tasks. It was liberating to no longer be dependent on a Friday's
results or on the reports emanating from the radio. In that sense
I felt insulated from the emerging bad news.

But at a deeper level I was very aware of the significance of
the prospect of having no Cork team in the LOI. It was as if we
were back in 1982/83 after the demise of Cork Alberts/Cork
United. Or perhaps it was just like the expelling of Cork Celtic
from the league in 1979, the resignation of Cork Hibernians
from the league in 1976, of Cork Athletic in 1957 or of Cork
United in 1948... keep going back and you'll find the same
story. It's as if we're powerless in the continuous cycle of
boom and bust. All of our efforts on the pitch to win leagues
and cups, to do well in Europe... all of that momentum we'd
built, the relationship with our fans, our identity as a proud

sporting community – it was all being washed back down the swanny.

As had been the case with the demise of those earlier clubs, I felt the impact on the footballing people of Cork would be severe and long-lasting. I was also concerned about the loss of footballing knowledge and the damage to the credibility of the game that can occur when a club folds – even if a new club replaces it. But what could I do? Nothing, it seemed.

Thankfully we had a group of committed fans who were about to do something. Something special and new. They knew that we needed a break from that cycle of boom and bust; they knew that what we needed most was a long-lasting club.

FORAS make plans as Cork are wound up

Next week's First Division game at the Brandywell between the new league club formed by FORAS and the recently-recreated Derry City will do well to match the twists and turns that led yesterday to the demise of Cork City. But there is consolation in the fact it is unlikely to contain quite so much of a farce factor either.

The order to wind up City was finally given yesterday afternoon by a High Court judge who Tom Coughlan, even as he complained the process was "horseshit", felt obliged to thank for her patience over the last six months. ...

Meanwhile, the couple of players still contracted to the club from last year, along with the dozen or so who had been lined up to play in the event the salvage operation was completed, began to turn their attention to the grim business of finding alternative employment in a league that is just 10 days away from starting.

A couple looked likely last night to move to clubs outside the area with, most notably, Fahrudin Kudozović talking to Galway United and Sligo Rovers, and Dan Connor on the brink of signing for St Patrick's Athletic.

But for most, FORAS's new operation looks likely to be the only option if they are to stay in professional football. Those who are offered contracts almost certainly face the prospect of more pay cuts and diminished conditions.

Notwithstanding the fact the Premier Division will now be more dominated than ever by clubs from Dublin and the east coast, the ramifications of City's demise – just over 25 years after the club was founded – will be felt around the country. While Coughlan has the right to appeal the High Court's action yesterday and those of the licensing committee the night before, even he didn't seem to hold out much hope as he spoke outside the Four Courts yesterday.

So, barring an astonishing turn of events, Bray Wanderers will be confirmed over the next day or two as a Premier Division side again and, a little further down the road, Dundalk will be offered the chance to compete in the Europa League this summer. ...

(Emmet Malone, *The Irish Times*, 24th February 2010)

Electric launch to new season

The chaos which has defined the past 12 months of the League of Ireland is represented by two pages placed side by side, due to the alphabet's sick sense of humour, in the comprehensive media guide produced for the 2010 campaign.

In the First Division section of the newly branded Airtricity League, the competitors from Cork and Derry are paired together.

The boxes for their 10-year record are completely blank, a stark reminder of all that has been wasted. ...

Certainly, this year's launch was markedly different to the more salubrious affairs of recent times. Managers weren't invited, while there were no press releases about prize money because the powers that be haven't decided whether they will reduce it or not.

FAI CEO Delaney defended the delay in an announcement until next week, in addition to arguing that the Abbotstown authorities were blameless in the Cork affair and an emerging controversy with respect to the transfer of Limerick FC's licence from one company to another, with Jack McCarthy, the original holder, claiming to be left in the dark.

"We've put a lot of money into the league over the last few years," said Delaney, with respect to the prize money. "We'll look at our overall budget in terms of what it costs to run the league next week. Club budgets have dropped."

Delaney accepted that the demise of Cork City did not reflect well on the league as a whole, but said that the fault essentially lay with Tom Coughlan, part of his oft-repeated argument that the actions of owners rather than administrators are the cause of the game's problems.

"The biggest success that we have to bring to bear is the culture of the owners," he said. "Cork was one example where the owner ran the club in a cavalier manner. He didn't listen and it was unfortunate what happened. Derry are another example of that.

"At the end of the season, we brought the disrepute charge (against Coughlan). I'm disappointed that the club wasn't taken over in that period.

"I think a deal could have been done and indeed should have been done."

So, was he saying that the FAI did nothing wrong?
"Nobody is blameless," he responded. "But what I see is a lot of improvements which I don't think have been recognised as well as they should be. The clubs had losses of €7m a few years ago, they are now down to €2.7m and they will be less next season." ...

(Daniel McDonnell, *Irish Independent*, 27th February 2010)

Friday 5th March 2010

League of Ireland First Division

The Brandywell, Derry

Derry City FC 1–1 Cork City (FORAS Co-op)

Derry City 1-1 Cork City FORAS Co-op

Derry City's relationship with the highs and lows continued on Friday night against Cork City FORAS Co-op at the Brandywell. On the upside, over 3,000 fans attended the game but were to be disappointed as the season opener finished 1-1.

The clash between the two demoted teams was a bit a like the New York pension investment fund for the North of Ireland in that it promised a whole lot but frustratingly, it fell way short of the mark. Cork took the lead through a stunning strike from Davin O'Neill in the second half but Derry debutant, Emmett Friars equalised for his hometown club just after the hour mark. …

Cork's style of play and choice of tactics were predictable. The Turner's Cross outfit played very cautiously throughout and it was understandable as manager Tommy Dunne was only able to name two substitutes. In recent days the Dubliner has signed several new players but because of registration problems they were not permitted to play. …

In essence, a draw was a fair result. Cork had clearly heeded the fact that Derry had a greater squad to call upon and with it being the opening game of the new season there was a sense of the indestructible.

Be that as it may, Cork defended tremendously. The former Derry City duo of Greg O'Halloran and Dave Rogers negated Derry's attacking prowess. Each cross and pass into the area was as quickly cleared as it was dispatched.

Cork City FORAS Co-op FC: Mark McNulty; Ian Turner, Dave Rogers, Stephen Mulcahy, Greg O'Halloran; Davin O'Neill, Paul Deasy, Cillian Lordan, Graham Cummins; Eoin

Forde, William Heffernan. Subs not used: Wesley Tong, John Dineen.

(From extratime.ie, 6th March 2010 – article courtesy of *The Sunday Journal* and Andrew Quinn)

~~~~

That was a great start, considering only 13 players were registered to play for the club, but as the season progressed, while everyone did their best, the team found it hard to climb the table. Cillian Lordan was particularly brave in taking the captaincy at such a difficult time in the club's history. While most of the rest of us, the more experienced lads, had moved on, he remained fighting for the club on the pitch.

I turned up occasionally to give my support at home games and I remember feeling very proud of Cork City on my first occasion back at 'the Cross' – looking around at the fans who now owned the club. Then, towards the end of the year, I got a call from Tommy: he wanted to meet me.

A few days later, in the comfort of Soho Bar in the city, Tommy made his pitch. He needed me back. The club needed me back. I'd finished too early, he said. The club was part-time now so I'd be able to make training in the afternoons and not miss college or work.

I told him I was interested but that I had some prior commitments. I'd gone back to my old GAA club, St Finbarr's ('the Barrs') and committed to their senior football team for the 2011 championship season.

'No problem, Hog,' said Tommy, 'sure we can work around it.'

'But Tommy, coming up to the GAA Championship, if there was a clash I'd have to play for them, you know that?'

'Sure, Hog, we can cross that bridge when we come to it. But we need you back. Now, what can we do for you?'

We discussed the payment situation: I'd taken the sportspersons' retirement scheme, which had helped pay for my Blackhall training to become a solicitor, '…so I won't be able to give that money back.'

'Don't worry – we'll look into that too. We'll get it sorted. And maybe there are some coaching courses we can put you on. You need to be a part of this club.'

'Sure Tommy, we'll see.'

'Hog, come back, play a few games this year. Next year we'll be getting new faces in. This club needs to go back to the Premier Division and we need you to be part of that, to help the club get back there.'

It all sounded very exciting, and I have to admit that it felt nice to be wanted again by CCFC. So I agreed to go back for the remainder of the season, just to help out, along with a few others such as Billy Woods.

However, it transpired that Cork City FC wouldn't be able to pay me anything; if they did, then my retirement clawback would kick in and I'd have to reimburse the Revenue, which I wasn't in a position to do. Other perks were mentioned by Tommy, but we settled on a new pair of football boots every now and then, which in the end suited me. I was enjoying playing the game for the love it again, without the chains that money could bring.

~~~~

I managed to play five or six games at the tail-end of the 2010 season as the team finished mid-table, with Derry City (who, unlike us, had kept most of their players together) going straight back up to the Premier Division as champions.

Tommy was anxious that I should play again next year.

'OK Tommy, OK,' I said.

Chapter Two – Interview with Sonya O'Neill, July 2019

Born and raised a stone's throw from Turner's Cross, Sonya O'Neill works in TV production with RTÉ and has been a Cork City fan since 1996. She served on the committee of the Cork City Supporters Club for a number of years before being a founding member of FORAS in 2006. She served as secretary and treasurer during her six-year tenure, stepping down just after City were promoted to the Premier Division. She was the spokesperson in the media during the foundation of the Trust, the dealings with the previous owners and the subsequent takeover.

Neal Horgan: Sonya, you were onboard when FORAS came in to take over the club in 2010; what position did you hold at the time?

Sonya O'Neill: I was secretary of FORAS in 2010. The chairman that year was John O'Sullivan, but the first chairman of the Trust was Kevin Lynch. That's very often forgotten. I think that came about because we went into the bank when we were first starting up and they asked, 'So are the chairman, treasurer and secretary here?' And we hadn't the structure at the time, but Kevin happened to be there, I was there...

NH: How long ago was that?

SO'N: Well, we had our official launch in 2008 but it was back in 2006 that we started the whole thing. We'd been in talks with Brian Lennox at the time, so this was pre-Arkaga and pre-Tom Coughlan. The idea was to set up a more structured supporters' club. We were hoping to make a tangible difference by providing facilities and eventually a base that we would keep separate from the daily running of a football club, which just eats money. So back in 2006 we were working with Brian in a supporting, ancillary role. The idea was that the Trust would purchase and retain ownership of anything that it provided to the club, such as a treadmill or maybe a training ground, and then lease it to whoever was in charge of the club at a minimum fee. So if anything happened to the owner or the club, then all that base, including those facilities, would be preserved. That was the fundamental idea behind it all.

NH: So who were the people involved in FORAS at this early stage?

SO'N: Well, there was Kevin Lynch, John O'Sullivan, Jonathan O'Brien, Kevin McCarthy. Paul Hartnett was involved, Pat Shine was there, Seán Ó Conaill, Cathal O'Driscoll and myself. As time moved on there was also Catriona Golden, Laura Barry, Joe Hurley, Bernard O'Donovan… loads of great people.

NH: Where did you meet?

SO'N: Usually the Turner's Cross Community Centre; we used to rent a space there. But the very first meetings were actually at the Garda Club in Penrose Quay and the Telecom Club on MacCurtain Street, where we were trying to get expressions of interest. I remember the very first meeting; we asked if people would be interested in putting money into this idea every year, and we only had 40 expressions of interest. The supporters' club had met in the Telecom Club up to that point and so I suppose it grew out of that group really. I think it was Pat Shine who suggested the idea of a trust. Pat was a huge force behind FORAS; I'm not sure we'd have a club today if it wasn't for Pat. Anyway, a couple of us had watched a documentary about Luton Town where a fans' trust had been formed to wrestle back control from their owner to save the club. It really showed me the effect the fans could have if we were organised and structured. At the time we had Brian [Lennox] so there was no worry there, but we wanted to help if we could – and to work in tandem with Brian.

NH: That was 2006, so what happened from there?

SO'N: Well, we slowly and steadily went through all the red tape to become an industrial and provident society. There was a lot of work and it took us ages. But there was no need to hurry as things were going fine at the club under Brian. Then, in or about 2007, Arkaga entered the scene and, as you know, they were talking about spending huge money and building a big stadium, so we took a back seat. But in the background we kept slowly putting the formal pieces together. Then, when things started to go wrong, we had more people getting involved – and the people already involved were putting more work in too.

NH: When things started to go wrong... you mean in 2008 when Arkaga pulled out?

SO'N: Yes, and I remember the time it happened. The day the news broke that Arkaga were after pulling the plug and the club was going into examinership, I happened to be at work [in RTÉ studios, Cork] and Derek Mooney was actually interviewing the court-appointed examiner, Kieran McCarthy, in our studios. They were talking about what was going to happen to the club. Someone told me that this was happening downstairs in our radio studios so I thought I'd better go and introduce myself. So I went down and told him I was on the board of FORAS and he said, 'I've been thinking about [FORAS]. I really want you guys involved.' And from that moment on he was always interested in what we were doing. We had some money in the bank at the time from membership fees – a couple of thousand quid. Actually, I remember saying to Brian Lennox at the beginning, 'This is what we have in the bank,' and him saying it wouldn't last until the next week!

NH: [Laughing] Typical Brian!

SO'N: [Laughing] Yeah, he played it down a bit. But the examiner was interested and kept us involved. I remember another local businessman, Danny Drew, was interested in taking over the club, and the examiner asked us to meet with him and we did. He then asked us to meet with Tom Coughlan and we did that too. We had our doubts as soon as we met Tom as to whether he knew what he was getting himself into. In the meeting with him, Tom seemed to read back to us what we'd written in our manifesto. It was along the lines of, 'For the people, by the people; I'm only going to mind the club for you to take back.' That sort of thing. And that set off a few alarm bells. But the situation was getting drastic and we weren't in a position at that point to step up. We were set up to support rather than take over the club. But I did think Tom was looking for something himself, and maybe we could've ridden on his coat-tails and it might've worked out… but, in short, that didn't happen.

NH: No it didn't, but you were involved in helping Tom run the club at some point?

SO'N: Yes. Tom took over at the end of the 2008 season and we began assisting him in the off-season for 2009, getting committees in place so that FORAS had an involvement in how the club was run. We'd also become more visible around the city in many ways by that point. We had an official launch in the City Hall, and we had your testimonial match…

NH: Yes – thanks again for that!

SO'N: We were delighted to assist. Plus it all helped to get us out there into the public. But while we were doing all this we could tell it wasn't going to work out with Tom. I'd say we knew by about April 2009 that things weren't going to work out.

NH: What happened?

SO'N: Well, I remember there was a ceremony – I think it was in the April – in the city for the Cork City underage team. They'd won something and I went along to represent FORAS as I was working in town. The Lord Mayor gave us a nice mention, saying the Trust was doing great work in the background, and I remember Tom turned and basically told us that if we were getting the credit we'd have to start stumping up the cash. So it was quite clear he was looking for money from us at this point.

NH: And this was only one month into the season?

SO'N: Yes. It wasn't a good sign. So we told him how he could access the money or how he could get use of the money in the way we'd planned. We'd buy what was needed and lease it back to him or to the club… and he responded by saying this wasn't what happened in real life. But we weren't going to back down; we told him we were doing it differently as the funds or facilities could just disappear with the club, as had happened with Cork clubs in the past. This was the reason we'd set up the Trust in the first place. I think we had €60,000 in the bank at the time. It went downhill from there really.

NH: In what way?

SO'N: He stopped us from assisting at matches, on the turnstiles, etc. That was the beginning of the end of our relationship with him.

NH: And by the end of 2009 the club was on a precipice?

SO'N: Yes, and this is where it all went nuts. High Court proceedings, members' meetings, big decisions. I'm not sure who contacted who, but there was a discussion with Quintas [an accountancy and wealth management firm], who were representing a consortium that were interested in taking over and giving us a stake. Also, Tom had approached us with a deal regarding something called 'refundable shares', whereby we'd give the money to him and we would hold onto the shares, and then he'd buy them back from us – or something.

NH: Not sure about that one…

SO'N: No, we weren't sure either. Would our money have helped to save the club at that point? That was a difficult position for us to be in.

NH: I see what you mean. You felt FORAS could be risking the club by not handing over the money?

SO'N: Yes. It wasn't easy. In the end our rules wouldn't allow it to happen anyway. Decisions like that would have to be taken by the membership and Tom wasn't willing to wait the necessary time that it would take to call an EGM [extraordinary general meeting]. This is actually one of the strengths of the Trust model; it saved us from being left with nothing in the bank when the inevitable happened. And it *was* inevitable. And personally, I didn't think the Quintas option was the answer either, long-term. Overall it just felt like the club needed to go back a bit before it could go forward.

NH: To get back to base?

SO'N: Well, to have any future I felt we had to go back a bit – but we could never really pursue that as people's jobs were on the line.

NH: But that's how it played out in the end…

SO'N: Yes. I remember, just when the club licences were being arranged, Jonathan O'Brien and Paul Hartnett sitting down with Quintas, working on the takeover and trying to keep the entity alive. They were working through the creditors' list that had been provided by Tom to see if they could reduce the amount of money that the creditors would accept. But the other argument was that if we were struggling to deal with the money owed, where was the money going to come from to bring the club forward? Also, we had to be sure that there weren't any further creditors – i.e. further to the list we'd been given. Nothing was certain in that regard. Every day there seemed to be a new name added to the list.

NH: So there was a lot to consider in terms of keeping it going.

SO'N: Yes, and that's basically why in the end it didn't happen. We already knew then that we had to work on other options. We'd called a members' meeting and decided that we should apply to the FAI for a licence on our own, on the strict condition that if someone else got a licence for the club – be it Tom, Quintas or whomever – then we would withdraw. It was a back-up plan really, as at the time we were working hard with Quintas to see if we could get that deal across the line.

NH: What were the possibilities at that point?

SO'N: Scenario one was for Tom to continue running the club on his own, if he could work it himself. Scenario two was that he would agree to the takeover with Quintas and ourselves; and if all that fell through then the third scenario was for FORAS to come in and run it on our own, as we'd made the licensing application – but as I've said, that was only a back-up plan.

NH: And it was crucial that you had that back-up plan…

SO'N: Yes, or else there would've been no League of Ireland football in Cork City for at least a year. Although in a sense if that had happened it would've been a cleaner break.

NH: Yes, but the club could have lost all momentum.

SO'N: Funny you say that. Before I had my son, Sam, if you'd told me I wouldn't be at a home game for five, six months, I wouldn't have believed you. But then I had Sam and fell out of the habit as he wasn't sleeping well, so I didn't go for a few months. It struck me then that people can get out of the habit of going to games very quickly. Even now, when we have five or six weeks without a game it effects the crowd. Imagine if there'd been a gap of a year?

NH: Also, the fact that there was no gap in years means, to me, that it remained the same club. But anyway, who had come up with that idea to apply for the licence?

SO'N: It was Seán Ó Conaill, I think. As you know, he's a professor of law at UCC, so he knew what he was talking about. It's important to remember that all these key decisions were made by the members often during very difficult and emotional meetings. They voted to apply for the licence – but yes, that suggestion by Seán was vital, as things turned out.

NH: Yes, that was crucial.

SO'N: Looking back, having the FORAS trust properly set up in advance of any trouble, and having the licence application in the background… I'm proud of that. We all are.

NH: You should be; it was great forward thinking.

SO'N: It took some pressure off, having the formal stuff done. But there was still pressure in taking over, obviously. People's jobs were at stake. We weren't heavily involved with the players but we were getting wind of what was going on. Towards the end of 2009, everything was falling apart but the general public didn't really know what was happening. There were rumours of players not getting paid and all that, but nothing was out in the open until 'Busgate' – remember that?

NH: I do. Dan Murray decided enough was enough.

SO'N: That's right. And it changed everything; it was pivotal really. The fact that players hadn't been getting paid really hit home when you got stuck on that bus up at Silversprings. The public took notice – it was pivotal, what Dan did. We were brought on the radio to give our account. Money started flowing in to us.

NH: That's a huge gap in my knowledge right there. I hadn't realised Busgate had that effect on you guys, on FORAS.

SO'N: Yes – the players, you guys, had a completely different perspective.

NH: So what happened from there?

SO'N: Well, we went into overdrive really. We went on a fundraising drive and did our best to engage with the media and also with the FAI. After our own licence application had been submitted we met with a number of potential sponsors and with some experienced Cork City people asking about the ins and outs of running the club and what help they could give us in the event of taking over. People like Jerry Harris, Brian Lennox, Liam Murphy... Then we had to call a full members' meeting in advance of the end of the season so they could decide whether they wanted us to hang onto our funds or give our money – I think we had about €100,000 by then – to the consortium with Quintas, with businessmen Peter Gray and Michael O'Connell, as our stake in the club. The members were split at the beginning. We were careful to only give the members the facts and not try to sway people one way or another. Then one or two people spoke and it got sort of emotional. In the end it was almost unanimous that we'd go with the consortium. And that was the start of us thinking we might have to take a large part in running the club. As we'd agreed to go with the takeover, we had to prove we had the money – which we did. We had a team working on the licensing application for the consortium effort – Tom's licence, as such – but the deadline passed for this as debts were owed which meant the FAI wouldn't issue the licence. And the consortium was dependent on the licence. Then the FAI gave Tom an extra week to sort out the debts. Of course, FORAS already had a licence in the bag. But during that extra week we were trying to get the paperwork for the consortium licence sorted; trying to help figure out a plan of payment for the creditors so that the licence could be issued.

NH: So at that point, either scenario could happen for FORAS – the consortium idea or go it alone?

SO'N: Yes, and as we already had our licence sorted, we were helping Quintas sort the consortium takeover.

NH: When did you find out that the application for the consortium licence had been refused?

SO'N: Well, it was actually Tom's licence that was refused, which meant the takeover couldn't happen. We were in the solicitor's office – McGuire Desmond – in Cork with Quintas when we found out. Apparently Tom didn't provide the accounts until late on the Friday of the extended week and the FAI said it was too late, game over. And they were right. That was far too late.

NH: So the club was gone, after you'd worked so hard with the consortium to make it happen? That must've been upsetting.

SO'N: Yes, it really was. Even though we knew and had always stressed that it was just the company that was gone, not the club, it was still very difficult as people were going to lose their jobs. The guys at Quintas were very frustrated too. I came out of the offices and called Pat Shine – who'd left earlier – to tell him. But then we started saying, 'Well, that's it – it's down to us. Let's knuckle down, lads.' We decided we were going to have to step up – even though our eggs had been in a different basket right up until that moment and it was now a mere nine days until the first game of the season.

NH: Christ...

SO'N: Yes, it was a very short timeframe.

NH: I had known it was a short timeframe but I hadn't realised FORAS had gone from being part of a consortium to being so suddenly on their own. I'd thought you had more time to plan for it.

SO'N: But the thing is, we'd done everything well and in advance; we'd dotted our i's and crossed our t's, got the licence and put it away. The Trust, the licence, the members… they were all there. So we could worry about other things now. We had the advice from Brian Lennox as a former chairman; Jerry Harris was very helpful about the day-to-day stuff and players registrations; Liam Murphy had been helping us to get players… We knew that we could only enter the First Division, but that was OK. However, we needed to find a manager. And that was really, really hard.

NH: But Roddy Collins had been appointed by Tom at the end of 2009, after Doolin left…

SO'N: Yes, but this was a new start. Roddy was never going to be our choice. No disrespect to him – and maybe we should've thought more about him, as we'd been very conscious of players being left go – but ultimately we wanted to go in our own direction and we had bigger fish to fry at that point. We got Éanna Buckley onboard and Kevin Mullen and they based themselves and the club office in the Turner's Cross Tavern. And as a board we used Turner's Cross Community Centre as a base… and that's where the heated discussions started. We were trying to figure things out.

NH: You had to get new gear too, didn't you? I know the gear they used for that first game was new and different.

SO'N: You've got me there: I can't remember any of that now. We all had different jobs.

NH: What was your job?

SO'N: Crying…

NH: [Laughs]

SO'N: [Laughing] Not really. But I do remember there being tears and I remember feeling the weight of responsibility. We had all those moments. One minute we'd be feeling brave and inspired, saying, 'We have it now. We have the club we love; it's our responsibility,' …and then a few hours later we'd be saying, 'No, that's it. We can't do it.'

NH: There was doubt, understandably. It was a huge burden to be landed with so suddenly.

SO'N: It was, and in addition the club's assets were stuck in liquidation, because the holding company had gone into liquidation. So we couldn't get the club's name or the players transferred over to us.

NH: You had to figure out all these things in just nine days… *and* get a manager and players?

SO'N: Yes. We had anticipated the name change and in fact the members had voted on a name and crest at a previous meeting. But the biggest thing was the players. We didn't anticipate that we wouldn't be able to access our own players. We'd hoped the FAI would help us with this, but it didn't happen.

NH: Really?

SO'N: Yes. To me it felt like doors were being closed in our faces. We hadn't asked for special treatment, but the problem was this: when the licences were being issued the FAI gave Tom a week's extension to see if the takeover could happen. During this week the transfer window closed. Once we took over we asked the FAI if they'd open the transfer window for 24 hours so we could get access to our own players, etc., and they declined. This put us under significant pressure.

NH: That's shocking, that they didn't try to help you with that at such a crucial juncture.

SO'N: Well in my opinion they made things very difficult. Regardless of all the disturbing revelations with the FAI at the moment – my mind had been made up about them long ago.

NH: So how did you get players?

SO'N: Well, we found a manager and he got players that were free and not attached to any clubs.

NH: Tommy?

SO'N: Yes: Tommy Dunne. I'd spoken to a few ex-players about taking over and while they were very supportive the timing was wrong – so we were getting nowhere. But then Jerry Harris called in and said he'd been talking to Tommy Dunne. Tommy happened to be in Finland but was willing to take a call.

NH: Great! Do you remember meeting with Tommy?

SO'N: Yes, but before that I remember the call to him. Paul Hartnett rang him and Tommy was great. He's a huge part in it all and has been somewhat forgotten, but I think he was brilliant, the way he bought into it…

NH: I agree; he bought into it and managed the situation very well with very limited resources.

SO'N: He did. He managed the position brilliantly, especially in his dealings with our board and with the players. Tommy looked after getting players and all the logistics for the players. But going back to those initial negotiations with him: one day, during a second or probably third call, we were working through a deal – remember Tommy was living in Finland, so it was a big move for him to come over – and the person negotiating was saying something along the lines of, 'Yeah, a car? We might be able to get you a car, Tommy…' and Pat Shine jumped up and said, 'Hang up! We can't afford a car!'

NH: [Laughing] But it worked out well?

SO'N: It was great. Once Tommy came in we didn't really have to worry about the players as he looked after that. We'd been talking to some sponsors – the radio partner Red FM, and we spoke with Clonakilty Blackpudding I think, and I remember speaking to McCarthy Developments to strike a deal and ensure we could still use the training ground at Bishopstown. Those relationships had been built up previously. As I mentioned, Éanna Buckley and Kevin Mullen stayed on working for us, and Jerry Harris. Also, the accountant Alan Whelan pulled in to help Laura Barry. These were all crucial people. You know that while it was a really stressful period I remember it fondly, the way everybody pulled together to make it work. To prove that the people who loved the club the most – i.e. the fans – were the right people to take care of it.

NH: And that first game against Derry…?

SO'N: I remember there were a couple of friendlies during the lead-up to it. Paul Hartnett and Jonathan O'Brien took over the football part with Tommy. It looked like we hadn't enough players at one stage. But we were able to get a few more at the last minute and in the end 15 players travelled to Derry on a bus that was christened 'the golf buggy'. It was a very small bus to be fair and didn't have a toilet. Tommy still talks about it. The Board travelled on the fans' bus and I remember Éanna meeting us as we arrived and telling us that two of the registrations hadn't gone through and so we had only 13 players – two of whom were goalkeepers.

NH: Mad stuff.

SO'N: It was. But we'd done it. And during the game… I'll never forget that goal, that first goal by Davin O'Neill up in Derry that night – still my favourite moment of all time. That and the goal by Cummins against Shels few years later. Absolutely fantastic moments that made it all worthwhile.

Chapter Three – 11th January to 9th July 2011

Dunne Expects More New Faces, Lordan Leaves

Cork City return to pre-season training on Saturday, with manager Tommy Dunne expressing optimism that there will be further additions to the squad in the near future. ...

With thirteen players now contracted to the club for the 2011 season, Dunne is still keen to add a number of new faces to the squad. ...

"We all know the importance of this season, when we will be one of a number of teams with aspirations of promotion, but we have to be diligent and prudent in our dealings and remember that this is about the future of the club, not just one season. I am currently speaking to four or five players that I would like to bring in to the club, and it is now about trying to get those deals over the line, and I hope that I will have news on these later on in the week."

Dunne also confirmed that captain Cillian Lordan will not be with the club for the 2011 season, after accepting a job offer abroad. The City boss said: "Cillian has been offered a job in Holland, which he has accepted, so he will not be back with us this season. He is a true professional and from my point of view, he will be badly missed. He's a good player, but he is also a positive influence in the dressing room and on the training pitch. The fact that he played with a knee injury last season and never complained shows the character of the man for me. Although he was a full-time pro for a number of years, he continued with his studies and he is leaving to further his own career. ..."

(<u>Cork City FC website</u>, 11th January 2011)

Saturday 15th January 2011

Tommy arranged for our pre-season training to begin today but I nearly didn't show up. Last night I was totally stressed out. It's been building for a while; I've been worried over the inevitable conflict between GAA and soccer. There wasn't a clash at the end of last year, but I know there will be this summer when the GAA Championship starts. So during the night I decided I'd meet Tommy before training and suggest that he doesn't really need me, given the new lads coming in, and tell him that I won't be able to get the Barrs to change their policy of not allowing fellas to play matches near their championship games – and so maybe it'd be best for both of us if I left now.

But then I chickened out and said nothing.

In truth I enjoyed meeting and training with the lads again – Danny Murphy, 'the Cockney Rebel', is back; Timmy Kiely too; and Greg, Davin and Nults are set to continue on from last year. A Frenchman named Vincent Escudé-Candau has been drafted in to bring some continental flair to the midfield, while our top striker from last year, Graham Cummins, is still with us and he's been joined by the wily Waterford man Vinny Sullivan. There are other additions, with the experienced Kerry winger Derek O'Brien signing from Galway and a young Cork lad named Gearóid Morrissey joining after coming home from Blackburn Rovers. Morrissey might form a youthful and energetic midfield partnership with Shane Duggan, who has remained at the club since 2009. At the back the sole Dubliner in the side, the strong Gavin Kavanagh, will probably be paired with young Mul, who did so well to break in under Doolo.

As Cillian Lordan has stepped away from football, Greg has taken over the captaincy. Even allowing for the loss of Cillian, we have a much better squad this year.

We've been told we'll be spending most of pre-season at Carrigtwohill AFC's all-weather pitch just east of the city, which is where we trained today. Tommy also told us before we began that Woodsy is now his assistant. We wound Woodsy up, telling him he can't talk to us players anymore.

Tommy continued, 'And there's no more bleedin' talk of us being a young team; no more excuses. We're gonna be ready for it this year. We're gonna be a good squad and youse need to be on top of your game to get into the team, I'm telling youse. With the players we have now, we should be challenging to go up, and this club needs that.'

He sounded a lot like Doolo.

Everyone enjoyed training, which was a light session, easing us back as all managers tend to do these days (in stark contrast to 10 years ago when the first day back would be sheer hell). I imagine that Tommy's training sessions will be unchanged from last year, with loads of passing drills, which I love. Passing drills are training exercises focused on passing the ball and running in predetermined directions and shapes that revolve around cones, with a number of balls in action at once. You go on a journey of sorts as you weave and twist and turn between and around the cones before arriving back at your starting point. From my earliest playing days, passing drills were always a rudimentary part of sessions – but the type that Tommy and Paul Doolin have introduced to us at Cork City over the past few years are more elaborate and challenging. They often progress into increasingly difficult drills, perhaps using your weak leg, or at greater pace or distance or with a higher frequency of passes and balls coming at you. Anybody who happens to be passing overhead in a hot-air balloon might look down to see an army of ant-like footballers creating shapes with the balls and running around crazily in various directions, following the man in front of him. Apparently Tommy, and Doolo before him, used the Arsenal training drills – which is evident in the fluidity and movement involved. Quite often you can have most of the squad moving at once but with each player involved with his particular ball throughout. That's why I love it. I love touching the ball. Feeling it, caressing it, manipulating it so that it spins back to you or stops dead, or – as is needed in many of the drills – cushioning the ball so that you've taken the speed from the pass and moving it about a foot and a half (but no more) in the direction in which you're now looking to move or pass. I'd be happy to do these drills forever. There's something almost hypnotic about them when they get going, the players falling under a spell concocted to keep the ball flying around with a smoothness and beauty all of its own.

After the passing drills we generally have some sort of training match and today was no different. I was selected on the same team as Murph, which was great as we could read each other's play like in days of old. I immediately knew what his shouts meant; I instinctively knew his next move and he knew mine. We began a waltz of sorts, keeping the ball between us and away from the others with skill and speed of thought. Partly because of this, our team won handsomely.

It was a nice feeling, and as we were leaving the pitch you could tell there was excitement in the camp. However, we were all sobered a little by the crazy pre-season training schedule that Tommy handed out afterwards on A4 pages: he had us down to train almost every day – which was a lot for us part-time and amateur players.

We were discussing this in the portacabins as we got changed when young Ian Turner (who'd played at right-back for most of 2010), who hadn't trained, came in. All the lads gathered around him and listened intently – whatever he had to say was clearly serious. Turner explained how less than a week earlier, he and his girlfriend had stayed in a hotel in Kinsale. Shortly after arriving into their hotel room his girlfriend began to feel sick, and so they decided not to go out for a drink as planned but to stay in the room instead. However, his girlfriend deteriorated and so Turner decided to call SouthDoc, who sent an ambulance. The paramedics arrived and checked her out; she was deemed to be OK and the paramedics departed.

Not long afterwards, Turner's girlfriend was sick again. Crucially, he decided to call SouthDoc again. That was the last thing he remembered before being woken by the paramedics. This time they were brought to hospital, and they later found out they'd suffered carbon monoxide poisoning. Tragically, a girl in the room below them had died as a result of the same thing. So that second call to SouthDoc before he passed out had saved Turner's and his girlfriend's lives. It was hard to fathom.

Thursday 10th February 2011
A familiar story is dominating the sporting headlines in Ireland today. Another LOI soccer club in trouble, teetering along the edge of existence.

Sporting Fingal on verge of collapse as contracts cancelled
Sporting Fingal are on the brink of collapse after the club cancelled all of its players' contracts yesterday afternoon. The FAI promptly confirmed that the club has pulled out of the Setanta Sports Cup with UCD being parachuted in to meet Lisburn Distillery in the opening game on Monday.
Abbotstown will continue talks with Sporting Fingal today when a decision may be made on whether they can continue as an Airtricity League club. Club licences for the coming 2011 season, which starts on March 4, will be issued after the Independent Licensing Committee meets on Sunday. The club, who won the FAI Ford Cup in 2009 and played in the Europa League last season, was launched just three years ago tomorrow. …
Speculation had been rife in recent weeks concerning the club's financial viability following the ending of benefactor Gerry Gannon's backing at the end of last season.
On a day of intense talks yesterday, the club's 13 players, including new signing Greg Bolger and Colin Hawkins and Gary O'Neill, who had re-signed from last season, had their contracts cancelled. …
The players' union, the PFAI, said it was "massively disappointed" that contracts, some of which have been signed very recently, would not be honoured.
(Paul Buttner, Irish Examiner, 10th February 2011)

~~~~~

Another one bites the dust. It's terrible for the players, fans and everyone who worked hard to bring professional football to this particular community. And while the Anglo Irish Bank debacle and the recession may have been important factors in the demise, in my opinion the continued absence of an overarching plan for professional football from the FAI is appalling. Clubs will continue to die, and the FAI will continue to take praise for things that are going well whilst stepping to the side when things go wrong. Nothing has changed.

~~~~

Early season 2011

Over the first few months of the season, Tommy's prophecy that we'd challenge for promotion appeared to be well founded. We won five and drew three of our first eight league games, putting us just behind early leaders Shelbourne. However, that didn't stop Roddy Collins – now manager of promotion rivals Monaghan United – from having a go just before we hosted his team at Turner's Cross...

Roddy rubbishes Cork boss Dunne as "a boy doing a man's job"

Wherever Roddy Collins goes, controversy is rarely a million miles away. Ahead of Friday evening's Airtricity League First Division fixture between Collins' Monaghan United and his former employers Cork City, the outspoken Dubliner has slammed his opposite number Tommy Dunne, dismissing him as little more than "a boy doing a man's job".

The surprising attack on Dunne appears to stem from some ill-will which exists between the pair since the former Shamrock Rovers defender stepped in to the Turner's Cross hotseat in February 2010.

Though Collins had been in charge at City for a two-month period prior to the club's winding-up in early 2010, he was overlooked by the reborn FORAS Cork City FC who instead opted to promote Dunne from his position as the side's assistant manager.

Collins, who claims to have given up his post at Maltese side Floriana to take over at Cork, remained out of work for almost a year until he was appointed by Monaghan United shortly before the start of the 2011 season.

Collins told Paul Dollery that the new board had made a mistake in appointing Dunne.

"Cork are a good unit. They have a great set-up, fantastic training facilities, a big catchment area and a fine squad. But unfortunately they have a boy doing a man's job as their manager.

"The job is too big for him and that will prove itself. He was only an understudy to me. It's a pity, because it's a massive club. It's a Premier Division club, they shouldn't be down in the First Division."

Despite the fact that he was overlooked in the past, Collins was quick to stress that he would not necessarily turn down any approaches from the club in the future, describing himself as "made for that job".

"I would absolutely love to manage that club," he said. "If the lads from FORAS had given me the opportunity last year I would have gotten them promoted."

(From *The42* – www.the42.ie – 30th March 2011)

Friday 1st April 2011

League of Ireland First Division

Turner's Cross, Cork

Cork City FC 2–2 Monaghan United FC

Honours even, with our top striker Graham Cummins and Davin O'Neill on the score sheet for us, leaving both sides unbeaten so far. I felt it was important for Tommy that we didn't lose. Crowd numbers are rising slowly also.

Friday 8th April to Thursday 5th May 2011

In our next game we beat Waterford 2–1 away, coming back after being 1–0 down at half-time. That was a hugely important result and was followed up by good wins against Finn Harps at home (5–0) and Salthill Devon away (5–1), which pushed us right up the table, but we're still on the coat-tails of Shelbourne who seem to be winning every match and look very strong even at this early stage.

League of Ireland First Division standings, 5th May 2011

Pos	Team	Pl	W	D	L	GF	GA	GD	Pts
1	Shelbourne	8	6	1	1	17	8	+9	19
2	Cork City	8	5	3	0	17	5	+12	18
3	Longford Town	9	6	0	3	12	6	+6	18
4	Monaghan United	8	5	2	1	16	10	+6	17
5	Limerick	8	4	2	2	12	5	+7	14
6	Athlone Town	9	3	3	3	4	10	-6	12
7	Mervue Utd	8	3	1	4	13	13	0	10
8	Waterford	8	3	1	4	6	7	-1	10
9	Wexford Youths	8	1	0	4	8	17	-9	3
10	Finn Harps	8	0	3	5	14	3	-9	3
11	Salthill Devon	8	0	2	6	3	18	-15	2

Friday 6th May 2011

League of Ireland First Division

Turner's Cross, Cork

Cork City FC 1–1 Longford Town

Tonight we managed to salvage a one-all draw against a Longford Town side containing former Man United and Newcastle winger Keith Gillespie, with young Jamie Murphy scoring in the last minute to keep our unbeaten run going. When your team scores last-minute goals like Jamie's, you get the feeling there might be something in reward at the end of the season. Last-minute goals are so telling – they show that the team is determined to succeed and that it believes in itself right to the end, so Jamie's equaliser felt very important to all of us and our fans too. People are now starting to believe we can do it this season. Tommy's delighted but is keen to keep us focused and in control. He knows things are going well though. Next up: Shels in Tolka next Friday – the first time we get to stare them down eye-to-eye this season.

If Monaghan and Limerick were fancied to do well this year, then ourselves and Shels are probably fancied to do even better and perhaps win the league. So we'll all be nervous but excited arriving in Tolka. In a way we're already carrying the expectations of our fans – can we get back to the top table of Irish football?

I love playing in Tolka Park. Even though Shels had a great side a few years back which turned us over a few times, overall the matches there are some of the best moments I've experienced in football. Dalymount has a sparkle when Bohs are doing well, and a sort of understated history, with the abandoned stands and rotting seats of the old stadium behind two sections... St Pat's has a charm of its own, with players often having to walk into the ground through what has always seemed to me to be someone's living room; the team bus pulls up outside an innocuous mid-terrace house, we enter its front door and walk through the living room to get to the ground. When Pat's are going well, Richmond Park (the ground at which I've scored a quarter of my league goals) can be electric. But for me, Tolka can offer something even better.

Tolka has always felt to me like a real, football-designed stadium, one of the first to have four sets of seated stands all around the pitch. The dressing rooms, upstairs in a stand behind one goal, are also decent and there's something professional about the whole set-up. The seats look well maintained, and the pitch is generally in a great condition. The crowd are as tight to the pitch as they are at Turner's Cross, and the Shels side of circa 2004–2008 was a top-class LOI side which came closer than anyone to reaching the group stage of the Champions League. I remember well the days of chasing the likes of Mark Rutherford, Stephen Keddy, Richie Baker, Ollie Cahill, Bobby Ryan and Wes Hoolahan around the pitch. Keddy was technically good and clever, while Rutherford was very quick and ruthless – he could leave you for dead. Baker was combative and brave with an eye for goal. Cahill, who I'd played with at Cork City back in 2000/2001, was athletic and aggressive and a smart winger. Ryan was pacey, slick and tricky, while Hoolahan was innovative with a gifted left foot. Of all these players, of course, it was Hoolahan that went on to make a career for himself in the UK. And while Wes was excellent, I know he would take no disrespect from me stating that on any given day I wouldn't put a lot of difference between him and any of those other wingers. It goes to show the small margins – and sometimes the luck and timing – that play a part in football. No doubt Wes Hoolahan deserved everything and more from his career, and he certainly did everyone in the LOI proud, but if I had to choose prior to a match who I might prefer marking, I'm not sure who I'd pick. It might very well be Wes as we shared the same low centre of gravity, as well as the same pace, and so I enjoyed marking him. Others, such as Cahill or Rutherford, had such pace that you needed to be careful how close you got to them at all times. If you got too close, the space behind you was a real danger point. In any event, such was the level at Shels over a number of years; they had that quality of player, two or three players deep in every position each year. That's one reason, I suppose, that they ended up overspending and that they're back playing in the First Division with us. How the mighty have fallen.

Friday 13th May 2011

League of Ireland First Division

Tolka Park, Dublin

Shelbourne FC 1–1 Cork City FC

Tonight I played left-back as the Cockney Rebel (Danny Murphy) had picked up a red card in the last few minutes of our league cup game against Wexford a few weeks back. Tommy was irate with him as the red had been for foul-mouthing the ref when the game was nearly over. I was displeased also: I might love playing at Tolka but I don't love playing left-back.

When I started out with Cork City in 2000, my chance in the first team had only arrived because I could play with my left foot. Back then, Brian Barry-Murphy had left to go to Preston. Damien Delaney, who was younger than me, was on his way to Leicester. We had some good young defenders coming through – the likes of Alan Bennett, Alan Carey and Damian O'Rourke. Greg O'Halloran also was around, playing in different positions including midfield. These young lads were competing with the established defenders such as Declan Daly, Fergus O'Donoghue, Stephen Napier and Derek Coughlan for a place in the team. Anyway, I got in at left-back under Derek Mountfield, and his assistant and successor Liam Murphy also liked how I played there.

As a right-footed full-back I could do one thing a little better than most left-footed left-backs: I could curl the ball with my right foot over the opposing centre-back's head and behind the opposing right full, for our forward or left-winger to run onto. This type of ball was called 'hitting the corner' and was used a lot more back in those days. It may seem like a fairly agricultural thing to do with the ball, but when you consider the pace of the game, and that you need to be able to pull it off as and when the striker or left-winger makes the run, then you might come to understand that it's not such an easy thing to do. The advantage for a right-footed left-back is that when he hits this ball it curls away from where the opposing keeper would be coming to claim it. A left-footer, on the other hand, hitting the same ball from left-back, will need to be very accurate so that the ball doesn't go too long and into the keeper's area. That nice little deftly-hit curler into the pocket behind the full-back – I mastered that ball.

I played the next few seasons alternating between left and right, but when Pat Dolan came in circa 2004 he had a chat with me about settling into the right-back position and it worked out well, with me playing there ever since.

And now, 10 or 11 years after I mastered that pass, I needed to unveil it once more. I asked myself, 'Can I still hit that ball?'

Thankfully the surface in Tolka was decent tonight and I felt comfortable dropping a few deftly-curled beauties over the right-back as of old. However, I'm not as effective in attack on the left side.

A big part of a good full-back's role in this league is putting decent balls into the box. A simple roll-back from a deep-lying striker or left-winger would allow a left-footed full-back to knock the ball into the box first time with comfort and accuracy. But this requires a high enough skill for one's non-preferred foot. I have a decent enough left foot, but roll a ball back to me (while I'm on the run) to hit into the box and it's 50/50 as to whether the cross will be a good one or not. And if it's not, it'll be either really bad to the first man's feet, or a balloon effort that goes off towards the opposite corner flag. There's always the option of playing it with the outside of the right foot – but that's heavily reliant on the ball back being either totally smooth or predictably bouncy. Most rolled balls in the LOI are neither of those things. So despite the advantage of the ball into the corner, a right-footed left-back is really a limited sort of left-back (with some notable exceptions, such as Denis Irwin) – they're somewhat incomplete and never fully comfortable.

I made sure to thank the Cockney Rebel during the week: 'Can't keep your mouth shut, can you Murph?' Murph, to be fair, had a chuckle as he knows my pain. Anytime I play left-back he can see what I do a little better even than him (those deep-curled balls), but he can also see how my legs get tied up in the final third – whereas he can be excellent attacking in the final third (though I wouldn't fancy his chances doing the same with his right foot!).

Another thing Murph does really well as a full-back is to slide-tackle low and early. I'm different in that I prefer to stay on my feet and marshal the winger backwards or towards the line before engaging with a body movement or a poked-out leg without warning. A great trick is to put your leg through the legs of a player who's attempting to shield the ball; it's a trick that requires balance, timing and patience. Overall I rarely fully commit myself to a tackle if I can avoid it. Murph, on the other hand, would prefer to fully commit, crunch the player and ball in a tackle and then run away with the ball himself. Murph's ability to crunch-tackle and spring up is his masterpiece. It's nearly Roberto Carlos-level in its execution.

In the end I quite enjoyed playing left-back for a change and we saw out a nervy 1–1 encounter with our rivals for the top spot. They looked us in the eye and we didn't blink.

Sunday 15th May 2011

There was a Munster Senior Cup game today against junior side Carrick United. It was an important game for the fringe players, but everybody else was trying to avoid getting picked (most of us had played in Friday's draw against Shels). So at the ground tonight Tommy named a weakened team but still included a few lads who'd played on Friday. Greg was particularly pissed off that I escaped whereas he had to play two games in 72 hours. I did have to sit on the bench, though, which is never much fun.

Munster Senior Cup semi-final

Bishopstown, Cork

Cork City FC 0–1 Carrick United AFC

Coming off, nobody seemed too bothered that we'd lost, but Tommy was on the warpath. He was particularly angry at a few of the fringe players. Woodsy calls these types of games 'career-enders': play badly and you'll be asked to move on. But nobody played well today.

Monday 16th May 2011

The word on the grapevine is that after yesterday's loss Tommy has told a few of the lads that he doesn't want them around anymore. Timmy Kiely, who came back to the club this year on a one-year contract, is apparently one of them. I think it's harsh on him – he has the ability and he's proven it in the past. But sport can be cruel.

The same sort of thing has happened to a lot of the lads when they were in the UK; they were brought into a room by some coach who told them they were no longer needed or wanted. Everyone seems to remember the precise details of who told them and where. There's an acceptance that football is about success or rejection, and rejection means you have to leave. It seems overly harsh to me though. Surely a guy who signs for a year should be given the chance to see out his year?

It may be a coincidence that 'Ding Dong' Denis Behan and 'No-Show' Joe Gamble have recently been released from Hartlepool, but some of our lads reckon there's something in it.

Tuesday 17th May 2011

Today Tommy made us watch the video of our match against Shelbourne. At one point he stopped the tape and announced that he'd been over watching Aston Villa recently and that the keeper had been able to start play by passing the ball on the deck to a dropping midfielder.

'What do yees think of that?' he asked.

Cummins answered for us: 'But that's the Premiership, Tommy.'

'I know, but youse can do it. Yee have to try it at least. That's the problem with this country – youse don't want to try it. So, what do youse think?'

The boys were generally sceptical.

Cummins again spoke for the group: 'We tried it last year Tommy and I think we made too many mistakes from it.'

'Ya, but we're better this year.'

Tommy looked towards me for my contribution, and he could probably tell from my expression that I was sceptical too.

'It might be OK in Tolka or Turner's Cross on good pitches, but not on other pitches in this league,' I said.

'We'll work on it in training and see how it goes from there,' Tommy said.

A bit later, during our training match, goalkeeper Mark 'Nults' McNulty tried passing to our midfielders from the back, but the ball was given away each time. It seems Tommy wants us playing like Ajax, but I don't think we should overcomplicate things – especially not in this league.

Friday 8th July 2011

League of Ireland First Division

Turner's Cross, Cork

Cork City FC 1–0 Salthill Devon FC

Cork City 1-0 Salthill Devon
Shane Duggan's 15-yard strike was enough to give City all three points on the road to promotion. Salthill made it difficult for City on occasions, with the Leesiders found lacking in front of goal for the majority of the game.

Tommy Dunne's men incredibly had seventeen corners to Salthill's one, a statistic which highlight's City's dominance of the game. Newcomer Daryl Horgan was handed a starting place on the right wing, leaving Derek O'Brien on the bench.

The home side should have taken the lead inside the opening minute. Davin O'Neill jinked his way past Salthill's motionless defence, but from five yards out he could only curl his shot onto the upright. …

After the break it was more of the same, with City dominating possession and peppering Salthill's goal. Cummins headed off target again shortly after the restart, but the goal eventually arrived midway through the half. Shane Duggan latched onto a loose ball from 25 yards out, he charged through on goal and his shot bobbled and bounced into the bottom right-hand corner, much to the relief of the 1,700-plus City fans in attendance.

(From www.corkcityfc.ie, 8th July 2011)

We were all over them but struggled to score. Duggy is on fire now after scoring two last week also.

Saturday 9th July 2011

Things are still going well for us in this middle part of season. Even though we recently lost our unbeaten run at home against Waterford, we've managed to win more games in the second third of the season than in the first third and we seem to be motoring along nicely. However, Shelbourne have continued to do even better than us, and seem to be pulling out of everyone's reach.

Our near neighbours and promotion rivals Limerick have just made some interesting signings. After weeks of speculation linking Joe Gamble and Denis Behan to Cork, in the end they've signed for Limerick. Rumour has it that the millionaire businessman JP McManus is involved with Limerick in some way, and so with these signings we now see them as real contenders for promotion. It looks like it'll be ourselves, Limerick, Monaghan and Shels fighting for the two promotion spots, with Shels currently well ahead of the lot.

Meantime, Woodsy's tribulations as assistant manager over the last few weeks have kept me entertained. First he had an altercation with the Mervue manager and ended up with a cut on his head (while Tommy fought off the Mervue manager for him); then last week up in Donegal, in our win against Finn Harps, he had a fracas with our main striker Graham Cummins.

Cummins, it turned out, had been pissed off that Woodsy had shouted at him over something. When young Shane Duggan scored, Cummins came to celebrate with all of us around Duggy, but instead of celebrating with us properly he turned to face the dugout and started pointing and shouting, 'F**k you Billy!' I pushed him back into the celebration huddle and tried to get him to shut up, while being mildly amused by it all.

In the dressing room afterwards, Woodsy had a go at Cummins – rightly so in my opinion. You can't be shouting back at an assistant manager like that. In the showers after the game I took the piss out of Cummins about needing to apologise to Woodsy, but I was half-serious about it. You don't need fellas fighting amongst themselves.

Cummins did eventually apologise to Woodsy in training the following week, saying to me afterwards, 'I told Woodsy that I overreacted alright Hog, now leave me alone ya pr*ck.'

On Tuesday we were brought to training at the Fota Sheraton Hotel to help them learn how to deal with a football team in advance of Birmingham staying there next week before they play us in a friendly. The training pitch at Fota was outstanding, but it was difficult to find, and as a result a few of the lads – including me – were late. I half-expected Tommy to have a go at me, but it was Woodsy – who was also late – that was the focus of Tommy's ire while the rest of us were sent to warm up.

Running around the pitch, we all looked back and laughed as Woodsy got his ear bent. When we finished our lap and arrived back to them, things were tense and remained so for the rest of the session. Poor Woodsy.

We're still in with a chance of promotion, and to help matters Tommy's signed two new players. One of them is a lad from Galway named Daryl Horgan, who played in front of me yesterday and looked good. He's a proper winger – likes to get wide, take his man on and get a cross in. I think he'll do well with us. The other is a striker from somewhere in the UK and he looked good in training though he didn't tog out yesterday. He turned up in a leather jacket to the bus and Greg asked him where he'd parked his bike, while Woodsy suggested we should have a fashion test for new players before we sign them from now on.

Over my years at the club, as may be the case in many other clubs, I've noticed there's always at least one player that's fighting hard to get back from an injury – and in doing so may be fighting for his career. Just lately, that person has been Cathal Lordan.

The younger brother of Cillian (Lordy), Cathal made his way into our first team back in 2007 during Damien

Richardson's time at the club, following his return from an FA Youth Cup-winning Ipswich side. However, after falling out of favour with Rico he left the club (and football) back in 2008/2009, only to return last year. He's a very creative player and extremely comfortable on the ball; the kind of player that has the vision and ability to see a subtle and penetrating pass before others – and to pull it off too. But, devastatingly for Cathal, he ruptured his ACL last year which ruled him out until now and he's been trying to make his way back under Tommy recently – with no little difficulty. I've been doing a little extra with him after training, trying to help him turn, but he's still somewhat uncertain of his knee, which is terrible for the guy. I'm hoping he still has a long career ahead in the game as he's a proper ball-player when he gets going. However, I'm not sure Tommy will allow him much more time, given his swiftness to let go of other players recently.

Chapter Four – Interview with Cathal Lordan, February 2019

Neal Horgan: Cathal, explain how you started out…

Cathal Lordan: I played with Ballincollig underage. We had a very good side; there were a couple of good sides in the league during that time, with strong players all over Cork. We had some brilliant footballers at Ballincollig, and I remember once getting an invite to a five-a-side game at Ballincollig Community School where the likes of Colin Healy, Liam Miller, Alan Carey, John Cotter, Mark McNulty and my brother Cillian were playing. There were other groups with great footballers that we used to play against on the street or in the green – a guy named Paul Fenton who signed for Nottingham Forest, and also David O'Sullivan who was an Irish underage international – football was constantly competitive in Ballincollig at the time, which was really great.

NH: That's a high concentration of good footballers; you were lucky to be exposed to that volume of talented players.

CL: Yeah, it was excellent… there was a lot of talent around the place… The cul-de-sac where I lived was quite something also. You had a guy named Darren O'Connor who went to Colchester, ended up coaching in the US; you had Susan O'Donovan and Zoe Murphy, both of whom became Irish underage internationals; you had Patrick Cronin who became Cork's hurling captain. We used to play every sport – we had nothing better to do at the time. It was great, but it's not the same now.

NH: How did you end up moving to Ipswich?

CL: In or around Kennedy Cup time, when I was 14, a few lads from the Cork Schoolboys League were asked by a scout to go to Leicester, then after the Kennedy Cup I ended up going to six clubs overall: Man City, Wolves, Ipswich, Forest, Leicester (again) and Southampton. In general, they were really good experiences. You're quite young and you're out of your comfort zone and there's a lot of emotion you go through, but I think that's really important and a lot of that stood me in good stead when I finally moved over to England. At some of the clubs on trial you could find it quite difficult to get through the week, but they were all unbelievable experiences really; extremely challenging, especially at such a young age.

NH: Were there a few of you, or did you go on your own?

CL: It varied. On occasion I would go on my own, but usually there were a few of us from Cork and Ireland that went together. We would spend days or a week there, and then the club would decide if they wanted you. I was lucky to have a choice between Nottingham Forest and Ipswich, and I chose Ipswich.

NH: Why was that?

CL: Even though one or two of the clubs we'd visited were quite good – I enjoyed Leicester and Southampton to an extent – Ipswich was by far the best. It was really homely and welcoming and there were lots of Irish there, and the English lads at Ipswich were really good lads, which was important.

NH: You discovered this during your trials?

CL: Yeah – we'd have a week here and there, between mid-terms first week of New Year and Christmas, etc.

NH: And who was interacting with you?

CL: My old Ballincollig coach, Paul Doyle. He became an Ipswich scout not long after I signed there, so anytime I went over, either him or one of the Dublin scouts – who were lovely guys too – came with us, so that made it a bit easier.

NH: Do you remember signing?

CL: Yeah, I think it was a trial during February mid-term break, or maybe later in the year, and they offered me a pre-contract. Paul had gone over with me and I spoke with him straight after it happened, and then I rang my parents. It was a year before I was to move over there; it was February 2002 and I was signing to move over in the summer of 2003.

NH: That must've felt brilliant…

CL: It was fantastic. I knew from the age of 10 what I wanted to do and who I wanted to be, and I became so focused on working towards that goal. Everything went into it – even to my own detriment. Education in particular took a back seat.

NH: So how long was your contract with Ipswich?

CL: I signed a three-year contract. We were the last of the three-year YTS – scholarship programmes. We were set up living with a family but there was a section separated for us players. There were other Irish there: Billy Clarke from Cork was sharing a room with me, Shane Supple was in the room next to us, and Michael Synnott, and then a year later Owen Garvan arrived. All of us and one English and one Turkish lad: it was great. When we started out it was under-16s, then under-18s, and then reserves. Later I think that changed to 17s/19s and reserves, but I could be wrong. So with the 16s you were trying to move to play with the 18s; that was the focus. We had training every morning, double sessions most days except for Wednesdays when we had school.

NH: Was that the only day you had school?

CL: Yeah.

NH: What was school like?

CL: It was quite poor overall. Later on there was a guy called Sammy Morgan from Northern Ireland who came in and changed everything for the better, and it's completely different at Ipswich now. But the education on offer was really bad when I first started.

NH: What did it involve?

CL: In the first year we went to a local high school, a local sixth-form class, and did basic maths and English, but we were more of a distraction and a disruption to the others in the class than anything else. So they don't do that anymore – it's now private schooling within their academy. In the second year we went to Otley College in Ipswich and did a course that might be the equivalent of a FETAC course over here, in anatomy and physiology and things like that.

NH: And none of that really helped when you came back to Cork?

CL: No. I was starting from scratch education-wise when I came back.

NH: But you got a brilliant footballing education at Ipswich?

CL: Yeah I did, and things went well on the pitch. In my second year things started to go really well. We won the FA Youth Cup; I scored two in the first leg in the final against Southampton and we ended up beating them, which was great. On the other hand, while I was doing really well with the youth team every week, the reserve manager wasn't giving me a look in – which was a problem as that was now my next step. I was getting very frustrated and I nearly left Ipswich at the end of my second year, as I knew the reserve manager wasn't a big fan of me as a player. I got in touch with an agent – it was Liam Miller's agent: Liam's mother had given my mother the agent's number, but the guy had a conflict of interest as he was involved in a deal with Ipswich at the time and he didn't want to mess with that by taking me from the club before my deal was up. Anyway, a move didn't work out for me at that point, but looking back I probably should have left then after the Youth Cup final when my stock was at its highest, as they say. When I went into the reserves in my third year the reserve manager still wasn't giving me a look in. It took me two or three months just to be part of his side... and it didn't really work out in the end. So I saw out the last few months of my contract and had an offer to come back to Cork.

NH: What was returning to Cork City FC like?

CL: Well, I came back on trial, in April/May 2006. You guys had just won the league and you had a very strong side. There were some exceptional players; the training ground wasn't fantastic but training itself was very competitive – but overall, looking back now, it was a bad decision for me.

NH: Why's that?

CL: Well, at the time the emphasis at Cork City FC was on winning and winning alone, and you had a very experienced team. Understandably, therefore, the interest in developing young players wasn't the priority. Rico [Damien Richardson] wanted to win the league again, which was fair enough. But that meant that with the likes of Joe Gamble, Colin O'Brien and George O'Callaghan still there from the year before it was going to be tough for me to break through, and as I've said I felt there wasn't really an emphasis on developing young players, like there might've been at previous times in the club's history.

NH: I didn't think about that at the time... In fact, did any young player come into that side?

CL: Roy [O'Donovan] did.

NH: But he was 20 or 21, wasn't he?

CL: Yeah, maybe.

NH: Timing is important. Also, the difference between being 19 and 20/21 can be a big thing. It was that way for me, actually – I couldn't get into the Cork City first-team squad back in 1998 and 1999 because Dave Barry's side at that time was trying to win the league. But then Barry left in 2000 and Liam Murphy decided to give youth a chance, and things changed for me at the age of 20.

CL: Yeah, I know what you mean, and I actually got into the side the following season in 2007 when I'd turned 20. I think I started the first five league games and played the Setanta Cup games and did well. We won all five of those league games and then Rico dropped me away up at St Pat's and we lost. In fairness to Mick Devine, I remember him in the dressing room afterwards saying to Rico in front of everyone, 'Why did you drop Cathal?'

NH: Good old Mick!

CL: Yeah, I felt at least someone had recognised my performances over the previous games. But it didn't make any difference – I was out of the team after that even though I was training really well. I remember wondering what I had to do to get back into the team. By that time Georgy had left but Joe Gamble was still there and you had Colin Healy and Gareth Farrelly becoming available, and Darren [Crazy Daz] Murphy joined. So then it was becoming more difficult to even get on the bench and it just made me question what position I was in.

NH: Three senior internationals and Crazy Daz in front of you for the central midfield spots?

CL: Yes, but after that I let myself down a little too.

NH: How?

CL: Well, I was young and a little stupid. I'd been away from home for so long; I kind of got caught up in the culture that your group had going at the time.

NH: The drinking culture?

CL: Yeah. You guys were able to enjoy yourselves at the weekend and I got caught up in that – but I wasn't an established player. I shouldn't have been going out with you guys, thinking back now; I should've just been training harder. I kind of got out of it though when a loan move to Waterford arose. Gareth Cronin was manager there and he looked out for me; I was playing and it was going well, and I was away from Cork a bit so that helped. But then the season ended and Rico released me from Cork. Waterford got relegated that season but Gareth still offered me a contract. But then Rico got sacked at the start of the following year [2008] and Alan Mathews came in, and I thought there might be a chance to get a contract. So I trained back with Cork under Mathew's assistant Skee McGee, who was doing pre-season for three or four weeks while Mathews was training his replacement at the bank up in Dublin. I was doing really well and I was super-fit; I remember being in the top five in every run, doing great in possession games. I thought, 'This is it now – someone's got to give me a chance.' Then Alan Mathews came back, played me in a pre-season friendly for about 15 minutes on the right wing away to Shels on some school pitch, and then told me the next day that I wasn't in his plans. I was gutted: I'd spent two months busting my balls and he'd hardly seen me play.

NH: Where did you go from there?

CL: I became disillusioned with the game and I hated Cork City. I felt I'd been rejected from football again and I just got a job at what's now Dell EMC and played football locally. I didn't enjoy that time looking back; it felt like bottom-of-the-barrel type of stuff. Not being given a chance, not knowing where to go or what to do, and I was annoyed with myself for getting caught up with the culture you guys had. When I'd first come back from Ipswich I remember I was always able to use my own strengths in training. Even though other lads were bigger and stronger, I was able to stamp my way of playing… but then that went and I lost my way. Myself and Cillian always butted heads on it, because he could see it happening and tried to help me, but I'd already taken a knock from Ipswich and when you get told this, it's not just your job – it's your identity being torn up too. It was very difficult for a long time.

NH: That's not surprising. You'd been focusing on this since you were 10; it had seemed to be making sense as you went on the trials, got offered a three-year contract, moved over, won a FA Youth Cup and got the pro contract with Cork City. Then within a year or two it's over and you're out of football. That's brutal.

CL: Yeah, it is. It's probably the biggest issue for young lads that leave the game – not knowing who they are or where they're going. And there's a real lack of support too.

NH: But then you came back to play with Cork City in 2011?

CL: Well I actually came back the year before, in 2010. I'd probably reached my lowest point just before that – I was 21, I'd dropped out of football and was just working. But then around early 2010 I was asked by Stuart Ashton and Paul Bowdren to play with Cork City in an under-21 futsal tournament in Limerick. Ray Lally and a few other lads were playing, and we won the competition in the Munster region and then did well afterwards in the All-Ireland series, getting to the semi-final. After that I got selected for the Irish under-21 futsal team for the European qualifying tournament. We went to Barcelona in a pre-season tournament – we played the

Barcelona reserves professional futsal team. They were incredible…

NH: Class.

CL: Yeah, it was brilliant. Dane Massey, now of Dundalk, was the captain of the Irish side and he scored when we beat the reserves one-nil. We played another Catalonia side too. They were class, all real footballers as well. It was a brilliant experience – futsal's big on the continent. We watched the senior Barcelona futsal team playing in an 8,000-seater stadium in the Barcelona complex: they were all fantastic footballers. Then we went to Andorra and did OK, played a class Dutch national side, but in the end we didn't qualify for the elite tournament.

NH: The Dutch were good?

CL: Yeah, they were. There was this one Dutch guy – we were looking at him before the game – he was a tall, heavy guy; he didn't look like a footballer. We thought he must've been the goalkeeper, but then during the game he was playing up front and he was unbelievable. His acceleration over three or four yards was immense and he got a hat-trick against us.

NH: You don't have to move around the pitch as much in futsal, right?

CL: Yeah, you just need to be really clever and skilful.

NH: So after that, how did you end up back with the senior Cork City side?

CL: Cillian was captain of Cork City at the time, in 2010, and had a good relationship with Tommy. About five or six games into the first season under FORAS, Tommy asked Cillian if he thought I'd be interested in coming back. He must've heard I'd done well with that Irish futsal team – but apart from the futsal, I'd been out of football a long time. Anyway, I came out training one Monday and Tommy asked me to sign amateur forms the next day, and I started a league game the following Friday against Athlone. It was great: I was playing and enjoying it again. I played the next 10 games in the middle of the park; there were three of us in the middle –

Cilly, Shane Duggan and me – and we were doing well and had a nice balance between us. I was finding myself again as a footballer really, and getting fit. Plus, I was just about to start a course at UCC [University College Cork] part-time, so for me it felt like I'd been given a second chance. Cork City were on the rise and we started to put together some good results, and it all seemed to be coming together for me both on and off the pitch. Even though I'd started in college, I felt like some of my performances had shown glimpses of the old me and that there still might be some sort of career in football for me. But then I got injured.

NH: It happened in training, didn't it?

CL: Yeah, it did. The last match I'd played before it happened was against Derry and I'd done really well, got man of the match – and that was the year Derry went on to win the First Division at a canter. It was one of the best games I'd played in years, and again I remember feeling things were coming together for me. At that point I came to a verbal agreement with Tommy that I'd sign part-time terms until the end of the year, so I was going to get a small amount of money to play football while I was in college, which was great. Then the following match was at home against Athlone; it was unusual for the fact that it was at the Cross on a Saturday afternoon at 4 or 5pm and we trained on the Friday night. On that Friday during a training game, Mul [Stephen Mulcahy] had the ball and Davy Warren was on my back. Mul passed it to my right and I went to chop the ball and spin Davy all at once but my foot stayed where it was and my body went the other way… and I heard a pop. Next thing I was on the ground and could feel myself getting sick. I was in agony. It was a big shock as I'd been doing so well. But they did a test on my knee and said it was just bone bruising, that it wasn't my ACL. I had an MRI, just to be sure, and the radiologist confirmed it was only bruising. I felt like I'd dodged a bullet. I spent the next six weeks doing rehab with our physio at the time, Rob Savage; he was great and spent a lot of time trying to get me back. Then, six weeks into the rehab I remember running around a cone one day, really just jogging lightly, and my knee collapsed. I went to a specialist the following week and he told me my cruciate had gone and I'd need an operation. I was devastated, but I got the op done the following week. They told me afterwards that when they'd opened it up, my knee was in a bad way. I took in my previous scan to show them and it turned out that the original radiologist had got it wrong – my cruciate had actually gone in training that day before the Saturday game some six or seven weeks previously, and I'd been running around on it since then. That was bad, but worse was the nine months that I was out after the op. I managed to get back for pre-season in 2011, but the knee still didn't feel right. I got another MRI done and was told that they'd missed another tear which was now catching between my joints and so I needed another operation, meaning another six months out. So by the time I made it back towards the end of the 2011 season, I'd spent the best part of 18 months out since that match against Derry.

NH: That's nightmare stuff.

CL: From a footballing point of view, yes it was. But even then I got back and played in the last few games of the 2011 season, including a win away at Finn Harps and another game – two 20-minute cameos. Of course, I felt like a newborn giraffe walking for the first time, falling around the place... you know the way the legs feel after a long-term injury. Then, to be fair to Tommy, he put me on the bench for the last game against Shels – which was great, but I'd missed out on the season really and Gearóid Morrissey had come into midfield and done well. Then we ended up signing Healers in 2012, so I struggled to get back in. For the first 10 or so matches of the 2012 season, Tommy would bring me on quite late in games. I'd started to improve again in training, but I needed game time. I was in that cycle where you're on the bench and not getting game time, with the first 11 or 13 players that were playing every week moving ahead. So I was always off the pace to a certain extent, but the big thing for me was that I'd just finished the first year of a sports studies/PE course, so things were getting back on track in that regard.

NH: How did you find the college experience?

CL: It was probably the most challenging experience I've ever had; I found it so overwhelming at the beginning. I'd been out of education for so long. I started with a night course, three hours a week at Colaiste Stiofáin Naofa, just to see how I'd find it. Small steps... It was really Cillian that had pushed me to go back to education after I left Cork City for the first time in 2008. He'd been in college during part of his Cork City career and he recognised how unpredictable football was as a career option in Ireland. He was the one who kept pushing me to look down different career paths in case football didn't work out. Looking back, I was lucky that I had him to guide me, along with parents who were extremely supportive throughout.

NH: So you went to Stiofáin Naofa and then to UCC after that?

CL: Yeah, after Stiofáin Naofa I started at UCC on a one-year part-time course. The careers office at UCC had told me I needed to build up my CV, do foundation badges in coaching, and do the one-year course as a mature student the following year. So I only did history for the first year in UCC. I'd been out of school since I was 15 or 16, and at that time it was only really in Leaving Cert subjects that you learned research, structuring, essay-writing skills, how to bring different information together... I'd not done any of that as I'd left school in fourth year. I'd signed a pre-contract by the time I was 14 or 15 and I wasn't focused on being academic back then. So this was really tough, seven years later. It helped that I'd made that smaller step back into it with just history to complete in the first year – but I still found it really, really hard. There seemed to be so much information in front of me; tonnes of books when I was only writing a 1,000 or 1,500-word essay. I remember wondering how the hell I was going to do it, to refine it. So much information to analyse and bring together… where would I start? It was difficult to find a process as this was so new to me, but I managed to get through it and became more confident in my own method. But I knew that if I passed history there was a good chance I'd get selected as one of the mature students for the sports studies/PE course. And that's what happened in the end. I completed a four-year degree in physical education; my career outside of football was finally taking shape.

NH: And so you ended up leaving Cork City at the end of 2012?

CL: Yeah. It was difficult, as I thought I'd been doing well – but that's football. And so I moved on to UCC's side.

NH: And John Caulfield was manager of UCC, wasn't he? How did you find football there?

CL: It was great, and it was really good to have Caulfield there. But it was a huge change for me overall. The first year was very good as I'd grown up in a soccer bubble with soccer friends – even my friends outside of soccer were soccer lads. Football had been my identity for a long time. Now I was meeting college guys from all different backgrounds. It was a fantastic and eye-opening experience for me… probably my favourite soccer experience since England, as I felt my horizons were broadening.

NH: So you were finally getting a broader view, discovering that there were other things out there that might be as rewarding as football?

CL: Yeah – and I hadn't been able to see that when I was in the soccer bubble. When I used to come home from England and my friends were in college I'd hang out with them occasionally, but I just didn't get the college thing. I used to think, 'That's not for me.' But when I became part of it, it was much better than I'd thought. I was 24 at this stage and luckily there were a few mature students, and lads like Stephen Mahon and Andy Neville, who I got on well with. It was a great time; I enjoyed the Munster Senior League and even won a Collingwood [Cup] eventually.

NH: And after UCC you ended up moving into teaching?

CL: Yeah, I did my HDip at Rochestown College and I've been working there ever since, teaching PE and history and also coaching some of the school teams.

NH: So you stayed in the game… was that important?

CL: For a long time I looked at it like that – staying in the game – but I've moved away from that mentality. I'm just coaching as I enjoy it now, and that's all. I also coached Cork City women's team and then the UCC freshers with you, and they were both enjoyable experiences.

NH: Happy days with the freshers…

CL: Yeah, they were. The lads were great, weren't they? And the women's team with Frank Kelleher – that was great too. Now I'm coaching with the Cork City under-17s, thanks to Colin Healy; he gave me the opportunity and I took it. And although I'm enjoying it all, at the same time I can take or leave my involvement with soccer now – which is a big change from when I was starting out.

NH: It's brilliant that you've picked yourself up after everything that's happened and can still enjoy the game.

CL: It took a long time, though. I didn't watch Cork City for years; I found that very difficult. It was a challenging transition but I enjoy coaching, and now that I'm back at Cork City I hope to help some of the younger players have some positive experiences in football. I'm very lucky to have parents that have supported me constantly and were behind every decision I made, and I was also fortunate to have someone like Cillian looking out for me; if it weren't for that I don't know what would've happened or what path I would've taken. So that's maybe something I can put back into the game – be a helpful voice for the up-and-coming players like Cillian was for me. I've learned a few hard lessons that I might be able to pass on. Thankfully I do enjoy watching Cork City these days, and in particular I love seeing young players coming through the club and getting a chance to become professional players while living in Cork. That's really great to see, and FORAS deserve great credit for the work they've done that's allowed it to happen.

Chapter Five – 23rd July to End of Season 2011

Saturday 23rd July 2011

Our mid-season break starts tomorrow and Tommy had been barking at us all week not to take our eyes off today's game at Longford. And despite us coming in one-one at half-time, Tommy nearly lost his head in the dressing room. He reminded me a lot of Doolo at his worst, jibing us for every little thing. Woodsy, for his part, tried to calm him down and in the end we went back out and won the game 3–1.

League of Ireland First Division

Flancare Park, Longford

Longford Town FC 1–3 Cork City FC

All the lads were delighted afterwards. Most of us have holiday flights booked for tomorrow, but Tommy warned us not to go overboard.

'We're playing Shels the week after youse come back, so youse better be right, I'm telling youse.'

I'm flying out of Dublin airport tomorrow morning to go to Oslo for the week with my girlfriend Caroline, so I arranged to catch a lift to the hotel with Tommy and his Dad as they were driving from Longford to Dublin – leaving Woodsy and the boys to take the bus back to Cork.

Oslo probably seems an unusual destination in comparison to most of the lads' choices (they're generally heading south) – and it'll seem even more unusual after the terrible tragedy that befell the city yesterday. When a colleague at work broke the news to me that a bomb had gone off there, I really thought she was joking. Unfortunately, it was true.

'Our hotel's near where the first bomb went off, but we're going anyway,' I told Tommy and his Dad as we headed towards Dublin.

Tommy's Dad, Theo, was to prove great company for the journey. A former Shamrock Rovers and Shelbourne player, he didn't let 10 minutes pass without mentioning the time his Shels team beat Cork Hibernians in the FAI Cup final, way back. He may have been trying to motivate either myself or Tommy, but instead I got him talking about the Dunne family, who are synonymous with the great schoolboy club 'Home Farm' in Dublin – and whose most recent celebrated output is Tommy's first cousin, Richard Dunne.

'Ah, Richard's done well. He's a good lad,' said Theo with understated pride.

He told me about the time he was managing UCD and they nearly knocked out eventual winners Everton (one of the clubs Richard played for) in the European Cup Winners' Cup. 'Peter Reid said afterwards that it was their most difficult game of the whole tournament,' he boasted – this time unreservedly.

As we were approaching the airport hotel in Dublin, Theo said, 'Ah, youse need Cork back in the Premier League for it to be a proper league.'

'But who will you support when we play Shels in the last game of the season?' I asked.

He thought about it for a second before winking at Tommy and answering, 'Cork, of course.'

I got out, thanked Tommy for the lift, wished his Dad good luck and went to get my bag out of the boot.

Then it hit me: I'd put the wrong bag in Tommy's boot. I was meant to put this bag – which held just my dirty boots, shin guards and used gear – back on the bus. My second bag, all packed for Oslo with folded clothes, was sitting on the bus back to Cork.

I felt a cold sweat breaking out on my forehead.

'What's wrong?' asked Tommy, noticing the look of horror on my face.

I told him what I'd done and he laughed his head off. He took my useless gearbag from me and jumped back into the car to tell Theo. I walked away, but then I heard the screech of his tyres and turned to see Tommy reversing the car at speed towards me.

He braked near my foot and as he did so his head popped out the window, 'And another thing,' he said, 'that's a bleedin' fiver for leaving your gear behind.'

Tommy drove away, he and Theo laughing into the darkness as it dawned on me that I'd be walking around the shattered Norwegian capital in my shiny Cork City FC tracksuit.

~~~~~

Elsewhere, No-Show was sent off for Limerick yesterday as he and Denis made their debuts in a loss against Monaghan.

The promotion race is heating up.

Sunday 31st July 2011

Oslo was beautiful; a city in mourning, but a beautiful city nonetheless. Walking through the sombre streets, we came across crowd upon crowd of mourners. Every one of them, from the youngest to the very oldest, was carrying a red or white rose in a show of unity and respect for the victims. It was so desperately sad, but you could really feel the strength of the city through its people – even on this, the darkest of days.

We got out of the city as soon as we could. This was no place for tourists. We travelled to Gothenburg in Sweden and passed their impressive football stadium. I thought about explaining to Caroline how Cork City had triumphed in the home leg against Gothenburg in the UEFA Cup in 1999, of how this was but one of many triumphs that we'd had over Swedish opposition (even if Gothenburg had won the tie 3–1 on aggregate). I thought of Liam Kearney's lovely volley in Malmo, of Neale Fenn's turn and strike against Djurgårdens in the Råsunda Stadium… but sensing that Caroline may not have been fully over my tracksuit and suitcase debacle, I held my tongue.

And it was a real bonus to come home to a suitcase of clean and folded clothes. Jerry Harris had a good laugh at me when handing over the suitcase. He said that while he'd recovered many interesting lost items for players over the years, this was a first.

Tommy had organised a double session for our first day back – in Cork's 'Collins' military barracks. Some of the lads feared we'd be put through military routines, but in fact we were just using their training pitch and Tommy took us on a light enough session with a bit of running in the middle.

During the running he jibed at me, 'Come on, Hogs – you're not in Oslo anymore.'

F**k off Tommy, I thought.

We finished at 12 and Tommy told us there were sandwiches organised for 12.15 but we weren't to be back on the pitch until 3pm.

'Three o'clock?' asked Davin in disbelief.

'Ya, three o'clock. Yez can eat your grub, have a rest and come back. It's bleedin' perfect.'

This *would* have been perfect if we were full-time, but everyone's part-time now and a few of us are amateurs, which is a different story altogether. If we trained at 3pm that would mean a 9.30–5.30 training day, on a Sunday. In our opinion this was beyond the part-time training limit – and Tommy knew he was pushing it. We ganged up on him so that we'd finish earlier, and in the end he agreed. 'OK, OK – back for two o'clock, yez moaning b*****ds, but youse better get up there quick and get fed so. For f**k's sake!'

~~~~

This evening the Cork senior footballers, in a surprise result, lost to Mayo in the quarter-final of the All-Ireland. Their defeat means that the Cork club championship (which as usual was suspended while the Cork senior footballers played in the All-Ireland) will restart and that my Barrs championship match will be played next weekend – meaning I'll miss the Shels game. Tommy's gonna have a meltdown.

Monday 1st August 2011

We trained this morning as it's a bank holiday. I felt it was best to tell Tommy now and get it over with. I told Woodsy first during the warm-up.

'F**k – he'll crack up,' was Woody's estimate.

'I know,' I said, 'but what can I do? I told him at the start that this would happen.'

'I know, I know,' said Woodsy, 'but he'll hit the roof – you know that, don't you?'

We did the warm-up and some passing drills, during which Tommy – only half-joking – shouted another jibe about my head still being in Oslo.

I didn't react.

After this, Tommy announced we'd break into a full-sided 11-v-11 game. I knew I needed to tell him before he picked the teams, as he might be preparing for the Shels match. I called him aside.

'Do you have two seconds, Tom?' I asked awkwardly as he was about to read out the team sheets.

'Ah for you Hogs, of course. What's up? Are you still blocked up from the Oslo sandwiches, is that it?' he asked, laughing.

'No Tom,' I said, pulling him aside. 'Did you hear how the Cork senior footballers lost yesterday against Mayo?' Maybe not. 'Well…' as I said this I noticed a distinct tint of red spread across his face, '…that means I'm probably gonna be stuck for playing next week.'

'Wha…? That's the bleedin' Shels game!' his anger increased.

'Ya, I know…'

'For f**k's sake, Hogs!'

'I know, and I wanted to tell you now before you make the teams out for this 11-v-11, in case you were preparing to…'

'For f**k's saaaaake! Can't they give me more f**king notice?'

'They only lost yesterday so…' I explained, turning to jog back to the lads.

'For f**k's sake! It's a bleeding joke – that's what it is!' Tommy ranted.

I didn't play well in the 11-v-11 game; in fact nobody did, and Tommy seemed very upset with us all afterwards.

When we'd finished the game he pulled winger Derek O'Brien aside and they soon entered into a heated argument about Derek's defending. Unfortunately I still needed to tell Tommy that I won't be able to make training tomorrow either as I'll be training with the Barrs, so I had to wait until he was finished with Derek.

Their argument grew into a shouting match, and at that point notorious local scribe Noel Spillane ('Spillachi'), crept up alongside me.

'Jesus, Noel,' I said, 'have you been hiding in the bushes?'

'Ha, no,' he laughed as he readied his 1970s audio recorder.

'I won't do a piece right now Noel, if you don't mind.'

'No bother,' he said, 'but what's the story? The Barrs championship will kick in now, won't it?'

I explained the situation to him briefly as Derek passed us, clearly enraged following his confrontation with Tommy.

Spotting his opportunity, Spillachi quickly finished with me and approached Tommy with recorder ready in hand.

I spotted my chance also: 'I won't be there tomorrow either, Tom!' I shouted from behind Spillachi while walking backwards.

But my trick didn't work. Tommy said to Spillachi, 'Just two seconds, Noel,' and came marching over to me so that he was out of Noel's earshot.

'I'm not f**king happy with you,' he said in a low voice.

'Sure there's nothing I can do about it; we knew this would happen from the start,' I countered.

'Ya, but it's the biggest game of the season, Hog,' he said.

'But every game is the biggest game – aren't you always saying that?'

'I know Hogs, but come on, for f**k's sake.'

We left it at that.

Thursday 4th August 2011

I received a call from the *Irish Examiner* this evening asking for an interview. I politely declined.

The guy continued, 'Well I just want to let you know that we're probably going to run a piece on you anyway, in relation to playing GAA over soccer.'

'OK, well thanks for letting me know, but I have no comment.'

Friday 5th August 2011
Horgan opts for GAA in fixture dilemma
GAELIC football has won out over soccer in an agonising battle for Cork City defender Neal Horgan's sporting affections this weekend.

Cork City host Shelbourne tonight in a key top-of-the-table clash in the Airtricity League First Division as Tommy Dunne's charges, currently in second place, seek to make inroads into Shelbourne's 10-point advantage.

But they will have to plan without their experienced defender Horgan as he is involved with St Finbarr's as they face city rivals Na Piarsaigh in the fourth round of the Cork senior football championship tomorrow afternoon.

Horgan is focusing his attentions on the Togher club's clash which takes place in Páirc Uí Rinn at 3.30pm. The 31-year-old, a key member of City's 2005 Premier Division-winning side, returned to the St Finbarr's senior football setup last season. He grabbed a starting berth at wing-back during their senior football campaign only for their county title hopes to be dashed when they suffered a final defeat to Nemo last October.

(Fintan O'Toole, *Irish Examiner*, 5th August 2011)

I've played for about 12 seasons at Cork City FC and it's unusual for me to get a headline on my own – particularly in a broadsheet. So it's going to be difficult for me to explain this to people around the city over the coming weeks. My reasons – that I had a prior commitment which Tommy and the club knew about, and that (apart from the free boots) I'm a volunteer, for God's sake, training every second day and travelling every second weekend to help put the club back where it belongs – are long enough to communicate.

And while I knew Tommy wouldn't be delighted with the headline either, today I didn't feel like defending myself to anybody. It did annoy me that the article said GAA had 'won over soccer', despite 'this weekend' being added at the end of the sentence.

I enjoy both sports – wouldn't that have been a better angle? It seems to me that we have a legacy issue with these two sporting codes (Gaelic games and soccer), and that we always seem to have to face one against the other as if they're opponents. And that legacy is being imposed upon me in this article.

Whatever the historical issues, it's just silly these days, and it's something we need to move on from as a sporting country.

Anyway, I turned up in the dressing room in my tracksuit (but without a gearbag) about an hour before kick-off to wish the lads the best. I felt slightly embarrassed, but f**k it. Tommy asked, 'How ya, Hog?' in a stressed-out-but-making-an-effort sort of way – which I appreciated. I sat down and picked up one of the match programmes. The league table illustrated the scale of the game, with Shels being so far ahead and Monaghan and Limerick on our tails.

Pos	Team	Pl	W	D	L	GF	GA	GD	Pts
1	Shelbourne	19	16	2	1	40	11	+29	50
2	Cork City	19	11	7	1	35	13	+22	40
3	Monaghan Utd	19	12	4	3	36	19	+17	40
4	Limerick	19	11	4	4	24	14	+10	37
5	Longford Town	20	9	2	9	24	23	+1	29
6	Waterford Utd	19	8	2	9	20	16	+4	26
7	Mervue Utd	19	7	3	9	24	29	-5	24
8	Athlone Town	19	6	4	9	11	24	-13	22
9	Finn Harps	19	4	3	12	16	27	-11	15
10	Wexford Youths	19	3	0	16	16	37	-21	9
11	Salthill D.	19	1	3	15	9	42	-33	6

I also noticed in the programme that Tommy wasn't hiding from the issue:

Tonight is a big game for us, and offers us an opportunity firstly to remain in the hunt for promotion, and also to close the gap on the league leaders. ... Prior to our last game against Longford I commented that we were now entering the business end of the season. ... Over the course of the season you will always have one or two setbacks or problems, but in general I am happy with the way the squad is shaping up. Neal Horgan's absence tonight as a result of his GAA commitments is an example of this but I believe we are in a much stronger position this year to deal with such issues. Neal's quality and experience are important to us, but the players we have available to us to replace him are certainly up to the standard required, which is a contrast from last season.

(*City Edition*, Volume 28 Issue 12, p.4, 'Tommy's Thoughts')

Not quite *'Everything is fine Neal, obviously, as we anticipated this before the season began'*, but certainly better than *'I'm not f**king happy with you'*. Anyway, Tommy's right: the squad is much stronger this year. He replaced me with Mul, who's being doing very well lately at centre-half. Unfortunately, and devastatingly for Mul, he seriously injured his knee after 10 minutes and was stretchered off the pitch in complete agony. He was replaced by young Turner, in his first real test since the gas incident.

Mul's injury looked bad. It happened – as it so often does – just as he was making real strides towards becoming one of our best players. We're all hoping it isn't going to be as bad as it looked.

At half-time I discovered that former Cork City FC legend and Cork GAA All-Star Dave Barry was seated behind me. We had a brief chat and he made a remark about my choosing the GAA over soccer.

You of all people, I thought, and started to defend myself somewhat aggressively.

He stopped me mid-flow: 'I'm only messing with ya,' he said, laughing.

I apologised, 'Sorry – I'm just a bit stressed and tense about it tonight.'

In the second half the lads, and in particular Turner, played great to win in resounding fashion. The crowd was as big as we've had in a while also, and they were rocking at the end which was great to see.

League of Ireland First Division

Turner's Cross, Cork

Cork City FC 4–1 Shelbourne FC

Afterwards, in the dressing room, Tommy was elated and tried to make a speech but his voice was gone. So he sat down and whispered to Woodsy, who echoed, 'Back in Sunday. And well f**king done lads.'

Saturday 6th August 2011

I was picked to start with the Barrs today, which was somewhat of a relief, all things considered. I played at half-back and we won well, which means that the fixtures might clash again soon. But I don't care tonight – I'm just delighted to be through to the next round.

Friday 12th August 2011

After two great results in the league against Shels and Longford, we also beat Limerick in the semi-final of the League Cup in midweek. So the city's been buzzing with talk of CCFC. The media has been reporting more and more about us lately too. Things are going well – although there's still a long way to go.

So there was a great crowd for our home game against Wexford Youths tonight. Tommy was unhappy that I wasn't available again as I have another GAA match coming up, but Turner's doing very well and I'm delighted for him – especially considering the terrible incident that he was involved in at the start of the season.

I had considered staying away from the dressing room tonight as I felt like a traitor, but when I arrived the lads were all nice about it. Mul was there too, on crutches. It turns out his injury was to his cruciate, which is an absolute disaster for him. I shook his hand and told him I was sorry to hear it. We had a long discussion about the injury and which specialist to use. It turns out he's out of work over it too, which is awful.

When Tommy came in he seemed totally stressed out. We said a tense 'hello' to each other and I asked how he was fixed for tonight. He told me he was down bodies: 'I've lost bleedin' you and Mul, and Davin's out now too.'

League of Ireland First Division

Turner's Cross, Cork

Cork City FC 2–2 Wexford Youths FC

Wexford were very motivated (as they always seem to be against us) and our lads were tired from the games played last week. This could turn out to be a very costly draw. Was it my fault? Tommy might be thinking that. But I was upfront with him from the outset…

I still feel bad, though, and I imagine a few of the lads won't be happy with me. Anyway, I'll get over it.

Saturday 13th August 2011

Shane Long moved from Reading to Premiership side West Brom today for €7 million. As far as I know, CCFC no longer have his sell-on clause. Who has it, then? Just a thought…

Shane, along with Kevin Doyle, was bought by Reading from Cork City midway through 2005. Two great and modest lads, they both quickly prospered in the UK and we've all felt a pride in their achievements over the years. We wouldn't mind the wages they're on either!

Thursday 25th August 2011

Europa League, third qualifying round

Partizan Stadium, Belgrade, Serbia

Partizan Belgrade 1–2 Shamrock Rovers FC

(Shamrock Rovers win 3–2 on aggregate)

Michael O'Neill's Shamrock Rovers did the unthinkable in Europe tonight. The seemingly unachievable.

I caught the last 20 minutes on Setanta Sports: they were lucky but they were also brave. Sully (Pat Sullivan) was unbelievable for them. For us, really. They all were. But Sully seemed to exemplify them. He didn't hold back; he was confident, aggressive, clever and really brave.

Muzza (Dan Murray) played well too and it's apt that he captained the team that finally broke the duck. Watching the replay, when Stevie (Stephen O'Donnell) scored the penalty that put them through you could see Muzza on his own at the other end punching the ground in celebration.

I felt part of that celebration, part of *his* celebration. Well done, buddy. All those years travelling under pressure to play all over Europe against teams far better financed and better prepared, getting stuffed. Well done, Muz.

As for Stevie, I never doubted him when he came forward to take it. And he stuck it. Fantastic – absolutely fantastic.

This result raises the lot of us. The whole league – even the First Division. The radio can't get enough of them and rightly so.

We'd all been getting closer over the years but we needed someone to do it, especially as it seems things have been going backwards lately. And Rovers did it. Fair play.

I see a Cypriot team have made it to the Champions League group stages this year too, which shows what's possible considering we knocked out their champions back in 2006. We were better than them in every sense a few years ago.

Shamrock Rovers make history and enter Europe League
An incredible night for Shamrock Rovers. A ground-breaking night for Irish football. Historic. Brave. Fearless. No amount of adjectives can do it justice.

With one swift swipe of his left foot, Stephen O'Donnell slotted away a 112th-minute penalty to deliver the League of Ireland champions the key to the promised land.

They are in the group stages of the Europa League and today, in Monaco, they will learn their opponents. It will

*present logistical questions that no club from this country has
ever had to deal with before.*

*Either way, Rovers have €1m in the coffers, with more to
come. A mere six years after they faced oblivion, Michael
O'Neill's team will return home today tired after giving every
ounce of energy in their bodies, and withstanding an onslaught
from a Partizan Belgrade side who have the budget to dine
regularly at the top table.*

The Northern Irishman was overcome with pride.

*"If I'm honest, I always felt it would be a step too far," said
O'Neill, when asked about crossing the hurdle into the group
stages. "We've got this squad put together for €600,000. They
probably had players out there who'll earn that alone.*

*"I would doubt whether a club has been able to progress so
far with that level of budget. But it's not just about budget. We
have to try and raise the levels. And the players raised it to
unbelievable levels.*

*"I would have been proud regardless of the result, because
of how they played, but to have players give what they did for
the club and each other, you can't ask for any more than that."*

And, for those endeavours, they will be greeted as heroes.

…

(From the _Irish Independent_, 26th August 2011)

Friday 26th August 2011

It's been a busy couple of weeks. I lost my GAA match to the
West Cork kingpins Castlehaven last week, which was very
disappointing, although in a sense it has made life easier. No
more clashes to worry about. I texted Tommy the next day and
he was good about it.

'I'm sorry yee lost but glad to have you back,' he said,
which I appreciated.

While I was playing GAA the lads had beaten Mervue
away two-one: a great result.

Then we had Wexford away in the FAI Cup tonight. I'd
been worried about Tommy putting me straight back in ahead

of young Turner, but that didn't seem to bother Tommy as he immediately selected me for the first team during training games. I told him after one of them that I felt like a pr*ck.

'Look,' he said, 'the young lad's done well, but I need you in there. If we get promotion then he'll learn even more, won't he? And anyway, I'm going to start him on wide-right against Wexford and I'll put you in at right-back.'

I still felt like a pr*ck, but we ended up beating Wexford.

FAI Cup fourth round

Ferrycarrig Park

Wexford Youths FC 0–1 Cork City FC

It was a tough game. We were struggling to score and then Davin came on and got a worldy. Our second-choice goalkeeper Bilko (James McCarthy) played in goal as Nults had 'been absolutely massacred', according to Tommy, in the game against Mervue and so was out injured. While Bilko did well, Turner was a revelation on the wing, so everyone was happy.

On top of that, young Kalen Spillane – a centre-half with a great left leg – finally started talking and dominating at the back, which was great to see. He's taking responsibility and trusting himself. I told him so afterwards. Talking is so important: not only does it keep you focused in a game, but the information you transfer to your fellow player, in a split second under pressure, can make all the difference.

Afterwards I had to wrench Tommy and the coaching staff out of Wexford Youths' restaurant/clubhouse as they were enjoying the pasta and free wine (as supplied to every team they host) way too much.

'Come on, Tommy,' I said, 'some of us have to work in the morning...'

Monday 29th August 2011

Tommy rang me this morning to ask if I'd rent out my spare room to a lad who's about to sign for the rest of season.

'I'll have to ask my flatmate, but I think it'll be fine Tom,' I said.

Tommy told me the lad was from New Zealand, which I figured would please my flatmate as he'd have an expert onboard for the upcoming Rugby World Cup. However, it also meant I'd have to paint the spare room, which wasn't so pleasing.

The kiwi lad was introduced at the start of today's training game and we were told he'd be around for the rest of the season. But then he played very badly in the training game and Tommy's decided not to sign him after all. My flatmate was disappointed, while I was relieved about the painting.

The real bad news is that I've hurt my knee again. It felt like just a simple twist during training, but it's blown up huge with the swelling tonight.

Tuesday 30th August 2011

At work today everyone was asking why I was limping around like a one-legged pirate. I told them it was just some swelling. I went to training to see our physio Rob Savage; both of us agreed there was nothing much I could do to improve it. The knee's f**ked.

'You'll just have to wait for the swelling to come down and do some exercises that won't hurt it,' said Rob, who's a real gent and very popular with the lads.

In a far worse position is Mul, who also spoke with Rob. He has to wait another three weeks for an operation, and the club has no insurance to pay for his wages so he's had to go on the dole (he's self-employed).

This is one of the downsides of being part-time. If you're full-time and you get injured then your wages have to be looked after by the club; but if you're part-time you're likely to be in trouble – especially if you're self-employed. Come to think of it, I'm not sure how much longer I'll continue to risk playing.

September 2011

During the month of September we won three out of four league games, drawing the first against Limerick. These were important results as they put us in with a shout of going up – especially since Limerick beat Shels, with a last-minute winner from Ding Dong Denis Behan. On the other hand we were knocked out of the FAI Cup by St Pat's, and beaten in the League Cup final by Derry (which was played in Cork).

That final attracted a huge crowd and was televised live, which was great exposure for the club again. In the first half I played better than I had in a while, which made me think I might have something to offer in the Premier Division if we do get promoted. However, my knee swelled up again in the second half – so much so that I had to come off.

In the end we lost one-nil to a penalty, which was no disgrace against Premier Division opposition. The lads were dejected afterwards but sometimes you need to lose the right games to be successful in a season. It's definitely the league games that are most important for the club this season.

The club organised a night out after the final, and as usual the lads took the piss out of what fellas were wearing. Derek O'Brien was dressed 'like a hillbilly', while Woodsy looked like the 'Red Baron' with his Luftwaffe-style leather jacket and comb-over haircut. My 'bowling shoes' took some mocking too.

We were excited to see Roy Keane – who'd been at our match – enter the bar with a few friends. Apparently he's friendly with Tommy from some underage Irish squad that they played in years ago. We were all too nervous to go over to him though, which was probably just as well. As the old saying goes, 'never meet your heroes' – and besides, half of us were balubas…

Neal Horgan

Friday 30ᵗʰ September 2011

Before tonight's match at home against Finn Harps, I told
Tommy that my leg wasn't right.

'OK,' he said, 'but I need you on the bench, and be ready –
we might need you sooner than you think.'

In the first half we were one-up and cruising. Then young
Turner, playing at right-back, made a mistake in attempting to
head the ball back to Nults. It was intercepted and they made it
one-all, and Tommy started to lose it.

'For f**k's saaake!' he roared, jumping all about the place.

Thankfully, young Kalen Spillane stepped up and hit a
rocket of a free kick, and then Davin scored to make it 3–1.
Shortly afterwards, Davin pulled his hamstring and Vinny
Sullivan, whose company I'd been enjoying on the bench, had
to go on even though he's got a cut on the ball of his foot
which made him somewhat limpy as he ran. They scored
again, making it 3–2 at half-time.

In the dressing room, predictably enough, Tommy had a
serious meltdown. He gave out to all the starting players one
by one, and then he started giving out to Nults, who responded
by shouting back. Then Tommy and Nults stood up and were
almost head-to-head before a few of the lads pushed them
apart.

After things had quietened down a bit, Tommy said to
Nults, 'Take your top off Mark,' and then turning to Bilko he
said, 'Go out and warm up; you're coming on, son.'

Woodsy tried to intervene: 'Tommy, it's a f**king
argument! Don't lose a sub over it!'

But Tommy was adamant. 'Out you go Bilko, get warmed
up.'

Bilko duly headed out to warm up in front of the Shed End.

A few minutes later Tommy had calmed down and he
asked Nults, 'How do you feel, Mark – are you up for it?'

Nults, who had thrown his jersey onto the ground,
answered, 'What?'

'Are you up for it? I need you to be right.'

Nults grabbed his jersey off the floor. 'Yeah, damn right I am. Come on then.'

'OK, put your jersey back on.'

Noticing that nobody had thought to tell him, I took it upon myself to break the news to poor Bilko, who was still warming up in front of our main bank of supporters at the Shed End.

'I f**king knew it,' he said, understandably disgusted.

Tommy also had a go at Turner for his part in their first goal, but to be fair I didn't think Turner was doing too badly. From where I was watching, it seemed he just needed to read the game a bit better – including reading his teammates, and in particular our other full-back Danny Murphy.

Danny and I have been two of the main full-backs at the club every year since he arrived back in 2003. No one welcomed his return this year quite as much as me. Murph brings a natural balance; he likes to go forward a lot while I'm more conservative. I like to stay back, especially now. You can't both be up the pitch, as your centre-backs need you.

We always used to play like this, with one full-back tucking in when the other went forward. It's basic enough, adopted by most teams playing 4-4-2, and it worked well for us – particularly in 2005 when we won the league. But some time afterwards, Rico, in an attempt to emulate the way Slavia Prague had played against us, sat our defenders down and told us he wanted both full-backs to stay pushed on from now on. It was a positive move based on the premise that our centre-backs wouldn't need too much help, except from a deep-lying holding midfielder.

We (the full-backs), he explained, could run up and down the wing almost as wingers, which was becoming a fashionable thing for full-backs to do. It was considered an advanced, confident move at that time, especially in our league. The problem was that our squad had been weakened that year and we couldn't really pull off such risky efforts.

In any event, while the combination between myself and Murph normally works, Turner is more like Murph: he likes to attack. So when they're both playing, there are times when they'll be up the pitch together, and losing the ball at those times creates a dangerous situation. This happened a bit today against Finn Harps and contributed to us conceding.

Tommy whispered to me in the dressing room at half-time, 'Get yourself right. We'll definitely need you at some stage.'

On 65 minutes Derek O'Brien was injured by a bad tackle and had to be stretchered off. It looked like Tommy was going to take Turner off – which would've been a shame as he was doing very well in the second half and could do without the knock to his confidence – but instead he moved him upwards when I came on and we ended up winning 5–2 with Turner and myself combining very well down the right-hand side.

League of Ireland First Division

Turner's Cross, Cork

Cork City FC 5–2 Finn Harps FC

Tuesday 4th October 2011

Huge game tonight, at home against Monaghan. On top of the fact that we needed a win to get ahead of them – and they were in a rich vein of form having beaten Shels last week – their manager Roddy Collins had been mouthing off in the papers again.

Tommy didn't seem too bothered, though. 'Let's not get involved in that, lads; just go out and play. The way youse are playing at the moment, I think youse are the ones on fire, not them.'

We were 2–0 up at half-time and Cummins in particular was causing them serious problems. We were without Davin, Derek and Greg (amongst others), but Daryl Horgan and Turner were flying on the wings and the two young lads in the middle, Gearóid and Duggy, were in control and knocking it about. Cummins got hacked down a few times and seemed hurt. At half-time he told me he was in real pain and I told him if it was really bad he should come off.

Tommy's response was different to mine. When approached by Cummins, he asked him somewhat aggressively, 'Is your leg broke, ya?'

'No...' said Cummins, clearly sensing the backlash.

'No. Then f**king get back out there!' Tommy shouted in front of all the lads.

Cummins came off after 20 minutes of the second half, but his injury wasn't too bad in the end. We won in front of a big crowd and it was a huge result.

League of Ireland First Division

Turner's Cross, Cork

Cork City FC 3–1 Monaghan United FC

Further good news is that some random lady has recently started waiting for us after matches with bowls of homemade chocolate Rice Krispie cakes. She was there again tonight. Tasty stuff.

Saturday 8th October 2011

League of Ireland First Division

Salthill, Galway

Salthill Devon FC 0–4 Cork City FC

Cummins played and scored, as did Vinny. To top it off, the Rice Krispie cake lady had travelled and I took a lorry load for the bus home.

'Come on the Blues!' Greg jibed Vinny in a Waterford accent when we heard that Shels had lost to Waterford, putting Shels within our reach.

Vinny reminded us that Waterford had also beaten our title rivals Derry back in 2005 a few weeks before we won the Premier League. 'You had us to thank then too, I'm telling ya.'

My knee felt very sore and I was limping a lot, but we've got no match next weekend, which is a blessing.

Friday 21st October 2011

League of Ireland First Division

Turner's Cross, Cork

Cork City FC 3–1 Longford Town

Another great result tonight; we're flying now. We just need a draw next week at Shels in the last game of the season to get second place and promotion. Shels will just need a draw at Tolka to be champions. If we lose, Monaghan could take second place and the automatic promotion spot instead of us – and Limerick could enter the equation at that point too if they win. But if we win, we take it all.

Saturday 29th October 2011

There was a huge contingent of Cork fans at Tolka tonight. Those who travelled are unlikely to forget it. The game was a thriller; lots of chances, and end-to-end stuff throughout. We scored first, young Daryl Horgan living up to his growing reputation with a smart finish after a cross from Gearóid Morrissey fell nicely into his path. After that, Shels had a lot of chances and they equalised before half-time. In the dressing room at half-time Tommy and Billy were impressively cool and composed. That's what we needed. They were happy with how we were playing; we were expressing ourselves in the game. To be fair to Tommy, he always wants you to play football if you can. At Tolka tonight, under the pressure of it all, that's what came across to the players. Just keep playing. I suppose, in the end, that's why a conservative right-full felt the need to get the ball from his keeper late in the game, when it would've been easier to allow Nults to hit it long and high and hold on for the promotion spot. 'Keep playing, be brave,' Tommy and Woodsy had said. And we followed their instructions.

League of Ireland First Division

Tolka Park, Dublin

Shelbourne FC 1–2 Cork City FC

Cork crowned champions at Tolka Park
Cork City have been crowned Airtricity League First Division champions after a Graham Cummins' 94th-minute winner sealed a 2-1 victory for the Rebel Army over Shelbourne at Tolka Park.

Cummins' dramatic headed winner saw City clinch promotion alongside Shelbourne who had to settle for second place following tonight's defeat.

Before a crowd of 3,277, Daryl Horgan delighted the big Cork following to fire City in front after just four minutes. But Shels responded and deservedly levelled through captain David Cassidy just before the half hour. ...

Even though the draw would suffice, Cork pressed until the end and got their reward in the fourth minute of added time.

Substitute Derek O'Brien beat his man on the left wing to cross and Cummins, who'd been relatively quiet throughout much of the game, beat Dean Delaney with a downward header for his 23rd goal of the season. ...

Cork, reformed two years ago following their financial collapse, are back in the top flight.

Shelbourne: Delaney; Matthews, Boyle, Ryan, S Byrne; B McGill (Mulhall, 90+3), Dawson, Sullivan, Clancy (C Byrne, 79); Cassidy; Hughes (Gorman, 77).

Cork City: McNulty; N Horgan, Kavanagh (O'Brien, 70), Spillane, Murphy; G Morrissey, O'Halloran, Duggan, D Horgan (Turner, 90); O'Neill (Sullivan, h/t), Cummins.

(From RTÉ – www.rte.ie – updated 30th October 2011)

Sunday 30th October 2011

When the final whistle blew last night, our hysterical Rebel Army fans invaded the Tolka pitch. These fans, who own the club – this was their triumph as much as ours. In fact, on this occasion it's fair to say it was their win even more than it was ours. And to get the winner so late on… It honestly didn't feel like winning a football match or even a league; it felt like the winning of a war that's been fought out over the last four or five years or even longer. A war for the soul of the club and a war for Cork football. And we'd won that war. All of us.

For some reason I often try to run away from crowds. It's probably a good impulse. I ran when we won the league in 2005 and the huge crowd in Turner's Cross invaded the pitch at the final whistle. On that occasion myself and George O'Callaghan had ended up in the dressing room and realised that all of the other players were still out on the pitch. We then tried to make our way back out, through the hugs and hand-slaps of fans and family, to where the league title was being presented in the centre of the pitch – but we didn't manage to make it on time. That's why you won't see George or myself in many photos as the 2005 league trophy is being lifted by Dan Murray.

Pitch invasions on those rare nights are brilliant things, though. Swarms of people, fans flashing up and past you, thanking you, hugging you, picking you up – the joy, relief and thanks on their faces. You try to get by them but you want to share it with them too. You also want, when you get a chance, to share it with your friends and family.

In 2005, as myself and George tried to make our way back out to the temporary stage that had been set up in the centre of the pitch for the trophy presentation, we met my uncle Martin with his then 14-year-old son Patrick. As we wrestled past them and the other fans, Martin gave me a big hug and said, 'Well done, Hog.' A few months later, Martin would take a fall and enter a coma for a few weeks before tragically passing away. So one of the very last times that I'd met him was on the pitch during that invasion. 'Well done, Hog,' turned out to be a goodbye as well as a 'well done' and is a memory that I cherish.

Another lovely memory of that night occurred after the trophy had been presented when my own group of friends from Glasheen caught up with me and carried me on their shoulders down to the rest of our players, who had approached the crowd behind the goal at the Shed End to celebrate. There I was left down off their shoulders so that I could join with the other players climbing into the Shed. It was a very fitting and brilliant end for that older version of the Shed on its last night before being replaced by a modern stand. There, in the darkening night, we sang and sang, fans and players together, the league trophy being tossed around as if it were a bouncing ball.

But I mean it when I say last night in Tolka Park was on a par with that night in 2005. Again I felt the need to run to the dressing room when the crowd invaded. This time, being in Dublin, there weren't as many people to evade, although we still had a few thousand travelling fans because of what was at stake. The dressing rooms in Tolka are upstairs behind a stand at one end of the ground, so I had to run a bit of a distance to get there; then I entered the stand, climbed the stairs and opened the dressing-room door. What I found there was… peace! Nobody in the room but me. I sat down for a minute and looked around at the gearbags and the clothes hanging on the hooks. I looked at the tactics board that Tommy and Woodsy had used earlier, the discarded bottles of water and empty Jaffa Cake packets. I took the chance to take it in. *Yes*, I said quietly to myself with a clenched fist. *Yes!*

The I grabbed my phone and rang my brother Eoin. He was, of course, in Tolka. I told him to make it towards the dressing rooms and went back down to the pitch to meet him. 'Jesus – the end was brilliant!' he shouted. 'And to win it like that! I haven't enjoyed a game so much since… 2005… or even Bayern!'

I ran back into the mass of pitch-invading Cork fans and made it just in time to see Greg lifting the trophy high.

League of Ireland First Division – 2011 final standings

Pos	Team	Pld	W	D	L	GF	GA	GD	Pts
1	Cork City (C) (P)*	30	29	9	1	73	26	+47	69
2	Shelbourne*	30	22	2	6	62	24	+38	68
3	Monaghan United**	30	21	4	5	60	27	+33	67
4	Limerick FC	30	20	6	4	49	22	+27	66
5	Waterford United	30	13	3	14	37	31	+6	42
6	Longford Town	30	12	4	14	38	41	-3	40
7	Mervue United	30	10	4	16	37	45	-8	34
8	Athlone Town	30	9	5	16	25	53	-28	32
9	Finn Harps	30	8	4	18	29	45	-16	28
10	Wexford Youths	30	4	2	24	29	69	-40	14
11	Salthill Devon	30	2	5	23	18	74	-56	11

*Promoted; **Qualifies for playoffs

Cork City V Shels Footage
If you haven't already seen the footage from last Saturday night's league decider at Tolka Park … then you really should.

A few weeks ago Shelbourne were sitting pretty with a ten point lead at the summit of the Airtricity First Division. By kick-off on Saturday night Shels were guaranteed promotion to the Premier Division but Cork City had reduced the gap to a single point. …

A draw would have been good enough to see the Rebel Army through but an injury time screamer from Graham Cummins will go down, certainly as one of the biggest moments in the club's history, if not in Cork sporting history too. …

Most fans are reporting something close to an out-of-body experience from this point on: a blur of emotion, singing, chanting, screaming and roaring. Grown men hugging each other, overcome with tears of joy.

Somewhere in this lucid Rebel dream was the sound of a final whistle and the barely believable reality that eighteen months after TNB and 'The Troubles', Cork City FC had regained Premier Division status under their own steam. What an achievement.

This time there are no mysterious shady investors, hedge funds, snedge funds, IOUs or dubious red money behind City's glorious win. The club is now owned by its fans, sponsored by Beamish and other local businesses who didn't give up on CCFC when all looked lost.

Even players like midfielder Greg O'Halloran are sponsored by the Sultans of Ping FC (yes, the band). How much more local can you get?!

While blurred memories of Graham Cummins's winning goal can be sharpened by [the TV footage], the emotional memories for dedicated fans who have been through the mill over the last two seasons will be crystallised in fans' memories for decades: the time we won the First Division in the dying seconds. …

(From www.thepeoplesrepublicofcork.com, 1st November 2011)

There's extended footage of the game online: '2011.10.29 - Shels v Cork' by @shelstv on Vimeo (https://vimeo.com). There's also footage of the game's closing moments from the Cork City fans themselves on YouTube (www.youtube.com).

All the work of FORAS, of Tommy and the players and the fans… it all came down to the last seconds of the match. The nerves and the growing tension. *Blow the f**king whistle, ref!* And when he finally did, it was euphoric, and we're still celebrating.

But away from our celebrations, other clubs, like Galway United, are facing the same old problems.

Troubled Galway opt out of league for a year

AFTER A rough season that ended in relegation from the Premier Division and continuing difficulties off it, Galway United's directors announced yesterday that they are taking at least a year away from senior football to reflect on their position. The Supporters' Trust that funded the club through much of last season has confirmed it has applied for a league licence of its own.

"People will ask: 'How can you walk away from your club?'" acknowledged Vincent O'Connor of the Trust yesterday, "and I'd have to say that it has been one of the most difficult decisions I've ever made in my life. But the level of the debt and some of the dealings we've had with the directors have made our position untenable. We felt that we couldn't bring the club as it is forward."

Instead, the Galway United Supporters' Trust (Gust) has decided to attempt to gain a licence itself so it can enter a newly formed club in the league. Taking their lead from supporters in Cork a couple of years back, Gust have been taking advice from the UEFA-funded organisation Supporters Direct, a group established to promote "sustainable spectator sports clubs, based on supporters' involvement and community ownership".

Gust's decision to go it alone has, however, raised the possibility that the longest-established of Galway's three Airtricity League clubs will be lost to the city and senior football next year, with the directors of the official club announcing yesterday that they have now withdrawn their own licence application. ...

(Emmet Malone, *Irish Times*, 14th December 2011)

Chapter Six – Interview with Graham Cummins, January 2019

Neal Horgan: That goal against Shels, to win the league… it must still be a highlight?

Graham Cummins: Of course, it's still my most important goal. It meant so much to the club to get back to the Premier Division – people still say that to me.

NH: And a few weeks later you were gone to Preston.

GC: Yes, it was exciting. But I was 24, which, looking back, I think was quite old to be going across the Channel. I'd say 20 or 21 would have been better; the club you go to will work on you for a few years at that age, but if you're 24 they expect you to be the finished product. And I got a massive land at Preston as I was going from part-time to full-time football. Preston were in League One, but they were at the extreme level in League One in terms of training. They would train from 10am until 4pm, as that's what the manager at the time, Graham Westley, wanted. Most other clubs would finish training at 1pm. At Preston on a Monday after a match on a Saturday we'd have a yoga session, then maybe weights, and then we'd have three 30-minute games – so a full 90 minutes – just 48 hours after our game on the Saturday. If we'd lost on the Saturday he'd be trying to change the team in the Monday game, reacting to what had happened. It was always the subs that were better on the Monday than the lads who'd played 90 on the Saturday. And we'd do something similar on a Tuesday. We were picking up injuries left, right and centre, getting home at 6pm and going to sleep wrecked. We didn't rest enough, in my opinion. It was such a change from Cork City under Tommy where we trained a few evenings a week and then played on a Friday.

NH: What else was different over there?

GC: There was a lot to get used to. I remember going over I wasn't in good shape – my diet wasn't great. Under Tommy back in Cork I'd come home every day after training and eat chocolate bars. Seriously – chocolate bars. And the clubs I played with over there didn't really teach me how to eat properly either. I moved on from Preston, played with Exeter and Rochdale and most recently St Johnstone. One club just had volunteers cooking for us; mostly it was just pasta and cheese, nothing else. The day before a game I remember getting frozen burgers... I'm sitting there thinking, *If this is what the club is doing it must be right.*

NH: Chocolate bars after training: even I wasn't that bad! I'd learned about sports nutrition back in 2003 when we first became full-time under Pat Dolan. Suddenly, after Dolan took over, what, when and how we ate (and drank) became very important. Looking back, it seems Dolan and some of his successors knew what the players at the top clubs in England were eating and tried to replicate that over here. Obviously when you were with the club in 2010/11, we were back part-time again and some aspects of the professional game fell by the wayside or were less of a priority. Ironic that those little lessons on how to be a good professional footballer tend to slip down the pecking order when a club's struggling to survive. But anyway, if you didn't learn how to eat properly at Cork City or at those clubs in the UK, how did you learn? How did you change your diet?

GC: When I was at Exeter, I lived with two guys; one of them was Christian Ribeiro who'd played Championship with Bristol and been capped for Wales. He changed my whole diet. Sometimes, living with other guys can be the best thing for you. I didn't necessarily like living with other footballers, but he was great, teaching me about types of sauces to use, portion sizes, etc. And it's unbelievable what a difference it makes.

NH: So you had those spells with Preston, Exeter, Rochdale and St Johnstone before returning last year to Cork City. Has the club changed a lot since you left in 2011?

GC: Yeah, it has. Obviously the club's gone full-time again and so there's a greater number of support staff, which is brilliant as you really need more off-the-field assistance when you're full-time. Back under Tommy in 2010/11 the club just didn't have those kinds of resources. Don't get me wrong: I loved playing under Tommy, and credit to him, he tried to make it as professional as he could within a part-time club. You'll remember Tommy trying to get the part-time guys to train as much as possible, which was difficult for everyone. And the money just wasn't there, so lads weren't going to commit to full-time. They couldn't really be expected to. That didn't stop Tommy from trying, though…

NH: Do you remember going to the Collins army barracks?

GC: I do. We had three or four days there during the mid-season break. Double sessions. And we were going mad at a double session at the time…

NH: Do you remember one of those days – it was a Sunday – we trained in the morning and finished about 12, then Tommy said we wouldn't be starting again until 3pm?

GC: [Laughing] Yeah. Davin went mad. I remember him saying, 'I need to see my kids, Tommy!' We were all giving out, asking to go back earlier. So Tommy wilted and we went back just after 2pm instead. But do you know what? I think Tommy's double sessions at the barracks helped us. The week after, we played Shels in one of the biggest games of the season and we beat them.

NH: I missed that Shels game as I was at a GAA match.

GC: Oh yeah, I remember that. Tommy was screwing. But the main thing was that we won. They'd been so far ahead and with that result we started to catch them. And we caught them in the end.

NH: The very end…

GC: Yeah, well it's a nice way to do it. And as I said, it's still my most important goal to date. Funnily enough, probably my second or third favourite goal was for St Johnstone against Rangers at Ibrox just before I came back to Cork. I remember my agent ringing me on the Monday morning and telling me that the goal would change absolutely nothing; that I'd be pulled by the manager and told I wasn't wanted. That meant after eight seasons in the UK I'd be moving back to Cork, as John Caulfield had already been onto me. St Johnstone were surprised I'd already spoken to Cork, but obviously I was well within my rights to do so as there wasn't much left on my contract. Even still, they got a bit annoyed that they hadn't known about the discussion with Cork. They even pushed for me to go to other clubs after that, but I said to the manager, 'This is the way it is; I'm going back home to Cork.'

Chapter Seven – January to 2nd March 2012

So we were back in the top tier of Irish football. And while this was obviously great for the club, Tommy and the players, I had some concerns about the increasing demands it would place on my body. The First Division is a good division; some teams are very fit, and I'd done fine, managing to keep myself on the pitch in the league games (aside from my absences due to GAA matches) when it mattered most. However, I knew that the Premier Division would be much more demanding. The top teams in Ireland such as Shamrock Rovers and Sligo were pretty much full-time outfits – although Michael O'Neill's Shamrock Rovers were unconventional in that they trained mostly in the evenings to allow players to work full-time jobs during the day. This didn't stop them from making the group stages of the Europa League, illustrating the huge unfulfilled potential in Irish football. Imagine if the FAI truly did support full-time football in Ireland… imagine what could be achieved in Europe by Irish sides. Rovers and many other clubs before them have done their best in Europe without the benefit of regularly playing other full-time teams in Ireland. That makes Rovers' achievement all the greater.

In any event, the likes of Shamrock Rovers and the other top sides we'd face this season in the Premier Division would be moving around at a proper pace, with a lot of physicality. In the few weeks after we were promoted I'd begun to worry about whether I'd be in a position to get myself up to speed. In addition, I was coming to the end of my legal apprenticeship and was scheduled to qualify as a solicitor in April 2012. Whatever leniency I might have enjoyed over the previous few years as a trainee solicitor was about to evaporate; I'd be joining the ranks of the newly qualified and I'd need to show I was worthy of being kept within a firm or of hiring. Whatever chance I had was dependent on me spending more time in the office – particularly as we were in the middle of a recession. It was a difficult time for everyone in Ireland.

I also had real concerns about how my right knee would respond to the higher level of intensity. I didn't want to have to pull out during an important match, which is effectively what I'd had to do against Derry in the League Cup final. The issue with my right knee was longstanding. I'd started having problems with it during City's part-time era, undertaking my first keyhole surgery around 2002. I seem to remember someone falling on my knee as I cleared a ball, which afterwards caused a click or pain anytime I tried to kick the ball. The problem didn't go away, so I had keyhole surgery to remove the cartilage that had been damaged and was causing the problem. It worked very well and things seemed fine. Then, seven years later, I started getting more pain in the knee. It was 2009 and we'd been doing a lot of training with Paul Doolin on AstroTurf. I eventually had more keyhole surgery to remove more cartilage. After that operation the surgeon told me I should retire as soon as possible. It was clear that my knee would be fighting a losing battle if I continued to train at that level.

So I took his advice and retired at the end of 2009 – only to come back as an amateur at Tommy's request. But that was the First Division, where the intensity is lower. Now that we were going back up in intensity in the Premier Division, I became concerned. So in late 2011 I decided to get another opinion, this time from a more sports-related consultant than before. He confirmed that there was indeed no cartilage left in my right knee, as a result of the two operations. He said this could cause difficulty down the line and one option would be to stop playing so as to avoid the risk of needing a knee replacement before the age of 40.

However, as he could see I was adamant about continuing to play, and relatively young and healthy, he said I might consider an operation called 'microfracturing'. This is a procedure that has had some documented success with basketball athletes in the US who'd also lost the cartilage in their knees. The surgery involves causing bleeding in the knee (by punching little holes into the bone), and once the new blood has hardened it can act as a new cartilage – albeit not quite as good as the previous one. It sounded interesting but risky.

I did some research on the internet and asked some other medical professionals. There were some good stories and some bad ones. What was clear, though, was that it was a significant operation that would require an intensive rehab programme including a six-month recovery period. Crucially for me, some of those who'd undergone microfracturing swore that they'd enjoyed the benefits of their operation for a long time afterwards – even some 15 or 20 years.

I spent a few weeks considering it. I spoke with Tommy and Woodsy in the off-season; they both expressed reservations about undergoing such a big operation but agreed that if it could help my knee in the long term, as it might well do, then it was obviously worth considering. Tommy said he'd be happy enough to take me back mid-2012 – if I made it back. 'An experienced player like you coming back into the second half of the season would be terrific,' he said. The fact that I was unpaid also helped matters. If I'd been seeking a contract or tied to a contract, perhaps I wouldn't have been in a position to make such a decision for myself.

So I went under the knife at the beginning of the year and then got stuck into active rehab while the lads began their pre-season. Tommy had been busy seeking new, higher-quality players for the Premier Division, but before the arrival of any new recruits came the news that we'd lost our captain from the previous season. This would be a significant loss around the dressing room and to the team in general.

O'Halloran quits after 'laughable' offer
Cork City captain Greg O'Halloran has quit the club after describing a new contract offer as "laughable".

The defender led the Leesiders to promotion last season, but will not play in their Premier Division campaign due to his fury at the offer presented to him.

"I was offered a near 80pc reduction in wages and, in a recession like this, that was just not feasible for me," said O'Halloran.

"To be honest, the terms were laughable, and for a player who played over 60 games for the club (in its current guise), it's a big disappointment.

"It's a disgrace what I was offered, having captained the team to promotion, but I know from experience that you never know what's around the corner in this game. I wish the club the best of luck for the season ahead, but they will be doing it without me," he added. ...

(Daniel McDonnell, *Irish Independent*, 11th January 2012)

Thursday 12th January 2012

The first day back for everyone today. I was looking forward to seeing the lads but I was also quite anxious regarding my body fat. I knew we'd be having those awful body fat tests today – I absolutely hate them. But they're part of the modern game, unfortunately. When I first started out in 2000, the club was part-time and these tests didn't feature at all. Back then, you'd have a fitness test at the start of the year, normally a bleep test, from which your general level of stamina and fitness was registered and understood.

At that time, what you did on the pitch was what mattered most; a few extra percentages of body fat didn't matter if you could bend one into the top corner or if you could dominate the opposing winger. On days like today I long for those simpler times.

However, there's no denying the plain logic that the less unnecessary fat you carry, the easier it is for you to get around the pitch – and the more likely it is that your performance will improve as a result. As football is played over 90 minutes at high pace I can't argue with this, and in any event I know that resistance is futile. It's just no longer tolerated to be carrying a little bit of flubber.

When they first started subjecting us to these tests, around 2003, I didn't think it was futile to resist. In fact a few of us tried to beat them. There were different ways of conducting body fat tests, but at the University of Limerick (UL) where we had our first testing under Pat Dolan, they used a handheld device that apparently sent some kind of sonar around your body and came back with the result. Some of the lads heard that if you were dehydrated at the time of using these devices, your body fat score would appear lower than it really was. So rather than scoring above 12% body fat (and being subjected to months of scornful running under Dolan) you could achieve something like 9% and be deemed in tip-top shape. How to get dehydrated, then? Hmmm... Some players, in an alleged attempt at lower readings, would have a few drinks the night before the testing. However, this risked an under-par performance in the 6 x 150m indoor running test that always took place shortly after the body fat readings.

I found the best preparation was to rest up the night before but to hold off drinking liquids on the two-hour journey to UL from Cork. On arrival at UL I'd take a few trips to the toilet (as many as possible) before the body fat test, and then have my water or energy drink ready as soon as the test was over. Looking back, the fact that our scheming went to such lengths illustrates the pressure – for better or worse – that Dolan had us under at the time.

After a few years the handheld sonar device was deemed deficient and the older but more controlled testing with steel callipers was introduced. At that point there was nothing much we could do but go to the toilet beforehand and breath in as much as possible during the testing. Anticipating an inevitably high reading as the club's representatives heartlessly clinched and prodded the cold, stainless-steel pronged callipers to the fat just above our hips, myself and Dan Murray (who also tended to come out high in the body fat test scores) would adopt our usual defensive approaches.

'Maradona did OK on the pitch, didn't he Muz? And he was somewhat heavy,' I'd say.

The fitness instructor would interject, 'Maybe he would've been even better if he'd reduced his body fat to optimum levels.'

'Maradona?' I'd say, 'Maybe he would've been worse. Look at what he did: World Cup, Serie As…'

Muz (who's English) would add something like, 'I'm with you Hogs. Glenn 'oddle did OK, didn't he?' as the callipers tightened, making us feel like pieces of meat.

Obviously there's little merit or point in that argument. The rising tide of knowledge in relation to sports science has increased everyone's level of fitness. This side of the game is becoming more important than ever, even in the League of Ireland. In truth, every player needs to embrace these changes; it would be fatal to their individual playing careers otherwise. And it is really great to see LOI teams bringing greater fitness standards.

For my part, as the knowledge of sports science and nutrition has permeated the game, I've certainly changed the way I've eaten – particularly with regard to fatty and processed foods. Chocolate has been reduced to minimum levels; fizzy drinks cut out completely. The education we received when we became full-time, from nutritionists employed by the likes of Pat Dolan, Rico and Mathews, has meant we're familiar with what's good and what's generally bad to eat as an athlete. Over time, this stuff has become less optional and more of a basic requirement at top-tier clubs.

The world of so-called performance-assisting products has also made its way through the dressing room door. When I started playing with the first team we'd have bottles of water, maybe some oranges and Jaffa Cakes (if Noelle Feeney was around), and that would be that. Now lads have their own containers in their bags for rehydration solutions, protein shakes and all the rest.

I've tried to stay away from these things in general, although some additions I've welcomed – in particular recovery drinks. I'll happily take the recovery drinks provided to the team after training, given the frequency of matches during the season.

That being said, I'm still quite conservative. Akin to my reluctance to wear flashy boots or hairstyles, I'm also very protective of what I do before a game. In fact I still have the same 'night before a match' meal that I had when I first started playing. Call it a superstition if you like, but if I don't have my usual food, then I don't feel right during the match the following day. It's a routine and a dish that's survived since the old days when we were part-time, before all this full-time nutritional stuff kicked in. It involves a takeaway chips and chicken dish from Jackie Lennox's on Bandon Road. And being a grandchild of the founder and a nephew of the owners, I'm often spared from paying for my meal – a lovely family tradition that has lasted well over 50 years.

Over the years I have tried other things – the obvious chicken and pasta, and other high-carb dishes recommended by our nutritionists – but I always felt I had more energy the next day after a Jackie's. Given that it's my family's business, this might sound like a product placement, but it's true.

However, as the years have passed and the optimum sporting diet has become a matter of common knowledge, this ritual has become more and more tricky. It's not so appropriate to be seen in the queue of the chipper the night before a game. I've had to employ stealth tactics – particularly in the Pat Dolan days – and organise my friends or flatmates to go in while I sit outside with a hat on in the car. In fact in the Dolan days I often got my friends to drive to the chipper alone, and I'd ask them to check their rear-view mirrors to make sure they weren't being followed, while I'd be waiting in disguise in my front room, just in case!

Pat was the most forward-thinking and unforgiving manager in terms of players' nutrition. The culture change that had been occurring in the English Premiership after Arsène Wenger's arrival made its way through Pat to us. Before Dolan, so long as your diet wasn't too outrageous you were fine. After Dolan it was considered unprofessional to have anything other than the diet of an elite athlete. That was an important change.

However, circa 2003, the pasta dish wasn't as common on Irish menus as it is today. As a result, when we had our pre-match back then, in hotels of varying quality all over Ireland, the pasta dishes were some of the worst meals I've ever eaten. And because it was the day of the game, you'd have little choice but to eat it. I remember some players simply couldn't face it and would just have cereal or toast. It wasn't that they didn't like pasta; it was that this 2003 Irish version was horrific.

Luckily for me, my Jackie Lennox's from the night before would serve as a buffer. My carb store would still be quite full – no matter what dose of experimental pasta and chicken was being administered on match day. I didn't really require the top-up, and I believe this has played a part in my performances on the pitch remaining steady enough that I've managed to be first-choice full-back, more or less, for the past 12 years.

And while in the years since then the standard of pasta dishes provided to us around Ireland has improved dramatically, I still haven't found a better 'night before the match' meal than a Jackie's.

This routine may well be a factor in my history of high scores in the dreaded body fat tests. Even when I was only a few years in, aged 23 during the first tests under Pat Dolan, my readings were higher than the other lads' most of the time. But after the embarrassment of the test results being read out, I'd beat them all (apart from Alan Bennett) in the fitness tests that would be held later the same day. Perhaps I would've been even fitter if I'd eaten better, like the fitness instructor suggested. But I was in the team week in, week out and it worked for me.

Today, given the fact I was on crutches for a few months after the operation and have fully enjoyed Christmas, I knew my body fat reading would be off the charts.

When we arrived for training Tommy welcomed everyone back and we were given our new Umbro gear. It was pretty haphazard: 20 guys grabbing stuff as our Polish kit-man Rafa desperately tried to keep count of what was being taken. 'Juuuust dtoow traeening tops... deee reddd ones are for staff only!' he shouted, but it was a losing battle. While he was doing this a member of the FORAS committee was trying to print squad numbers on the gear. It was all very disorganised and it took a long time. We'd met at 6pm but it transpired that training wasn't until 8pm, some 20km away in Mayfield. A bit of disaster for everyone except Tommy, who had planned it well to allow extra time for the shambles.

Finally the body fat readings were taken for most of the lads, but I made an effort to stay out of sight. I thought maybe I could get away without doing it... *Do I really need this at my age?* I made a move towards the exit but Tommy clocked me and said, 'Will youse just get it done? I know they'll have to get a second machine for you, Hog.' He laughed.

Woodsy also got in on the act: 'You've an ass like J-Lo there, Hog.'

'Thanks Bill,' I said.

I took my shirt off and the callipers were applied to the usual spots. There was no chat about Maradona or Glenn 'Oddle, as Muz is still at Shamrock Rovers. So I just breathed in as much as I could and hoped for the best. As I'd feared, the results were not good. My body fat score is very high – off the charts in comparison to most of the other lads. Weight is down, however. 'That's the diet showing there, Bill,' I quipped to Woodsy, who was speechless at the reduction in my weight.

After the handing-out-of-gear debacle, Tommy called the lads in together.

'Is everyone here? Who's missing?' he asked the group.

I wanted to shout, 'Greg! Where's Greg [O'Halloran]?' for the laugh, but I restrained myself.

I miss Greg. Greg and I would often reply to such a question with something like, 'Where's Andy Packer, Gaffer?' or 'Don't forget Michael Nwankwo!' or 'Where's Osvaldo Lopes?' These were players from the past that only a few of us would've played with. The manager would look puzzled for a moment while Greg and I (and perhaps a few others) would be highly amused with ourselves. Sometimes we'd shout the name of a player that had only just left the club; the comedic effect of this would depend on the manager at the time and the circumstances of the player's departure. That was riskier.

However, the situation with Greg is far too sensitive. Tommy wouldn't appreciate the joke. Sad that this tradition is over. If I were to shout, 'Where's Joey Gamble?' very few would get it; the culture has moved on. Besides, these days most of the lads wear headphones when we're on buses, and even in dressing rooms too, so they'd miss out on the joke. Another old ally gone in Greg – but that's football.

Once all the (current) lads were accounted for, Tommy showed us a video – on our new projector – of our win on the last day of the season against Shels. He started at the end of the match, just as the whistle is blown and the fans invade the pitch. After a few failed attempts he finally found the slow-motion control on the remote. He pointed at the screen amongst the hundreds of invading fans and picked out one person coming at pace from the dugout. 'Look, that's Billy,' he said. 'Keep your eyes on him.'

We watched Woodsy sprinting towards the main cohort of players who were celebrating on the pitch.

Then Tommy said, 'Wait now… wait for it…'

A young fan enters from the bottom of the screen and runs towards Woodsy. Woodsy attempts to sidestep him, only for the two to become tangled and fall on top of each other. It's very funny and a great spot by Tommy, to be fair. All the lads had a good laugh.

'He nearly clothes-lined ya there, Bill! Ha-ha – brilliant,' laughed Tommy.

A few seconds later Tommy reverted to a more serious tone. 'But seriously, lads. I'm telling youse: the work starts here and now. If we want the same next year, youse'll need to be right from today until the end of the season.'

Afterward the lads went off to training on the AstroTurf at Mayfield while myself, Mul and young Eoin McGreevy remained to see Rob Savage, our very friendly and helpful physio. He's a nice guy who brings a caring side – which is useful given Tommy's matter-of-fact attitude to the lads.

Saturday 21st January 2012

This morning I went out again to training in Bishopstown to see the lads as I haven't been with them for a while. I've just been following a rehab programme at home. When I arrived I was delighted to see Muzza back. He looks fit too. Seems he wants to move back to Cork, his adopted homeland. There are also a few new faces – as usual for this time of year.

I chatted with the new fitness guy, Paudie Horgan, while he was working on Kevin Murray. Paudie says we're 10 years behind the GAA and rugby, fitness-wise. Not so a few years ago, I told him as he called the lads out for warm-down stretching.

'Do we really f**king need this?' asked Muz, angrily.

'I'm glad you're back, Muz,' I said – and I meant it.

Saturday 28th January 2012

I saw the consultant again last week and he said I'm still four months away from full recovery. He's happy with my knee at this point, though, and says it's up to me whether I play on. He said if I don't, however, it might be the difference between needing a knee replacement in my 50s rather than my 40s.

I took a few days out to think about things. I figured maybe I should just pack it in – but then I spoke to a few people and felt more positive about the situation.

One of the people I spoke to was Colin Healy. Gamble had told me that Colin had had the operation and gone back too early. I texted Colin and within 10 minutes he called me from Ipswich, which was very good of him. He told me he'd been out for 11 months after the op, but that his operation was different to mine as he'd had a stress fracture of the knee. He did a lot of cycling and swimming for rehab but said it was hard coming back from the surgery, although in the end he was able to get back to a high enough standard. I asked him how he was getting on at Ipswich but he didn't seem too happy to talk about that, so I dropped it. I asked if he'd ever consider coming back and perhaps going to college, like Woodsy has done recently. 'No,' he said, 'because you need your Leaving Cert.'

'I don't think you do,' I told him. 'Cathal Lordan is doing it – I think he got in as a mature student.' The call ended with my thanking Colin for ringing me so quickly and for his advice, and he wished me well. I took encouragement from the fact that after the operation Colin was able to get back to playing at Championship level in England. If he could do that, maybe I could make it back to the League of Ireland Premier Division.

So I told Tommy I'm still four months away and he was again positive, saying it'd be great to have an experienced player like me coming back in June, which was what I needed to hear. I still had to tell my GAA club that I won't be playing this year, and I wasn't looking forward to that. I walked out to their training at the Barrs and asked to speak to manager Bill O'Connell away from the lads. Thankfully Bill couldn't have been nicer: 'It was a pleasure to have you with us, Neal. Best of luck for the year and you can always come back.' He then gathered all the lads in, explained the situation and asked them to give me a round of applause. They all wished me the best, which was really fantastic.

Saturday 4th February 2012

The lads were training at Fota again this weekend. It's a top-class set-up. I went out to touch base today and met Woodsy on arriving. I told him what the specialist had said, and I mentioned my conversation with Colin Healy and that he'd been out for 11 months but with a different injury.

'Ya, I remember he fractured his kneecap,' said Woodsy. 'By the way, Colin's coming out here at 11 o'clock and might be signing…'

Jesus Christ – brilliant!

In the dressing room at Fota I asked Rafa, 'Are we paying for training here?'

Rafa wasn't sure. 'Maybe now we have no sponsor they become shirt sponsor again?' he suggested.

The squad went training on the lovely secluded Fota training pitches while young McGreevy and I went to LeisureWorld to use the gym. He asked about Healy as I drove there. 'He'll be class,' I said. 'You'll learn a lot from him. Also, I bet we'll get a good sponsor if he signs, with Muzza in the team already.'

Happy days – very exciting.

The Great Big LOI Season Preview – Premier, Part I
There is an air of optimism in Cork these days. Why, you ask? Well they make their return to Premier Division football with an impressive looking squad at Tommy Dunne's disposal.

I think the general opinion of League of Ireland fans is that they're happy to see Cork's re-emergence as a Premier Division side. Their fans bring much noise, colour and hype and their continued support even [during] the dark years of the First Division proved their love for the club didn't die, attracting up to 3,000 fans for a game at one point during the summer.

The squad consists of a lot of new faces, but perhaps the two outstanding acquisitions are the familiar faces of Colin Healy and Dan Murray. Another player the Rebel Army will be delighted to have for the season is Daryl Horgan. The winger proved to be revelation when he arrived on loan from Sligo Rovers last year, and [Cork City] have now secured him on a two year contract.

One problem Tommy Dunne may face however is a lack of firepower up front. He looked set to be able to rely on Graham Cummins to find the net for his side, but with a late move to Preston they will now rely on loan signing Tadhg Purcell to step up to the mark and fill the big boots left by the young striker.

The Leesiders look too strong to face a relegation battle, in fact, they may even be a good shout for a top four spot if they can find the goals in Cummins' absence.

(Alan Finn, from 'Balls Out In Public' – https://ballsoutinpublic.wordpress.com – February 29th 2012)

Friday 2nd March 2012

The league started again today, and there's a lot of excitement around the city about us. I got a text from superkeeper Mick Devine: 'Best of luck today, kid.' A nice touch from the guy but I let him know that I'm a good few months away from playing at this point. Apparently he's currently centre-forward and top scorer for Abbey Rovers GAA team.

I had felt out of it somewhat, just at home doing my rehab, but then I watched Shamrock Rovers on TV beating Drogheda and I got a little excited. It's starting to feel fresh to me again. I know I'm in the twilight of my playing years, but if I get my leg right later in the season then maybe I can still contribute something. For all the knocks it takes, and the untapped potential of the LOI – even in its current state – it's a brilliant league to be part of if you're doing well. When you're travelling around the country, representing your city, being a member of the team can be really amazing and deeply fulfilling.

The hope is that we'll do well this year, and I'd love to be part of it. That's a motivation when I'm on the static bike or doing small exercises day after day. The colour and noise and feeling of playing at Turner's Cross, at Richmond Park, at Tallaght, at the Brandywell… all that spurs me on.

Neal Horgan

Chapter Eight – 13th April to 19th June 2012

Friday 13th April 2012

I trained last Tuesday on a high, having felt I'd got some clearance from the specialist that morning. I'd made sure to say only positive things about the rehab and the state of my knee; he did a few checks and we parted with a handshake, which seemed – to me at least – to mean 'Well done, off you go.' So off I went, and told Tommy that in four to six weeks I'd be ready. Problem is that despite Tommy's warnings to be careful, I couldn't stop myself after the warm-up from joining a possession game. I love possession games.

I was fine for a while but after about 15 minutes my knee suddenly felt weak, then a minute later it felt unstable and after another minute I felt a piercing pain which made me stop completely.

Today, three days later, it's still a little swollen and I'm really worried. Either I've defeated the whole purpose of the microfracturing by knocking the scab off, or it's just a minor setback. Only time will tell.

Tommy and the lads have also had a difficult start to the season. Last week's loss to Bohs left us with only two points after six games, putting us second from bottom; and the bad start was compounded by an embarrassing 3–0 defeat in the League Cup against Limerick in midweek.

Pos	Team	Pl	W	D	L	GF	GA	GD	Pts
1	Sligo Rovers	6	5	1	0	10	3	+7	16
2	Shamrock Rovers	6	4	1	1	13	8	+5	13
3	Drogheda United	6	4	1	1	11	6	+5	13
4	St Patrick's Athletic	6	3	3	0	10	3	+7	12
5	Derry City	6	3	1	2	7	3	+4	10

6	Shelbourne	6	2	1	3	8	9	-1	7
7	UCD	6	2	1	3	8	9	-1	7
8	Dundalk	6	1	3	2	2	6	-4	6
9	Bohemian	6	1	1	4	1	6	-5	4
10	Bray Wanderers	6	1	1	4	7	14	-7	4
11	Cork City	6	0	2	4	4	9	-5	2
12	Monaghan United	6	0	2	4	4	9	-5	2

The mood at training reached quite a low, with Nulty even suggesting on one of my morale-checking visits that it was the lowest ever.

'No, at least you're getting paid, and on time.'

'Ya, you're right there,' he corrected himself.

Also, there's apparently been a decline in Tommy and Danny Murphy's relationship. I spotted Murph looking down and dejectedly dropping his boots on the floor.

Muzza and I tried to inject some focus during the week in the lead-up to tonight's game against bottom club Monaghan: 'Just concentrate on the next match, and win it.' Same as ever.

League of Ireland Premier Division

Turner's Cross, Cork

Cork City FC 6–0 Monaghan United

Cork find their form
Davin O'Neill scored a hat-trick as Cork City gained their first Premier Division win of the season against Monaghan United at Turner's Cross last night.

Both sides had chances in the evenly-contested opening period. But City slowly began to take control and they went ahead just before the half-hour when Daryl Horgan cut in from the left and his 25-yard shot took a deflection and looped over Monaghan goalkeeper, Chris Bennion.

Four minutes later, the lead was doubled as Bennion spilled a Gearóid Morrissey free kick and O'Neill pounced to apply the finish. It was 3-0 after 49 minutes, Vinny Sullivan touching in another Morrissey free and Keith Quinn, who had been booked for the initial foul on Horgan, received a second yellow card for dissent.

O'Neill got his second and his side's fourth on 65 after Horgan broke well following Monaghan pressure in which Darragh Reynor hit the crossbar. Sub Tadhg Purcell made it 5-0 with 13 minutes left.

In the 87th minute, O'Neill completed his hat-trick from the penalty spot, the win equalling City's previous biggest in the Premier Division.

CORK CITY: McNulty; Kavanagh (Turner 70), D Murray, Spillane, D Murphy; G Morrissey, Dunleavy, Duggan, D Horgan (O'Connor 75); O'Neill, Sullivan (Purcell 70).

(From <u>The Irish Times</u>, 14th April 2012)

Thursday 3rd May 2012

Things have improved all round. Even though the lads lost last week to Sligo, they followed it up with a win away at Shels, with Vinny Sullivan scoring both goals. I'm delighted for Vinny; he's definitely one of those strikers that works hard for the team without getting the credit his work-rate deserves. No matter what anybody might say, a striker is judged by his goals. Tadhg Purcell – who came in on loan this season from Shamrock Rovers – also pitched in with two assists, and I'm glad for him too. I still think we could have a shout at the end of the season, particularly if we pick up a few results soon. Tomorrow at home against Dundalk, we need to win.

My leg is feeling better today. I partook in a training session and was happy that I completed most of it, including a game at the end. I still need another month, though. Off the field, I've finally qualified as a solicitor and that's given me a boost. It's possibly not the best time to be qualifying, in the middle of a recession, but I'm going to keep going with it and I'm delighted to have gotten to this point.

Football-wise, the only real negative has been the loss of young Eoin McGreevy, a small but talented midfielder with two great feet. He was included in training at the end of last season and did well in that before getting injured this year. Then he had a falling-out with Tommy and has now left. I used to give him lifts to training and I enjoyed his youthfulness. In my view he's the kind of player that Cork City should be protecting and developing. He's also from my GAA club, so I might be somewhat overprotective of him (just as fellow Barrs man Noel Hartigan had been of me when I was starting out). Anyway, I gave Eoin a call and told him he's definitely good enough and to keep playing. 'Not all managers are like Tommy when your injured,' I said. But truth be told, a good few of them are. From Tommy's point of view also I can see how it's very hard to keep a young, untested player on the books when you need to strengthen the squad in order to stay in your job.

Friday 4th May 2012

League of Ireland Premier Division

Turner's Cross, Cork

Cork City FC 3–2 Dundalk FC

An important win in torrential rain. Vinny with one and Davin scoring a brace.

Monday 7th May 2012

Today I met with freelance journalist and schoolteacher Edward Newman to discuss the idea of writing a book. Edward had helped me back in 2005 when I wrote a piece for the *Irish Examiner* which was published just after we won the league. I later approached him with the idea of a book recounting the 2008 season. He took a look at my notes and felt there might be something worthwhile and so we continued to discuss the idea over coffee over the subsequent months and years. These meetings culminated in my submission of a book proposal to a national publisher under Edward's guidance. As part of the submission I enclosed a draft chapter together with a list of contents and a rough description of the route the book would take. Furthermore, my cover letter emphasised that it was not my primary intention to attack former chairman, Tom Coughlan. As Coughlan's stewardship of Cork City – of perhaps the lack of it – was a popular topic with the national broadsheets and tabloids at the time, I was anxious to relay that this was not going to be a hatchet job on him. However, the publishers told me that without the Coughlan bits the story would lack the 'necessary teeth' to attract a national audience.

I was initially disappointed, but I was also relieved, given the personal nature of the book, that I hadn't lost control. I didn't want to embark on a pointless crusade against Coughlan. Edward pointed out that there were a lot of other publishers that might be interested, including more local outfits, but despite his encouragement I decided to concentrate on my solicitor role and I gradually lost contact with him.

Then, just last week, I ran into him again in the city and he expressed a desire to start up again. So today we met and talked about it for a good while. The conversation varied greatly, from the supposed 'greed' and 'horridness' of Premiership footballers – which I sternly reject as an unfair generalisation – to a comparison of the workings of the FAI versus the IRFU. I explained my theory in regard to the best strategy for Irish football (based on the work of others as well as my own thoughts) and he said I should write about it. He suggested that I set up a publishing company and we agreed to meet again in a few weeks.

Friday 18th May 2012

Today I arrived home from my solicitor graduation in Dublin still half-cut and had to make a beeline for Turner's Cross as we were doing a photo shoot in our new suits before the game. I arrived bang on time but wearing civilian clothes. Tommy stared at me in horror as I walked in.

'Murph's bringing my suit,' I muttered, 'as he collected it for me.'

'Whaa?' Tommy continued to stare.

I repeated, 'Murph has my suit.'

'OK', he said, 'but you need to get going for six o'clock.'

He seemed more than a little stressed. The match versus UCD later was a big game for him and for us. Three points and we'd be mid-table, and moving towards the right end of the league.

Murph arrived with the suit, I thanked him and got dressed pronto. Tommy went outside to the doorway and I heard him shouting to the photographers, 'We're nearly there, lads – just one to go.' Following which he came back in and said to me, edgily, 'Hoggie, hurry on fella, will ya?'

The photoshoot proceeded without further hitch and afterwards I did a warm-up with the lads. When the match kicked off I went in to have a shower in the empty dressing room – only it wasn't empty. Kitman Rafa and long-time volunteer Finbarr O'Shea were there, preparing for half-time and getting the dirty warm-up kit into baskets for washing and out of the way.

I had a shower and was drying myself while the Shed End above me sang, *'F**k the Dubs, f**k the Dubs, f**k the Dubs!'*

Rafa joined in: *'F**k the Dubs,'* he sang, laughingly.

It's good to be back.

Continuing the topic of strategic rivals, we discussed the end of World War 2. 'We finally get rid of the Nazis and then the US do a deal, and next the Russians come in and take over,' said Rafa. 'The Commies, we called them. They were terrible too,' he said.

I was about to question him on this but just then we were interrupted. From outside and above us there was a sudden elevation of noise followed by a very brief silence and then a loud roar.

Rafa clapped his hands. 'Brilliant!' And then: 'Shussh.' I hushed down and we waited in silence as the crowd sang madly.

A few seconds later the radio announcer, barely decipherable though the muffled tannoy speaker in the dressing room, said, 'DARYL HORRRRRGAN!! CORK CITY ONE; UCD NIL!'

Rafa raised a clenched fist and said a quiet 'Yes, yes' to himself. Finbarr commented that Daryl's flying at the moment and a great winger.

A few minutes later, though, there was a lowering of the noise and then some disgruntled voices could be heard above us. 'It's a penalty!' Finbarr shouted in from near the door.

'For f**k's sake!' grimaced Rafa.

Then a brief 'wowwww' before silence, which was inevitably broken by the radio announcer in a much more sober tone: 'Cork City one; UCD one.'

Rafa punched the dirty gear in disappointment before returning to the subject of 'the Commies'.

The lads won in the end and Tommy was almost delirious afterwards.

League of Ireland Premier Division

Turner's Cross, Cork

Cork City FC 4–2 UCD AFC

Thursday 24ᵗʰ May 2012

After a busy day at work I arrived into the car park at the Bishopstown training ground and was getting my gear out of the boot of my car when I heard a shout from inside: 'You're late, you fat b***ard!' It was Tommy. He was giggling away at me from the window of his office. It made me laugh.

The weather was great today and I was able to train, so I was absolutely delighted. The lads are playing Athlone in the cup tomorrow and this shaped Tommy's team talk after training.

'Lads, we're five games away from the FAI Cup and a day out at the Aviva. It seems the FAI Cup has a higher profile than cup competitions in other countries at the moment, so it's one to be up for. We'll need to be "at it" tomorrow though as Althone aren't bad. I'm telling ya, youse'll need to be right.'

After training, fitness coach Paudie pulled me aside and told me Tommy wants me to lose a stone. I had expected something like this; Tommy's banter on my arrival now being put to me formally... We discussed a lower-carb, higher-protein diet, together with using the cross-trainer for at least 20 minutes every day after training. I agreed as I'm happy to be part of Tommy's plans – particularly as it seems a few of the other injured lads are in the doghouse at the moment. Kevin Murray, Cathal Lordan and young Jamie Murphy have all had recent arguments with Tommy regarding their injuries.

Another lad on the injured list is young Shane O'Connor. He definitely seems to be sick of people asking about his ankle, so instead, as we were leaving the training ground, I asked about his time in the UK.

He was 15 or 16 when he went to Liverpool, he said. 'Looking back, I should've gone to a Championship club, but I was naïve enough to think I was going to play with Liverpool. I should've gone later; they might still have wanted me when I was 18. I was happy enough at the time to get out of doing the Leaving Cert, but really I should've waited. Even in Liverpool... I like accounting; I wanted to do it over there, to study it. I told them that, and my coaches, but they wouldn't allow me to do it as they said it would detract from my football. Looking back, I know it wouldn't have. It would've made me more balanced.'

In the car park I asked Shane how Liverpool had chosen him. He explained that he'd been on the Ireland underage team and loads of that team got picked up. 'Most of the schoolboy clubs got paid for their players,' he said, 'and the Dublin clubs actually paid some of it to the boys' parents.'

I told him that I think some the underage clubs in Ireland, particularly in Cork and Dublin, seem to have adopted as their mission the sending of players to the UK at 14 to 16 for financial reasons, and while the money generally goes back into club facilities, the clubs love the prestige of being associated with an English club. I don't like that and I think once a club gets too cosy with this type of scenario then the welfare of the player can come second – and obviously if that's the case it's not right. 'They don't seem to care about the players that *don't* make it; those that come back,' I said. 'They don't care anymore at that point, and nor, it seems, do the FAI. I remember asking if the FAI kept a record of players coming back from the UK, but it seems they only have a record of those leaving.'

'Ya,' said Shane. 'See the FAI, if I was to get a move back to the UK they'd start sniffing and scratching again about me. They don't give a sh*t now though. If I go to some other job now I'll never hear from them again. The English PFA are actually the opposite; they've been supporting me since I got back here.'

Earlier, Vinny Sul (who's from Waterford), Tadhg Purcell (from Dublin) and I had had a rant about how the Ireland under-21 manager had two LOI players on standby but when players got injured he called up lads from the UK instead. 'They don't give a sh*t about this league, except for the national team players,' we agreed.

Driving home, I listened to a radio interview in which Waterford men John O'Shea and Noel Hunt were talking about the upcoming Euros. Fair play to them. But there are six former LOI players in the squad and in my opinion not enough effort is made by the FAI to acknowledge the growing link between the national team and our league.

Tuesday 19th June 2012

More bad news today: Monaghan are pulling out of the league. You start to get used to the bad news after a while. As if this is what's acceptable or expected. It seems just part of the norm that clubs regularly have to pull out from our top league for financial reasons.

Monaghan forced to exit league

As 30,000 fans cheered on the Republic of Ireland in Poznan last night, yet another Airtricity League club was forced to withdraw from the domestic top flight due to a lack of support.

Monaghan United confirmed their intention to quit the league with immediate effect, stating "mainly but not only" financial problems [were] behind their decision. The club had struggled to find a title sponsor since rejoining the Premier Division after sealing promotion in a play-off against the now defunct Galway United last season, and with lower than expected attendances at Gortakeegan, couldn't make ends meet.

Chairman Jim McGlone said the club were left with little choice but to make such a difficult decision.

He explained: "In terms of trying to keep going, it would have stalled wages for players and would have built up debts that we could not honour. That's just not our style, so we felt the responsible thing to do was face it now rather than in six to eight weeks' time.

"Obviously the lack of a sponsor was the big blow. When we came into the Premier Division we were positive that sponsors would be found but it didn't happen. We were

seeking sponsors for the ground and the shirt but we couldn't find them."

The Professional Footballers' Association of Ireland claimed the club's players were not informed of the decision before Monaghan United officials ... issued a statement to the media yesterday morning.

"No player we have spoken to was contacted by the club prior to the statement being released and many players first heard that they had lost their jobs through Twitter," a PFAI spokesperson said.

"We find it extraordinary that no attempt was made to reach a solution with the players either directly with them or through this association. Situations like this have arisen in the past and agreements have been reached in order to keep a team in the league." ...

Meanwhile, after a board meeting in Poland following the announcement, the FAI declared that all results involving the club will be expunged, in line with the precedent set by Dublin City's disbandment in 2006 and accordance with rule 18.1 of the league's participation agreement.

Three teams — St Patrick's Athletic, Shamrock Rovers and Dundalk – had faced Mons twice, so now have a game in hand on the rest of league. Pats and the Hoops, though, have had four points deducted, while Dundalk lose just one.

Others to lose out include Cork City, who scored six against at home to United and drop down a place in the table, with Bohemians moving up because Mons had defeated the Gypsies at Dalymount Park.

Sligo, Drogheda, Shelbourne, Derry, UCD and Bray also woke up this morning with three points less on the board.

In addition to the league changes, one team will receive a bye in the third round of the FAI Cup due to Monaghan's removal from the competition.

(Alan Smith, *Irish Examiner*, 19th June 2012)

Same old story. And the loss of the points and goals scored represent an untimely kick in the stomach while we're trying to climb up the league table.

Chapter Nine – 25th June to 2nd December 2012

Monday 25th June 2012

There was a two-week break from fixtures for the Euro Championships, which meant that most players got a week off to go on holiday and then trained for a week on their return. However, I trained along with the other injured players while all the other players went on their holidays. We trained hard for four days solid and it was a good chance to catch up and get towards match fitness – although at times I felt slightly despondent. On the Monday I felt I couldn't keep up with the pace of things; I kept losing the ball in games and I could tell by Woodsy and Tommy's quietness that they could see I was all over the shop. I felt very down after that session, although the following day I was a lot better both in running and in the games.

During the last training session I felt really good. I enjoyed the session, knew what I was doing with the ball and felt comfortable and strong during the games. Then last Friday I played for the first time since my operation, during the last 10 minutes of a league game against Derry. We drew 2–2. It felt good to play but I might not get another chance for a while as Johnny Dunleavy returns from suspension this Friday against Bray, and he and Colin Healy (who's occasionally played at right-back) have probably been our best players this season. Either way, I was delighted to play my first few minutes since the final day of last season. I've been training hard and eating and resting properly and the body is getting there.

Meanwhile, Ireland were well beaten in the European Championships and the country is now more interested in what's wrong with Irish football. Everybody's questioning Trapattoni and the players and the FAI. How can we be so far behind not just Spain and Italy, but Croatia? However, the general public are not aware of how developed Croatian football is and how connected it is to the clubs on the continent. We were the worst team in the tournament, according to some. The newspapers are all concerned as to whether we'll get to the next World Cup in Brazil and whether we have the right management team to get us there. But I don't think these are the right questions for Irish football right now. The failure of the national team is the top end of the problem, the tip of the iceberg. The number of Irish players at English Premier League clubs has been decreasing for some time now due to the number of foreign players being brought in. There are fewer Scottish and Welsh players also.

Our approach to this new problem has been to do more of the same. We just send more over. But this approach misses the point. We're structurally defunct and relying on a pathway for producing players that is failing.

OK, it may still be the right thing for our very best to go, but at the moment it seems to me that we send far too many players across the Channel at a very young age rather than trying to develop them at home. Could we not develop a long-term strategy to deal with our structural issues rather than putting the majority of our efforts into trying to get a team together to qualify for Brazil in 2014? With Monaghan going out of the league the need for reform is clear, but those in the top seats at the Association seem to be focused elsewhere.

FAI chief takes 'grave offence' at Sopot criticism
FAI chief executive John Delaney has defended his much-publicised drinking sessions with Irish fans during Ireland's disastrous Euro 2012 campaign.

In weekend interviews, Mr Delaney claimed he had spent some €30,000 of his own money on fans during his reign and took "grave offence" at criticism of his socialising while in Poland.

The FAI chief said he was "entitled" to a night out during the Euro 2012 campaign in Poland.

"We worked very, very hard. And if I had a night out, with family, my sister was over there, my brother-in-law and some

friends, I think that's something I'm entitled to do on the odd occasion when I'm there," he said.

Mr Delaney also sought to address criticism of the incident where he was carried head-high by hundreds of Irish fans, who then removed his shoes and socks.

"What happened one evening on the way home to the hotel was a couple of hundred fans raised me up in the air and they carried me head-high home. Now, if that's a crime, I'm not guilty," he said.

The FAI chief described the incident as a "a bit of folklore" that had been blown out of proportion.

However, many of the fans who witnessed the event described Mr Delaney's behaviour as "embarrassing". On a separate occasion, he is believed to have bought a round for an entire bar in Sopot.

He admitted to spending €30,000 of his own money on fans in his tenure, saying there was nothing wrong in buying a drink for the fans.

"The Irish fans have been incredible and what's wrong with me buying them a drink? They invest so much in following the team. Just because other chief executives don't do it doesn't mean I won't," he said.

However, this seems to go against what the FAI chief said prior to the tournament. Speaking at the launch of the Drinkaware.ie Euro 2012 Survival Guide in May, he said there would be no repeat of the infamous "party train" for Irish supporters in Estonia last year.

Mr Delaney came under further pressure last night when the chairman of Monaghan United Jim McGlone, whose club had to resign from the Airtricity League due to financial issues, blasted his behaviour at the European Championships.

"There would be serious disquiet, not only within the Airtricity league, but within football in general over his behaviour," said Mr McGlone. "I suppose a man is entitled to a drink, and there would have been occasions in the past where I would have been glad nobody was around with a

camera to take a picture of me, but when you are representing
an association, images like that appearing do not look good."
…

(Conall Ó Fátharta, *Irish Examiner*, 25th June 2012)

Tuesday 26th June 2012

Tommy's been trying to bring in a few new faces to freshen
things up. Two young strikers from Limerick trained with us
today. Afterwards I gave one of them a lift back to the motel
he's staying in. On the way he explained how he'd recently
had a falling-out with the Limerick manager Pat Scully and
that he hopes to sign with us now.

I asked about his history and he explained that he's from
Listowel in Kerry and was over in Fulham in the UK for a few
years but got released. *Last-chance saloon*, I thought, but I
didn't say anything except that there seem to be more and
more Kerry players in the league. I dropped him off at the
motel and wished him luck. In truth I wouldn't like to be in his
shoes.

In other news, Muz, who's on the injured list at the
moment, has taken a job with Johnson & Johnson in Cork,
doing shift work. While this is a very good move for Dan – I
know they're a really great employer in Cork – it would be a
real shame to see man of his experience lost to the game
completely. We need to keep guys like him involved in the
backroom set-up if we're to build on the experience of the last
10 years or so.

In any event, while Muz recovers I hope to stay off the
injured list myself for a while.

Friday 29th June 2012

We played Bray away tonight. Bray is a lovely seaside town
and I enjoyed the spin from Dublin city centre knowing that I
could relax on the bench. I've been based in the Metropolitan
District Court in Dublin with work for the last couple of days
on a particularly emotional family law-related matter, so I was

really looking forward to the game – and especially from the recliner on the bench.

Bray's set-up is comfortable and especially pleasant on a sunny day. Their manager, Pat Devlin, is Damien Duff's agent and Bray have a tradition of playing attractive football and producing one or two exciting players every year – many of whom use Bray as a stepping-stone to clubs in the UK. They had one or two good players on show tonight, but we played really well for a change, scoring early in what proved to be a comfortable and impressive night's work for our lads.

League of Ireland Premier Division

The Carlisle Grounds, Bray, Co. Wicklow

Bray Wanderers FC 0–3 Cork City FC

Dan Murray and myself were unused subs and sat happily enough together on the bench, chatting away. Of course, we also encouraged our teammates during the game and added support to Tommy and Billy's message in the dressing room too. An experienced player or two on the bench can be of huge value to a manager and to the squad. At least that's what I told myself tonight.

I'd left my boots and half my training gear at Bishopstown last Tuesday, and as I was in Dublin already for work, Jerry Harris took it upon himself to get my boots looked after and my training gear washed. Good old Jerry.

~~~~

FAI chief earns €250k more than Spain and Italy rivals
FAI chief John Delaney earns €250,000 more than the soccer chiefs in Euro 2012 championship winners Spain and the runners-up Italy, it has emerged.

Angel Maria Villar, who is Spain's football boss, earns €152,000 a year and the FA boss in Italy, Antonello Valentini is on a salary of €150,000, the Irish Daily Star reports today.

Combined their annual salaries come to €302,000 – that's €98,000 less than Mr Delaney (44) who earns €400,000 a year.

Italy won the World Cup in 2006 and Spain won it in 2010 while Ireland was the first team knocked out of Euro 2012.

The Irish Times pointed out yesterday that he is paid twice the salary of Taoiseach Enda Kenny and €151,000 more than President Michael D. Higgins. Meanwhile, the FAI last night denied it had cut grants to clubs and leagues by €377,000 in 2011.

This figure was contained in an Irish Times report which said it had obtained a copy of the association's accounts to be presented to the AGM on July 21. Mr Delaney's €400,000 salary in 2011 was 7.2pc less than the €431,687 he earned in the previous year.

Whether the 'football family', as represented by the delegates to attend the FAI AGM, will have any issue with the chief executive's salary remains to be seen. No comment was forthcoming from the FAI on the salary amounts mentioned, but a brief statement refuted the notion that grants had been reduced in 2011, stating: "The FAI has not cut club grants by €377,000 between 2011 and 2010.

"In reality, the grants paid out amounted to €1.2m in both 2010 and 2011 and this can be vouched by the independent auditors." …

There is concern within soccer circles about the FAI debt on the Aviva Stadium, but in [a Sunday Independent interview on 24th June 2012] Mr Delaney repeated his confidence that it would be cleared within eight years.

"To talk about the debt of the Aviva is, you know… we had to find €95m for that stadium, and we owe €50m to our funding partners on that. And that will be clear by 2020," he said. …

(From the *Irish Independent*, 6th July 2012)

Sunday 15th July 2012

A young player named Brian Lenihan from local side College Corinthians has been training with us for the past few weeks. He's a shy lad but clearly has lots of ability and a great engine. Tommy's been impressed with him too and has signed him. I think he could be a really good player for the club in the future, on the strength of the past few weeks.

Cork City sign teenage midfielder Brian Lenihan

Cork City have announced the signing of 18-year-old central midfielder Brian Lenihan.

The teenager has joined the Turner's Cross outfit from Munster Senior League College Corinthians.

Lenihan, who has international experience at schoolboy level, is considered a versatile player and can also be called on in play in defence.

Cork manager Tommy Dunne is hoping this won't be his last business during the transfer window. ...

(From RTÉ – www.rte.ie – 11th July 2012)

Tuesday 14th August 2012

Unfortunately there's been a notable nose-dip in our results lately, not helped by my contribution to a Dundalk goal at Oriel a few weeks ago that allowed them to draw with us. I've been fairly despondent since then, even suggesting to Woodsy that it might be time to hang up the boots. But Woodsy told me to relax and that I have years left at the club if I want them. I then spoke with Tommy about the possibility of taking a break for a week or two and coming back refreshed. But he said I shouldn't do that, and that the best thing would be to stay involved – even when I'm not playing – and continue to help the others as someone who's 'been there and done it'.

Tommy encouraged me to start my coaching badges, and to go easy on myself as I've been out of action for a long time. He reckons the goal at Dundalk wouldn't have happened if I'd been fit.

Despite these supportive words I still had to watch a replay of the goal in front of all the lads, and endure the detailed analysis. It really is a type of torture.

And after the Dundalk match I'd trained terribly – which is what had prompted me to speak with Tommy.

However, I played the full 90 minutes against Blackburn Rovers in a friendly, and then Tommy left me out of the squad for the game against Pat's, which was just as well as my knee needed the recovery time. The lads lost 1–0, leaving us nearing the lower end of the table and in danger of being sucked into a relegation battle. In truth, the way things are going we're probably lucky that Monaghan have gone out of business as only one team goes down this year.

League of Ireland Premier Division, 14th August 2012

Pos	Team	Pl	W	D	L	GF	GA	GD	Pts
1	Sligo Rovers	19	11	7	1	33	14	+19	40
2	Drogheda United	20	11	5	4	33	23	+10	38
3	Shamrock Rovers	20	8	9	3	34	26	+8	33
4	St Patrick's Athletic	18	8	8	2	24	13	+11	32
5	Bohemian	20	7	5	8	19	18	+1	26
6	Shelbourne	20	7	4	9	24	27	-3	25
7	Derry City	19	6	5	8	20	22	-2	23
8	Cork City	20	4	10	6	24	24	0	22
9	Bray Wanderers	20	4	7	9	27	37	-10	19
10	Dundalk	20	3	7	10	16	36	-20	16
11	UCD	20	3	5	12	17	31	-14	14
12	Monaghan United*	0	0	0	0	0	0	0	0

*Resigned from the league

Tuesday 21st August 2012

The lads lost to UCD last Friday in what was by all accounts a fairly comprehensive beating (3–1); so we're heading towards a relegation dogfight – we're just five points above UCD, who are now second-bottom above Dundalk. I chose not to travel as I wasn't really in the reckoning to play and my knee hadn't settled since the Blackburn game.

Tommy was positively irate at training yesterday, using a replay to point out all the mistakes that had been made, as has been the norm since the Doolin days. He called the performance embarrassing. He then asked the younger members of the squad – about eight lads – to leave the room while he had a right go at the more senior players.

It wasn't pretty, but it led to a reaction as we went on to beat Drogheda 3–2 at the Cross in my first full competitive 90 minutes (100 minutes, in fact: the ref played an unbelievable 10 minutes of injury time, which I didn't appreciate) since my knee operation.

We finally showed some guts, holding on with 10 men for the last 20 minutes after Nults got sent off and conceded a penalty from which Drogheda equalised. It seemed harsh on Nults, as the Drogheda player had looked well off-side in the build-up, but we managed to hold on and then Davin got a late winner. It was a really sweet victory that moved us back towards mid-table, and I was massively relieved to play the full game.

I recently looked up Denis Irwin's statistics and it seems he played with United right up until he was 35. I'm only 32, so if my knee recovers I might have a few years left. A week is a long time in football…

Saturday 1st September 2012

Following our win against Drogheda we've lost twice to Shamrock Rovers – away in the FAI Cup (2–0), then at home in the league (1–2) yesterday. They totally dominated yesterday's game, and Tommy was exasperated this morning.

'We got absolutely savaged,' he declared in the team meeting. 'I had to switch the TV off for the last 20 minutes at home last night; I couldn't watch it. They were so far ahead of us.'

He asked us where our passion has gone.

'And another thing: if you look at our fitness, I'm telling youse, it's way behind theirs. Light bleedin' years behind. We got bleedin' savaged and that's it, youse can look at the tape yourselves. There's no other way of looking at it.'

Some of us replied, when invited, that we hadn't lacked passion against Drogheda and that things might have been different the other night against Rovers – we'd just missed a few good chances at the start. Woodsy added, in our defence: 'To be fair, Tommy, that Rovers group are one of the best groups in the LOI over the past 10 years; most of them are from the side that broke through to UEFA group stages last year.'

I added, 'Also, only four or five of our starting 11 yesterday have played in the Premier Division prior to this season, whereas almost every one of their players has three or four years' experience behind them – and experience at the top of the league too. Young fellas are still learning here but we're going in the right direction. It'll just take time.'

Whilst he acknowledged our points, there was no real change in Tommy's demeanour. He responded, 'I know what you're saying, fellas; we've got young lads and all that… but it doesn't change the fact that we got bleedin' savaged!'

The meeting ended shortly afterwards.

The teams below us have been winning; the next few results will be important.

Friday 7th September 2012

League of Ireland Premier Division

The Brandywell, Derry

Derry City FC 0–1 Cork City FC

Winning in Derry is never easy, and this was a massive win. I was absent at a friend's wedding but Tommy won't mind too much now.

League of Ireland Premier Division, 7th September 2012

Pos	Team	Pl	W	D	L	GF	GA	GD	Pts
1	Sligo Rovers	22	13	8	1	39	15	+24	47
2	Drogheda United	23	12	5	6	38	30	+8	41
3	Shamrock Rovers	22	10	9	3	38	27	+11	39
4	St Patrick's Athletic	21	9	9	3	25	14	+11	36
5	Derry City	22	8	6	8	24	22	+2	30
6	Bohemian	22	7	6	9	21	22	-1	27
7	Shelbourne	23	7	5	11	27	34	-7	26
8	Cork City	23	5	10	8	20	29	-2	25
9	Bray Wanderers	23	5	8	10	29	40	-11	23
10	UCD	23	5	5	13	23	36	-13	20
11	Dundalk	22	3	7	12	18	40	-22	16
12	Monaghan United*	0	0	0	0	0	0	0	0

*Resigned from the league

Thursday 20th September 2012

After the Derry match the lads beat Bray two-nil at home. Suddenly we're sixth and Tommy's beaming. 'We need to confirm that Setanta Cup spot now,' he said at training tonight, with an eye on tomorrow's game at Dalymount against Bohemian.

Friday 21st September 2012

League of Ireland Premier Division

Dalymount Park, Dublin

Bohemian FC 1–1 Cork City FC

I'm still on the bench since my hiatus for my friend's wedding, as converted centre-half Gavin Kavanagh is doing very well at right-back, with Johnny Dunleavy having moved to midfield where he's also done well. The draw is another good result.

On the bus home we discussed the recent luckless streak of Dubliner Keith Quinn, a left-winger who recently arrived from now-defunct Monaghan United. He's struggled to get on the bench after a few ropey early appearances, particularly in the game where we got savaged by Rovers. I'm hoping the guy gets another chance as he's had no luck at all since he arrived. After coming on at the worst time in the midst of that Rovers savagery, his car broke down the following week, and last Thursday our dressing room was robbed by an opportunist thief who decided to steal a good few of the lads' wallets, including Keith's. As the lads took stock of what had been stolen, Keith cried out in despair, 'Ah! They've only taken my runners too!'

Davin O'Neill was quick to take the opportunity: 'I can see why they didn't take your tracksuit, though!'

Yesterday at training Keith was talking about his nephew. The lads had seen a piece in the paper about this young kid and Keith explained, 'Yeah, he's off to Atlético Madrid; they're taking a look at him. He's only 14.'

When the lads quietened down I shared my concern with Keith: 'He's very young, isn't he? To be linked in the paper with a move to Spain?'

'I know what you mean, Hog.' he said, 'I was at [Manchester] United myself at 16. We'll look after him – don't worry – and it's better for any young fella to go to Spain than the UK these days. Imagine what he'll learn. His dad will be with him anyway.'

I didn't take it any further but I have concerns. I know Messi went to Barca at a young age, but not everyone is a Messi…

Friday 26th October 2012

It's one o'clock in the morning and we're on the bus home from Dublin. It was the last game of the season and the lads lost one-nil to Pat's at Richmond Park. I've been an unused sub for the last month or so. Results have been mixed – a draw against Sligo, a loss to Shels, another win against Dundalk – but we've finished sixth and got a Setanta Cup spot for next year.

Tommy's asked me to stay on for next season. Woodsy mentioned that there's a lot of running planned for pre-season at the Mardyke track – we've finally linked up properly with the UCC/Mardyke Arena. Sure I might give it one last push.

Sunday 2nd December 2012

I'm writing this from Vietnam where I'm on holiday. I received a text from club administrator Éanna Buckley a week ago saying our physio Rob Savage was in intensive care in Norway (where he'd gone to live with his Norwegian wife). A few days later Woodsy texted me to confirm, respectfully, that Rob had died. It's really shocking news. Poor Rob. He worked with me a lot over the past few years and I got to know him well. A real gem of a guy. I wouldn't be back running properly if it weren't for him. He even texted me from Norway after my first game back to say well done. He was a committed and talented physio with a lovely warm sense of humour. I'll miss him. Taken too early, at the age of just 31.

Chapter Ten – 14th January to 25th October 2013

Monday 14th January 2013

We're a week into pre-season and here's the news:

1. It appears our two strikers from last year, Vinny Sullivan and Davin O'Neill, aren't signing back. Davin is committing to his work as a fitter in the navy; and as for Vinny, I'm not sure he and Tommy got on all that well – despite Vinny being our top scorer last year. So they are two huge losses. Tommy's been busy trying to replace them. He's signed two new centre-forwards in Daryl Kavanagh from Shamrock Rovers and Danny Furlong from Wexford Youths. However, those signings have just been outshone in my eyes, as guess who turned up at training tonight… none other than 'Ding Dong' Denis Behan.

2. Centre-half Gavin Kavanagh hasn't come back from his home in Dublin to join us in pre-season yet and the lads found out that he's on the transfer list. It's a surprise to us all, as he and Tommy seemed to get on quite well (save for a few minor altercations) and he ended last year on a high, playing well at right-back. His absence might be related to the fact that Kevin Murray, after an injury-plagued season last year, has signed for the club again this year. Kevin was with the club back in 2005 and has spent the last few years at Cobh and Waterford. He signed back last year only to injure himself badly and played no part in the season. He's an excellent right-sided centre-back and will be a great addition if he can get fit. So perhaps Tommy's playing his cards close to his chest with Gavin.

3. Tommy seems to have had a bit of a falling-out with Colin Healy during the off-season. It's a strange one as

Colin's a brilliant guy to have around at training and is also always a top performer on match day. For the moment he's still training with us and he doesn't seem to be showing any signs of unhappiness, but some of the boys have noticed tension between him and Tommy.

4. During a crazy pre-season run out on the track at the Mardyke yesterday, Muzza told me it might be his last day at training. Tommy has signed Billy Dennehy's brother, Darren Dennehy – a 24-year-old 6ft 5" left-sided centre-back. Dennehy's making his way back to Ireland after moving to Everton as a 16-year-old. And so it's conceivable that Tommy may not offer Muz terms, as Muz was injured for a lot of last year. Muz wasn't at training tonight but I'm hoping he's just working nights or something.

Sunday 20th January 2013

There's been a bit of unrest in the squad. The lads have become aware of a difference in the way certain players are being paid. It turns out that some players have been paid from the first day of pre-season while the majority of the lads aren't going to start seeing wages until the first league game against Limerick on 10th March. So, effectively, some lads are being paid two months before other lads' wages kick in. Adding fuel to the fire is the fact that we're going to be playing competitive games in the Setanta Cup before the entire squad's wages start. While my wage of zero means I'm unaffected, I don't like the obvious unfairness – and I don't want it to ruin our season before we even get going. The discontented lads asked my advice about talking to Tommy and the club, and I reluctantly agreed to help. The last thing this club needs now is bad press. We typed up a document to give to Tommy and the Board.

We, the players of Cork City FC, would like to take this opportunity to express the following:

We feel that it would be only fair and right to receive our full wages from the start of the Setanta Cup until the start of the LOI season.

Considering that we have not been paid during the off-season (unlike some other LOI Premier Division clubs) or during pre-season (unlike most other PD clubs) we therefore feel that we greatly deserve to be paid this wage from the first Setanta Cup game until the start of the LOI season (roughly three weeks' wages). It should be noted that we are the only club in the Setanta Cup, as things currently stand, that are not going to be paid for competing in the first round of that competition.

We would like to make it clear that despite not being paid during the off-season or during pre-season, every player has put everything into training for pre-season and every player intends to continue to work hard for the club for the pre-season and season ahead. Players have also, of course, looked after themselves appropriately during the off-season.

It may be worth stating just what pre-season so far, and into the foreseeable future, consists of:

- *Training on five days a week (Monday morning, Tuesday and Thursday afternoon, Saturday and Sunday mornings). This is despite the fact that part-time contracts consist of four days.*
- *The training for six weeks (along with planned added sessions down the line) adds up to a total of roughly 34 sessions.*

- *There are also at least two games and probably more during pre-season.*

The start of national and international competitive club fixtures has always, in the past, so far as the players are aware, been the start time for payments to part-time players at the beginning of a season. We ask now that this continues and that our wages should start with our first competitive fixture in the Setanta Cup.

The players are making this approach to you now so that we can sort things out internally and hopefully without any difficulty. The last thing we want is a distraction from our pre-season. In that context we ask that you consider our request favourably in light of both the goodwill that we have shown so far as a group and our ambition for the year ahead.

Yours in sport,
The players at Cork City FC, Season 2013

Sunday 27ᵗʰ January 2013

It's done. A victory for all involved. Captain Kevin Murray, myself, Murph, Healers the rest of the players, FORAS board member Paul Hartnett, accountant Alan Whelan, CEO Timmy Murphy and Tommy have negotiated a truce. This victory, our first of the season, may be the most important of all. Players asked for respect for the training we've been putting in. Some were adamant that we should strike or go to the PFAI, but I didn't want that to happen. The club is just finding its feet and I thought a compromise could surely be reached – and happily now the matter has been resolved. In fairness to FORAS and Paul Hartnett (in his last week on the Board), they gave the players the respect we deserve. So it was agreed that we and the club would organise a charity/friendly game at the end of the year from which the players would receive some of the proceeds, and that the players would get an additional week's wages with a further bonus if we go through to the next round of the Setanta Cup. The lads were happy enough with this.

Murph is all about getting QPR or Liverpool over to play the friendly, but we'll see what happens. The most important thing was the open dialogue between FORAS and the players; this was refreshing and it disarmed the players in the end. It's a very welcome change from the previous interactions that the players were involved in under our last chairman and under Arkaga. FORAS seem to be on our side.

Tuesday 29th January 2013
We never threatened to go on strike, insists Cork skipper Murray
Cork City's new captain insists that there was never any threat of players going on strike during recent talks over Setanta Sports Cup payments.

Defender Kevin Murray was confirmed as Cork's skipper for 2013 yesterday and immediately set about addressing rumours of a player walkout.

The Rebels start their season when Cliftonville visit Turner's Cross on 11 February but there was speculation last week that the squad would refuse to play if they could not agree compensation payments for the two-legged cup tie.

The situation has now been resolved, Murray said on Monday, and insisted that the discussions between club and players always remained "amicable".

"Obviously we have engaged with the club over the last couple of weeks," he told CorkCityFC.net. "Representatives from both sides have sat down for discussions, and we are happy now that we have come to an agreement.

"I am aware that there has been stuff mentioned in the press and online, but there is absolutely no truth in any of it. The discussions that took place were always amicable and there was never any mention of any strike by the players.

"As a squad, we are happy to have it all sorted and we are now looking forward to getting back to competitive action." ...
(From *The42* – www.the 42.ie – 29th January 2013)

Saturday 2nd February 2013

Pre-season and transfer rumours are both progressing at pace. It seems that although Muzza and Gavin Kavanagh (who recently returned from Dublin) have both been training with us over the last week or so, only Muz is going to be signing – and even that's not certain as yet.

We've signed a left-footed Geordie winger from English conference side Darlington, named Adam Rundle. He's played a lot of football in the lower leagues in England and seems decent enough. It also seemed that our loanee striker from last year, Tadhg Purcell, was re-signing for us this year as Denis Behan and Tommy couldn't agree terms. Denis was doing very well in pre-season training until he came out to the track at the Mardyke. The rest of us were used to the track at this stage, but poor Denis really struggled, after which Tommy seemed to change his mind about signing him.

So the lads heard that Tadhg had signed, but then as I arrived at training last week in Mayfield I passed him as he was literally walking off the pitch and he said to me with a giggle, 'I'm off.' Before I got to ask him what was going on, Tommy called us all in and I had to jog off. The lads later told me that Tadhg and Tommy had disagreed about the amount that Tadhg would sign for, and Tadhg decided that he was leaving. According to the lads, Tommy called after him as he left the training pitch (just before I arrived), '...and you can leave behind the [training] gear as well!'

Welcome back to centre stage 'Ding Dong Denis Beehive Behan', who has now signed again for the club. Within a few minutes it was as if he'd never been away. He's as loud as ever but you can tell the older lads are delighted to have him back to entertain us. He's lifted the atmosphere already. The younger lads, however, clearly don't know what to make of him.

Denis started telling us about something he calls 'bonbongate' down in Limerick – an incident that occurred with their manager Pat Scully towards the end of last season:

'…you see, we were already running away with the First Division. So Scully was probably thinking about the following season already and laying down the law a bit. Anyway, we were on the bus to Waterford or Wexford, I can't remember which. The bus stopped at a garage and we all got off and went in. Then, I couldn't believe it: I hadn't seen green bonbons since I was in secondary school. But there they were. I think they must've come out in a different brand or something. So I said, "Right, I'm getting those."

'As we got back on the bus I told the lads about the jar of green bonbons. "I haven't seen them in donkey's," I told them, and they wanted to see for themselves. So, stupidly, I brought them out and tasted one. It was quality, I swear to God. They all wanted a taste and so the jar was passed around the whole bus. When it got back to me it was nearly empty, and they were laughing, the b*****ds.

'Anyway, we went and played the match and I don't think it went well; we must've drawn, I think. A few days later I got called into Pat Scully's office. There was a bit of an inquest going on as Pat wasn't happy with the result. When I entered his office he looked all serious and he had the sports scientist with him. And do you know what he said to me?'

'What did he say, Denis?' asked Murph, on behalf of all the older lads who were getting excited.

'He said, "I heard you were eating sweets, Denis… on the way to the match the other night." He was proper pissed off too. "That's not what I expect of professionals," he said, all angry-like.

'So I said, "Ah, stop there now Pat. It was a tub of apple bonbons and I had one. Then it was passed around the bus and those hungry f**kers ate the rest."

'Then Pat said, "But you can't be showing a bad example to the young lads, Denis. They can't be eating sweets before a match."

'I said, "It was one f**king bonbon, Pat. One f**king bonbon."

'And he goes, "Yeah, but it's a bad example and…"

'So I told him, "Pat, I can't believe you're blaming the result on one f**king bonbon."'

The older lads were all delighted by Denis' retelling of bonbon-gate – it captured him perfectly. 'It's great to have you back Ding Dong,' one of them said.

While the young lads laughed too, they did so somewhat nervously and then talked among themselves. 'He's got some shot though, to be fair to him,' I heard one of them say. 'And from either foot,' said another.

They'll soon get to know the complex creature that is Ding Dong Behan. I'm glad he's back.

Monday 4th March 2013

Setanta Cup – second round, second leg

Seaview, Belfast

Crusaders FC (NI) 1–3 Cork City FC (ROI) (agg. score: 1–4)

Tonight we qualified for the semi-final of the Setanta Cup by knocking out last year's winners, Crusaders, up in Belfast. The game marked young Garry Buckley's first start next to me at centre-half. He's fresh from a winning season with Cork City's under-18s and looks a good prospect. He did fine tonight. Also, Daryl Horgan got a nice goal and Daryl Kavanagh scored a beauty. This means the lads will get their bonus for getting through the round, as negotiated with FORAS a few weeks ago. The match highlights are notable for a fan falling onto the pitch following Kavanagh's goal (available on www.youtube.com).

Ultimately though, there is worry that the competition is becoming one-sided. Apart from our comprehensive win, elsewhere tonight Shamrock Rovers beat Linfield (NI) 4–1 while Sligo beat Glentoran (NI) 5–0. With the other quarter-final being played between Derry and Drogheda, it's likely that the semi-finals will be made up of four teams from the League of Ireland, which makes it all feel like a normal league cup competition for us. It doesn't bode well for the competition overall. It seems like the Irish League (NI) teams aren't taking it as seriously as they have in the past, perhaps because it hasn't fallen well into their season schedule this year. Whatever the case, I feel that if this were to be the main competition whereby European places for both jurisdictions are decided, things would be different and you'd see better performances and an increase in standards all round.

But that's another day's work. Today we're just happy with a good result which confirms we're going well after beating Cliftonville (NI) in the previous round. It's all good preparation for the start of the league campaign next week, when we'll face newly promoted Limerick – and Joey 'No-Show' Gamble. They've brought in some really experienced players so it'll be a tough game.

Sunday 10th March 2013

League of Ireland Premier Division

Thomond Park, Limerick

Limerick FC 0–0 Cork City FC

Limerick 0-0 Cork City

Limerick's return to the top flight ended in a grim 0-0 stalemate with Cork City in front of 3,578 spectators at Thomond Park.

Cork were on top initially, but Limerick improved as the contest wore on and could have nicked a winner.

There was plenty to admire in the defensive discipline of Stuart Taylor and Tommy Dunne's teams at the Limerick venue.

Chris Curran and David O'Leary went close in the third quarter for Limerick, but Cork, with Dan Murray solid at the back, defended well when put under pressure.

What should have been a pleasant occasion in front of a decent crowd was ruined by the wretched weather as the wind and rain disrupted both teams' passing approach. …

Limerick: Ryan; Nzuzi, O'Callaghan (Bradley, 68), Folan, Williams; O'Leary, Gamble, Tracy; Galbraith (Rainsford, 90), Curran, Bossekota.

Cork City: McNulty; N Horgan, K Murray, D Murray, Murphy; G Morrissey, Healy, Duggan; Turner (D Morrissey, 63), Kavanagh (Behan, 63), D Horgan (Rundle, 89).

(From RTÉ – www.rte.ie – 10th March 2013)

This was a tough game. I felt we had a lot to lose against this up-and-coming side. We're meant to be the kingpins in Munster, but they must have a bit of money if they've got in the likes of Ryan, Gamble, Folan and Stephen Bradley. These are all vastly experienced lads at this level, so tonight's draw was a decent start for us and a good point away. Unfortunately, Thomond Park has a capacity of 25,000 and most of the noise made by the 4,000 or so fans that turned up was absorbed into the surrounding emptiness of the stadium. Plus the stadium looked really empty on TV and with such a small crowd was somewhat eerie to play in as well. The conditions were wretched, with driving rain and wind, and so overall it was a bad advertisement for our league. We need to aspire to have nice modern stadiums with capacities of 7–10,000.

Friday 15th March 2013

League of Ireland Premier Division

Turner's Cross, Cork

Cork City FC 2–1 Bohemian FC

Our solid start to the 2013 campaign has continued with a good home win tonight. Good to see young Danny Furlong score, while Daryl Horgan is on absolute fire.

Cork City 2-1 Bohemians
A fine second performance gave Cork City an Airtricity League Premier Division 2-1 comeback win in front of 2,764 fans at Turner's Cross.

Owen Heary had headed Bohemians into a half time lead with his 41st-minute effort.

But Cork came out with all guns blazing and equalised through a Danny Furlong shot in the 50th minute.

The Leesiders struck the front just before the hour, the outstanding Daryl Horgan shooting to the bottom corner of Dean Delany's net for the winning goal.

Both these clubs have had bright openings to the new season. Cork are already through to the Setanta Cup semifinals after victories over Cliftonville and Crusaders.

Tommy Dunne's side also drew their opening league game in the scoreless draw with Limerick in the live televised match from Thomond Park last Sunday.

Bohemians had recorded two wins in the first week of their season. …

There was a fine atmosphere created by both sets of fans in the 2,764 crowd at the Leesiders' first home league game of the season. …

Cork, who failed to beat Bohemians in three league games last season, now have four points from their opening two league games.

Cork: McNulty; Murphy, D Murray, K Murray, N Horgan; D Horgan (Rundle 92) C Healy, Duggan, Morrissey; Furlong (Turner 85), Kavanagh.

Bohemians: Dean Delany; Derek Pender, Owen Heary, Roberto Lopes; Keith Buckley, Stephen Traynor (Scully 70), Ryan McEvoy, Kevin Devaney; Chris Lyons (Hanaphy 81), Karl Moore (Nangle 63).

(From RTÉ – www.rte.ie – 15th March 2013)

Saturday 23rd March 2013
Dunne seeking another City lift
… Cork City welcome Derry City to Turner's Cross tomorrow looking to maintain their own unbeaten start to the campaign. Brian Lenihan is Tommy Dunne's only definite absentee, though he has slight doubts over the fitness of both Daryl and Neal Horgan. Dunne said: "I think, at home, we can give anybody a match with the crowd behind us. It is important we perform well, and I do not see any reason why we cannot pick up the three points." …

(Alan Smith, *Irish Examiner*, 23rd March 2013)

Sunday 24th March 2013

League of Ireland Premier Division

Turner's Cross, Cork

Cork City FC 0–1 Derry City FC

I picked up an injury in my left quad in training during the week, so I wasn't involved tonight, which was disappointing but I felt I could probably do with the rest too after playing in all the games so far. John Dunleavy came in at right-back and did well but Derry still won with a last-minute penalty after new signing Adam Rundle handled in the box.

Monday 1st April 2013

League of Ireland Premier Division

United Park, Drogheda

Drogheda United FC 1–1 Cork City FC

I've been out of action for longer than anticipated. In the meantime on Friday we drew 1–1 away to Rovers with their equaliser coming in the 94th minute. Then today at Drogheda the lads conceded an 87th-minute equaliser to draw again 1–1. These last-minute goals are becoming a dangerous habit.

Monday 22nd April 2013

The habit continued last Friday at Shels; they equalised in the 94th minute. It was hard to take – although prior to that we'd won against UCD and had a good 1–1 draw at Rovers in the first leg of the Setanta semi-final, where I'd been able to make a return from injury. That had set us up nicely for the return leg today. Another all-Ireland final had seemed on the cards for us when we led 2–1. But it wasn't to be.

Setanta Cup – semi-final, second leg

Turner's Cross, Cork

Cork City FC 2–2 Shamrock Rovers FC

(agg. score: 3–3; Shamrock Rovers go through on away goals)

Late Dennehy goal sends Rovers through to Setanta Cup final

A late Billy Dennehy goal was enough to send Shamrock Rovers through to the Setanta Cup final on away goals against Cork City this evening, with the game finishing 2-2.

Having drawn 1-1 in the first leg, City got the advantage on 47 minutes, as Daryl Horgan opened the scoring, with goalkeeper Barry Murphy only able to help the ball into the net following his powerful strike.

A deflected Stephen Rice effort then brought Rovers level with just under 20 minutes left, as the game looked set to go into extra time.

Nevertheless, on 88 minutes, Daryl Kavanagh appeared to have put Cork into the final, as he got on the end of an Ian Turner corner.

Yet there was further drama, as Dennehy scored a last-gasp stoppage time free-kick, to send Rovers through and break City hearts in the process.

(From *The42* – www.the42.ie – 22nd April 2013)

That last-minute goal was especially difficult to take.

Tuesday 7th May 2013

Things have deteriorated rapidly. We've lost two league games on the spin in the last week, including a 3–2 derby loss at home to Limerick yesterday. Tommy's in a state of despair. He's been having regular fights with Danny Murphy and Colin Healy at half-time and after matches. Team spirit is low. The new signings, for whatever reason, don't seem to be working out and there's talk around the city that Tommy's under pressure. I think he's really feeling it now. I don't know how long we can carry on losing matches before something or somebody cracks.

The only good news has been in relation to our young winger Daryl Horgan…

Daryl Horgan Gets Under 21 Call

Cork City's Daryl Horgan has been selected to train with the Republic of Ireland Under 21 Squad prior to the forthcoming international versus Denmark.

The winger has also been placed on standby for the game against Denmark, which will take place in Billund on Friday, May 31st at 7.30pm.

(From www.corkcityfc.ie, 29th April 2013)

League of Ireland Premier Division, 7th May 2013

Pos	Team	Pl	W	D	L	GF	GA	GD	Pts
1	Sligo Rovers	10	8	1	1	21	6	+15	25
2	Derry City	10	7	2	1	24	5	+19	23
3	St Patrick's Athletic	10	6	2	2	13	7	+6	20
4	Dundalk	10	5	3	2	17	13	+4	18
5	Drogheda United	10	3	6	1	17	14	3	15
6	Limerick	10	3	5	2	15	10	5	14
7	Cork City	10	3	4	3	9	11	-2	13
8	Shamrock Rovers	10	2	6	2	14	7	-17	12
9	Bohemian	10	3	2	5	9	27	-8	4
10	UCD	10	1	1	8	10	24	-14	16
11	Bray Wanderers	10	1	1	8	7	26	-19	4
12	Shelbourne	10	0	3	7	3	19	-16	3

Friday 10th May 2013

League of Ireland Premier Division

Dalymount Park, Dublin

Bohemian FC 1–2 Cork City FC

Tonight, after the last few weeks, we were really desperate for a win. However, before the game I was busy in Waterford Circuit Criminal Court attending on counsel for a client who'd been charged with assault causing harm. The full hearing took place yesterday and the jury were to provide the verdict this morning. My boss thought the jury would be out with their decision by 10.30 or 11am and that I'd be on my way by lunchtime at the latest, still in good time for the game in Dublin. But at 3pm we were still waiting for the jury to decide. By this stage I'd missed the planned rendezvous (including pre-match food) with the team bus in Portlaois.

When I rang him, Tommy seemed relaxed about it so I assumed I was on the bench – which would've been the sensible decision as I still hadn't really recovered from last Monday's game against Limerick. I felt pretty wrecked to be honest. However, then Tommy called me back at about 3.15pm and sounded more focused: 'Just get to Dalymount as soon as you can, Hoggie fella.'

The jury finally came out at 3.30pm and found our client guilty as charged, with the sentence to be handed down at a later date.

Just as I was leaving the court at 4pm, Tommy rang. I answered, 'Hi Tom, just finishing now…'

'Where are ya?' he asked, sounding a little too concerned for my liking.

'Just driving now. I'll head to Dalymount directly. I have some food so I'll be fine.'

He rang again a while later: 'Where are ya now?'

'I'm by the Naas Road, coming into Dublin.'

'OK, OK, that's fine – just keep motoring to get here. And by the way, how're ya feeling?' he asked.

'I'm OK, I suppose,' I answered, half truthfully.

'Right well, you're starting. So get here as soon as you can.'

I arrived 20 minutes before the warm-up was due to commence. The lads were winding me up about my suit and asking Tommy to fine me for not wearing the club tracksuit and for being late.

Thankfully it all went well in the end and we won the match. I got through the game; in fact I really enjoyed it and played well in the circumstances.

It strikes me that when you're part-time there's a real beauty about playing that can become lost when you're a full-time player. Tonight I arrived at the game distracted by the court case. The match, when it started, was fresh and fun. When you're full-time it's a challenge to maintain that natural feeling of joy and freshness for a match. They say that's what makes the likes of Lionel Messi so exhilarating to watch and so effective as a player; for him it's still that game of joy and fun – at least when he's playing for Barcelona.

Looking back on my football career, the hours of video analysis, of practising set-pieces, the boredom of the coach journeys, the plain food served for pre-match meals, the feeling of enforced uniformity in wearing the club tracksuits, being subjected to inhumane body-fat testing… these are factors that took some of the joy out of the full-time game for me. These, along with the financial issues we've had. At times when I was a full-time player I probably should've looked for other ways to stay stimulated by the game. But I didn't need to do anything to enjoy the game tonight under the glorious lights at Dalymount.

Friday 17th May 2013

League of Ireland Premier Division

Turner's Cross, Cork

Cork City FC 1–3 Bray Wanderers FC

Having played the last two games and got through training during the week I thought I was a shoo-in to start tonight. But no: Tommy dropped me. I was severely pissed off when the team was called out. I'm not injured, and as Tommy and I had discussed before the season began, I'm looking to start as many games as I can. 'I want you to be pissed off if you're not playing,' he'd said. And tonight I was.

And then, for a few seconds that felt like longer, Tommy couldn't remember who he'd put on the bench. At the end of the team sheet he'd listed all the names togging out except one. 'And, eh… eh…' he stumbled, unsure of whom he'd left out. He turned to Woodsy: 'Who else is on the bench, Bill?'

'Hoggy, Tom,' answered Woodsy, matter-of-factly.

The f**ker Tommy. He hadn't given me any indication during the week that I might not be starting. F**k him. I should be playing. I broke my back to get to the game at Bohs and we won and I did fine. Now we're in Cork against Bray and he drops me. I was ready to win the game and see us move up the table. I'd been ready all week. But he changed the team and John Dunleavy was in at right-back.

In the dressing room and then on the bench I didn't look at Tommy at any stage. It may seem petty but this is how it needs to be. This is what we'd agreed. So tonight all my actions and inactions sent the message to him: 'Here I am Tommy, pissed off, as agreed.' Of course, I stayed professional but that's all.

We lost the game 1–3.

We never lose 1–3 to Bray at home. Never. That might sound disrespectful towards Bray – and to be fair there have been times when they've had particularly good teams. But those times have been very rare in my experience; usually, like this year, they stay near or just above the relegation zone. So it's probably fair to say we would never expect to lose to a typical Bray side, 1–3. Never.

Towards the end of the game the crowd in the Shed were singing, *It's time to go!* to Tommy. I'd normally attempt to console him but I didn't feel like doing so today. Afterwards he was a bit lost for words. Initially, he gave out to Kalen Spillane, saying we can't defend. I felt like jumping up and telling him, 'That's because you changed the f**king team, Tommy!' …but of course, I didn't.

After Tommy's speech I went out onto the pitch with the rest of the bomb squad to do box-to-box runs. While doing so the lads were discussing the possibility that Tommy's on the way out. I'll feel sorry for him if that happens, but I couldn't tonight. He should've played me. I know how to win these games. Obviously that's pride and ego talking to some extent; but in fairness I *do* know how to win these games.

Anyhow, I was so frustrated that I remained out on my own as the other lads headed back into the dressing room. The floodlights were still on but there were only a few people left in the stadium. A few minutes later the floodlights went out and it was just me in the dark under the stars, listening to my breath and the thud of my feet on the damp and somewhat upturned sod as I hurtled up and down the pitch in anger, thinking, 'I should've played tonight,' over and over.

I did a few final stretches and came down towards the tunnel that leads to the dressing room. The vultures had landed by then. There was a line of pretend-sorry-looking journalists waiting for Tommy to emerge… they could smell blood.

Spillachi, of course, was there and warned me about going into the dressing room. 'There's a bit of agro there I think. Be careful going in.'

'Thanks Noel,' I said.

When I did go in there was a lot of tension. There had clearly been an incident of some kind. The lads were either keeping to themselves or whispering in little semi-hidden groups. I found out later that Tommy had had a head-to-head with Daryl Horgan after he caught him laughing about something after the match. 'It got very nasty,' according to one of the lads.

Tonight I don't care.

Friday 24th May 2013

League of Ireland Premier Division

The Brandywell, Derry

Derry City FC 1–1 Cork City FC

There are disturbing rumblings and rumours afoot. Yesterday I overheard Daryl Horgan talking to Nults during our bus trip to Dundalk (where we stayed overnight before travelling to Derry today).

'I can't believe it, after all that's gone on over the last few years,' he said.

I interrupted, 'What can't you believe, Daryl?'

He leaned closer, across the aisle of the bus before answering, 'Me and some of the lads have heard there's no money to pay the wages.'

This is the rumour that's going around.

'No smoke without fire and all that...' Daryl added.

Then this morning, during breakfast, recent signing Adam Rundle looked at his phone and groaned loudly, sitting across the table from me.

'I can't f**king believe it mate,' he said, clearly distressed.

'What's wrong?' I asked, somewhat dismissively, fearing my Weetabix routine was about to be disturbed by some nonsensical and unnecessary pro-footballer 'drama'.

'I'm livid mate,' he answered, more firmly than I'd anticipated. Perhaps something was up. 'There's meant to be €1,900 tax back in my account from the club but it's not there; there's only €500,' Rundle said before going outside to make a call.

As he did so, a few of the older lads at the table next to me were telling youngsters Craig Byrne and Stephen Kenny that wages were paid every Wednesday last year but this year they've noticed it could be a Thursday or a Friday and they don't know why. They think something's happening. One of them even said he's heard there's a shortfall in the commercial budget and the club are going to try to renegotiate players' contracts downward.

Rundle came back in: 'I'm f**king livid mate. They've told me they're going to pay the tax that I'm owed back to me over four weeks. It's my money! They must be doing that to pay other players!'

Rundle, who seems to speak from experience having arrived from a financial nightmare at Darlington, summed it up nicely for all the lads: 'The club's in trouble; just you wait and see.'

My Weetabix routine had indeed been disturbed.

Thinking back, I was at Tommy's table for dinner last night and noticed that he seemed low. Maybe this is starting to add up now.

Anyway, Tommy named me back in the team and we drew 1–1, which I felt was a good result. As I sit on the bus back writing this, I'm hoping the rumours are just that.

Friday 5th July 2013
Text message from Tim Murphy, Cork City CEO: *There's been an administrative issue with the payment of wages, which means they may not have gone into your account yet. They will reach everyone's account by Monday at latest. Apologies for any inconvenience caused. If this causes any issue for you, please contact Kevin Murray.*

On receiving this message (despite not being on the payroll) I felt somewhat sceptical, given the rumours that have been circulating amongst the players – although apart from this issue there's been no actual problem with wages since Adam Rundle's warning back in May. Everyone seems to have been paid correctly. I called Kevin Murray to find out what's going on and he said it really is just an administrative error, and that there's no truth in the rumours as far as he's aware.

Saturday 3rd August 2013

After that Derry match we endured a very difficult summer. Tommy attempted to change the squad personnel and released many of the players that he'd signed at the start of the year. So Daryl Kavanagh and Adam Rundle were let go. Danny Furlong was placed out on loan with Waterford. Even Ding Dong Denis was released, which was a shame – but cry not for whom the Ding Dong bell tolls. The nine competitive games after the Derry match were made up of two wins, one draw and six losses – two of which were 3–0 hammerings. The fans were calling for Tommy's head long before the final straw which was a 2–1 defeat to local up-and-coming rivals Limerick yesterday.

A few weeks before his head rolled, Tommy managed to get the tall and skilful striker Ciarán Kilduff in on loan from Shamrock Rovers, and while (in partnership with young player Danny Morrissey) he would make an impression, it came too late for Tommy.

Cork City sack manager Tommy Dunne

Cork City FC and first team manager Tommy Dunne have parted company with immediate effect.

Dunne, who led the club back to the Premier Division in 2011, guided City to a mid-table finish last season, with the club currently sitting in seventh position in the Premier Division table.

Stuart Ashton will take over the role of caretaker first team manager "on a week-to-week basis".

Ashton, who first joined the club as a professional in the 1984 season, has won every honour open to Cork City FC underage teams, most recently retaining the Under 19 National League and Cup double.

"The board have not come to this decision lightly or hastily, and we are extremely grateful to Tommy for all he has done for us over the last few years," said Cork City FC chairman Mick Ring.

"We will always remember his time here fondly and wish him the very best for the future, but we feel our decision is in the best interests of the club.

"We must now look forward to our upcoming FAI Cup game against Kilbarrack and mid-season friendly against West Brom."

(From <u>*www.breakingnews.ie*</u>, 3rd August 2013)

So we arrived into recovery at the Mardyke this morning and were told by Chairman Mick Ring that Tommy had been sacked. To be truthful, it wasn't a huge surprise to anyone. Mick's a young enough fella and was nervous making the announcement in the statistics room. But he came out of it very well in my opinion and took the right approach. He asked us to respect Tommy for all the great work he's done for the club in taking us from oblivion with 13 registered players to the First Division title and back to the Premier League. He told us Billy Woods is to remain on as assistant under Stuart (Stewie) Ashton, who's acting gaffer until the end of the season. Stewie has the necessary badges and experience; he knows all the young lads very well and I think it just might work.

During the recovery session the young lads kept saying how weird it felt without Tommy. 'You'll get used to it,' I assured them. The first time your manager leaves or gets sacked is a disconcerting feeling. But if you can deal with it and move on, it helps remind you that your career is more about you, and more reliant on your decisions than those of any one manager.

I do feel sorry for Tommy, but overall I think it's probably for the best, both for Tommy and the club at this moment in time. He just wasn't having the same effect on the lads that he had three years or so ago, which is a natural enough thing for most managers. He may feel that his signings at the start of this year, coupled with the fact that he ended up shelving them, contributed to his downfall.

In any event, Tommy's gone. I tried to ring him a few hours after I found out but there was no answer, so I just left a voicemail thanking him for asking me back to the club as I've really enjoyed being back. I think he'll move on to better things. The rest of us now need to get on and keep the club in the Premier Division.

Sunday 4th August 2013

I've fallen sick with a flu. Part of me thinks it was brought on with the relief of not stressing about Tommy's position at the club anymore. For all the hatred when he dropped me against Bray that time, in truth I've played under him more as a friend than anything else. So the increasing pressure on him had an effect on me too I think. In any event, I went to training sick as a dog. I told Billy, and he said I should wait until after Stewie had spoken to the lads and then I could go home.

When the time came, Stewie spoke authoritatively and clearly. 'Working hard will be a prerequisite,' he said. 'We're going to play 4-4-2 and press high up the pitch. The back four will need to push out, and *if yee get caught once or twice, I don't mind. What's gone is gone. This is a new page for everyone. We need to stick together to get out of this.*' He also made his customary 'right time, right place' comment, which anyone who's ever played under Stewie will have heard at least a million times.

But overall his speech was just what the doctor ordered. Short and clear.

Then I went home to bed.

Wednesday 7th August 2013

On Monday the lads won in the FAI Cup against a Dublin Leinster Senior League team, Kilbarrack. It was important to have a positive reaction. I was still sick for the West Brom friendly yesterday, which was very disappointing as Nicolas Anelka was playing.

I went to the game though, and it was good to speak with Shane Long again after all these years. He's still a very nice guy.

'See that guy who just passed us there?' asked Johnny Dunleavy as the West Brom players were walking onto the pitch before the game.

'Yeah?' I replied.

'He's only captain of bloody Uruguay.'

It's not often that footballing royalty visits these shores, and when they do it's usually in meaningless friendlies like this one. Regardless, I felt rough and would've left before the game began, but Liam Kearney was back playing as a guest for us so I wanted to see how he'd do. And he did well, playing on the left wing. He's still got that footballing cuteness; he loves dropping inside from the wing to the centre of the pitch at opportune moments in order to find pockets of space and hurt the opposition. Maybe he'll sign, which would partially make up for the loss of Ding Dong Denis.

However, our attention shouldn't be on the likes of Nicolas Anelka (although he did play splendidly well last night) but on Friday when we play Bohs. It'll be a huge match and we'll need to be right.

Friday 9th August 2013

League of Ireland Premier Division

Turner's Cross, Cork

Cork City FC 1–0 Bohemian FC

Cork City 1-0 Bohemians

There was a dramatic finish to Stuart Ashton's first league outing in charge of Cork City, as Danny Morrissey finally broke Bohemians' resistance with a last-ditch header for a 1-0 win in Friday's Airtricity League Premier Division clash at Turner's Cross.

Bohs looked set to earn a valuable point in their struggle against relegation before Morrissey stooped to nod in Danny Murphy's left-wing cross in the 95th minute ...

Cork City: Mark McNulty, Ian Turner, Danny Murphy, Gearóid Morrissey, Shane Duggan, Danny Morrissey, John Dunleavy (Colin Healy 67), Dan Murray, Neal Horgan, Garry Buckley, Ciaran Kilduff (Stephen Kenny 80).

Subs not used: Rob Lehane, Brian Lenihan, Eoghan Murphy, Dave Ryan, John Kavanagh. ...

(From RTÉ – www.rte.ie – 10th August 2013)

Sunday 20th October 2013

After that absolutely huge win against Bohs we've been on a winning streak in the league (more or less) for the rest of the season – although we were knocked out of the FAI Cup by Sligo. Ciarán Kilduff has proved to be a revelation with Danny Morrissey up front. All those last-minute goals going against us for months and then they start going the other way. Hard to fathom why. That's football.

Friday 25th October 2013

League of Ireland Premier Division

Turner's Cross, Cork

Cork City FC 4–2 St Patrick's Athletic FC

It was the last match of the season tonight and I was on the bench. I sat back in the dugout with my feet resting at pitch level, turning my head to watch as the action moved up and down the field. I realised that this was probably my final game at the Cross. I was content with what we'd achieved since Tommy asked me to come back. We were back in the Premier Division and safe from relegation. I contemplated that it was a nice way to end it all, sitting back and watching the younger lads run around the now all-seater splendid ground. All I was missing was a cigar…

But then in the second half Woodsy told me to warm up. I didn't want to go on, so I sneakily got a few of the young lads to warm up instead, to make up the full quota of subs that can be warming up on the sideline at any one time.

'Go on Rob [Lehane], and [Shane] Duggy.'

The lads took my suggestion and went running off to the corner flag. When Woodsy turned around again I pointed at the lads. 'I'll go when they get back.'

A little trick leaned over the years, and it took some of the heat off. I was thinking I could do with sitting this one out. We were up 3–1 with about 25 minutes left. The reason Woodsy had called me was that at 3–0 young John Kavanagh had made a mistake at right full. And to be fair he was starting to look tired and the Pat's winger Chris Forrester was getting some joy down their left. Then they scored and I spotted Woodsy sneaking up to Stewie; he looked to be suggesting I should come on. Stewie appeared to concur, hence Woodsy being onto me.

F**k off Woodsy, leave me be for f**k's sake. There's nothing at stake here; it's the end of the year, we're safe, they're safe. Leave me be. My legs and body are sore and tired.

A few more minutes passed and it looked like the idea had faded, but then Kavanagh made another mistake and was clearly tiring. He's only played a few games at this level and looks a really talented player; tenacious with a lovely right foot (not something you normally hear said about right-footed players). But the recent games seemed to have caught up on him and the experienced Pat's players could smell blood. The second mistake nearly led to another goal.

After that chance I watched as Stewie turned to Woodsy, who turned to looked at me. Just as Woodsy turned I looked down to tie my shoelace, avoiding eye contact.

'Hoggie, warm up will ya?' Woodsy shouted, undeterred.

For f**k's sake. So I got up out of the dugout and ran towards the corner flag. A few of the other lads passed me on their way back to the dugout.

'You're going on are you, Hogs?' asked Duggy.

'I know, for f**k's sake,' I said. 'There's a full 25 minutes left.'

'Ah Hog, you'll be grand.'

I arrived at the corner flag, where a few more lads were warming up. I did my usual shuffling warm-up, half-sprint effort to the left and right, a few pretend headers, stretches, etc. Halfway through one sprint I saw Woodsy walking my way and shouting in my direction. I turned quickly in the other direction, pretending not to notice, but the other lads betrayed me: 'They're calling ya, Hog!'

So I turned back towards Woodsy, who was now beckoning me. He knew what I was up to. 'Hog, come on, for f**k's sake!'

'OK, OK Bill,' I shouted, and headed back towards the dugout.

'Tog off,' said Woodsy, somewhat curtly, when I arrived back – no doubt growing weary of my skilful evasion techniques.

So I sat in the dugout and began, very slowly, to take off my tracksuit, revealing the full clean kit underneath. In the meantime, and at great pace, Woodsy set off to get the attention of the fourth official in order to allow the substitution to take place at the next break in play. *There'll be no stopping this now*, I thought, fearfully.

Standing up and leaning forward, I subtly pleaded with my former roommate Woodsy (while trying to keep the young and impressionable subs from hearing): 'Just give him [Kavanagh] five more minutes, yeah?'

He didn't like that, our Woodsy.

'Are you ready?' he asked with rising aggression.

'Yeah, but give him five more minutes, for God's sake,' I pleaded.

'No. You're coming on. Get ready.'

Then the b*****d ball went out of play.

'Do it now, ref!' Woodsy shouted to the fourth official, beckoning me to the halfway point on the sideline.

There was a good home crowd, and when I came out of the dugout and onto the pitch they gave me a few cheers. I tried to acclimatise to the bedlam and rush of the game, to the pace of these fully fit young professional athletes.

First touch – no lie – I cued a deflected shot into the top corner for Pat's. It would've been a beautiful finish if I'd meant it. Christ, I felt like telling Woodsy, 'I f**king told you to leave me alone!'

3–2 and Pat's were at it now.

But then a few minutes later we broke down the right wing. I made a run and was found by my old buddy and centre-half Muzza, who'd read my run like days of old (after Ian Turner had made a run inside from the right, drawing the full-back with him). Muzza's ball, all texture and niceties, deftly spun over the Pat's players and I took it on my chest. The Pat's winger Forrester was chasing me but my next touch was good and I entered the Pat's box at pace. Without looking, my following touch knocked it low and across the goal where the incoming young Danny Morrissey arrived to find the net with a nice flick.

Muzza made a big deal about me in the celebrations and it felt good, getting tapped on the head by the lads.

In the showers afterwards the lads discussed what might happen next. As the season's over, everyone's on free contracts. Shane Duggan has already signed for Limerick, it seems. Some of our better players are said to be going to

England on trial. If they go we'll be left with the young lads and a few old lads. However, there'll be one less old lad: I don't feel like rebuilding again.

Chapter Eleven – 5th November 2013 to 27th November 2014

Tuesday 5th November 2013
John Caulfield named as Cork City Boss

Veteran player John Caulfield has taken the reins at Cork City in a two-year deal.

Caulfield, who replaces Tommy Dunne, is the club's joint-record goal scorer with 129 strikes and also holds the club record of 455 appearances. The former UCC manager says he will look to local talent to strengthen the side ahead of next season

"The most urgent thing is to talk to the players that were at the club last season and tie up the players that we can. I want a base of good, strong local players. We have a very good Under 19 set-up so we will look to promote players from within, and obviously attract players from the county and the province." …

Caulfield will be officially unveiled tomorrow afternoon at Turner's Cross.

"We finished sixth in the last two seasons and I feel that we can get higher," he said today. "The potential at this club is fantastic and I really want to see if we can get the crowds back in and make Turner's Cross a fortress again. I want us to be really competitive, have a passionate team and when people come in the gates at the 'Cross, see that these guys really want to do it for City. I want all of the people from West Cork, North Cork, East Cork, all around the county and the city too, to rally around and come back. We want to get back the support we have lost, the people who have stopped coming to games, because we all know that Turner's Cross, with 3,500 or 4,000 or 5,000 people in it, is a fantastic place to be. We've had fantastic occasions there and there haven't been enough of those this season."

(*Irish Independent*, 5th November 2013)

Stuart (Stewie) Ashton did a fine job in his interim role and must have been in the running for the permanent job. However, the Board decided to go with Caulfield. In my opinion either man would've been a great appointment for the club and Stewie can certainly walk away with his head high and an enhanced reputation following the upturn in our results at the end of last year.

As for Caulfield, I played with him at the start of my career and at the end of his, in 2000/2001. You could tell he had so much energy, even then as a 36-year-old player. I remember when he used to come on as a sub in those latter days of his career – he could play on the left wing or up front – he'd still make an impact and be a real menace to the other side's defenders. His partnership during his prime with Pat Morley will always be remembered fondly among Cork folk of a certain generation. Back in those days, when a centre-forward had a striking partner, Morley and Caulfield combined brilliantly for many great goals. That Morley was known as the classier of the two in terms of his touch and ability is slightly unfair on Caulfield, who didn't just bring energy and a fierce commitment; he had real quality and presence as a player. That quality was perhaps underappreciated, but maybe he'll make an even bigger impact as a manager. It's difficult to say how he'll get on at this point.

Thursday 7th November 2013
Caulfield called me and left a voicemail asking to meet up. I replied by text: *Hey Johnny, firstly congrats. Secondly, yeah I'll meet you next week for a coffee so. I'm working in town so just give me a bell and I should be about. I do have court Monday morning til about 12 though. You could always catch me later in the week too as you're probably under pressure. Cheers, Hoggie.*

Wednesday 13th November 2013

I met with John today at the coffee shop in the Cork School of Music. He's raring to get going – you can see it. He's looking at strengthening the squad and he wants me to be part of it. He said he can rely on me as a defender. The only thing is, he's changing training back to morning sessions. I told him this could present a problem for me and he said, 'Look, go see how your employers are and there's no panic at all either way.' I told him I'd love to help him, but I think it's going to be difficult to stay involved in a full-time training set-up, for obvious reasons.

I'm working at Healy O'Connor solicitors and both principals are fans of the club, which might help. They even sponsored the club for a few years; I'm sure they'll be as supportive as possible. Nonetheless, training in the mornings will present difficulties.

Wednesday 4th December 2013

I sent a text to JC: *Hi John, just to confirm for my bosses… Training apart from weekend will be at 10.30/11 on Monday, Tuesday and Thursday mornings, and I should make it back into work by 1.30ish. Is this right? They're happy to allow one morning a week but I'm pushing for a second. Thanks, Hoggie.*

He responded with a call to confirm that this is fine and again we can see how it goes.

Friday 6th December 2013

Text to JC: *John, sorry to get back to you so late. I haven't had a chance to confirm exactly when I can train with my bosses yet but I'm sure there's no problem with signing, in principle anyway, from their point of view. And as you already know, I'd be delighted to sign whenever suits you.*

Reply from JC: *OK great, we will do signing next week to maximise coverage.*

I'm not sure I'll really play any part, but it's a privilege to be asked and I'm really happy to help John out if I can.

Wednesday 1st January 2014

Text from JC: *Lads, pre-season training starts next Monday. Report to Bishopstown at 9.45am. – JC*

New Year's Day and he's texting us! He really is mad for road.

Thursday 2nd January 2014

Text to JC: *John, next week I'll be there full day Tuesday, Thursday morning session and possibly Friday morning but not sure about Friday yet. I'll be there Saturday too.*

Wednesday 8th January 2014

Text to JC: *John, I'll be training on Friday instead of tomorrow [Thursday]. I'm sorry but some court work has come up that I need to be there for tomorrow morning. Also, my Achilles is a bit sore and it might be better for the extra day. Obviously I'll still train Saturday too. Hoggie.*

Reply from JC: *OK, no prob.*

Tuesday 14th January 2014

Text to JC: *John, Liam Kearney is coming back to Ireland late Friday. He would be interested in talking with you. Hoggie.*

Reply from JC: *Tell him to ring me.*

Friday 7th March 2014

Liam ended up signing, which is great. The return of the 'Conna Maradona' is a big thrill for many fans who've witnesses his clever feet and smart football brain over the years. Another former teammate of mine has come back also; John Cotter has returned to the club as Caulfield's assistant. I can see already that they'll make a solid team.

For pre-season they had us doing some serious old-school running at UCC's facility, 'the farm', in Bishopstown. Unfortunately my fitness levels aren't what they used to be, and I can see that the lads are moving on while I'm struggling.

One of the morning sessions stands out in my mind. I'd arrived from work, joined in training and the warm-up. Then we did more running before a particularly tough run around the farm's heavy pitches. Myself and the recent signing Anthony Elding were well at the back of the group and came in to the finish line a few minutes after the rest of the lads. It's embarrassing and so far away from how it used to be when I was one of fittest. Overall, I'm finding it very difficult to marry full-time training and full-time work – which is to be expected, I suppose.

I'd say Caulfield might have thought my fitness levels would be better, but having worked in an office the past four years it's very difficult to reach the level he requires. He seems OK about it though, and happy enough to have me as an experienced player in the background.

He's arranged for me to train during the evenings also, with local side UCC under Noel Healy. It's very good of UCC to allow me to do so, but it means I'm more removed from Cork City matters.

In one of our early-season friendlies at Bishopstown I was on the bench. Caulfield was trying young Brian Lenihan at right-back. After about five minutes it was very clear who'll be the right-back for the season, as Lenihan was amazing – sprinting up and down the pitch, fantastic on the ball and clever in defence. John asked me did I want to come on near the end. 'There's no need really John, is there?' We laughed.

My biggest contribution, besides being a trusted head around the place, has probably been an article I wrote welcoming John back to the fray.

Cork City fans hoping good old days are back with return of club icon 'Johnny C'

Fans of the League of Ireland could be forgiven for thinking that 2014 rather than 2013 is the year of 'the Gathering'. The last few months have seen the return to the League of some very talented players from overseas. Chief among them is Irish international Keith Fahey who has returned from Birmingham to St Pat's.

Another former Irish international coming home is Stephen McPhail who, after a very successful career, most notably with Leeds United and Cardiff City, has signed for Shamrock Rovers. Both Fahey and McPhail are highly skilled, 'ball-playing' central midfielders.

The presence of Colin Healy in the centre of midfield for Cork City FC means that there will be no shortage of international-level pedigree in the Airtricity League midfield this season.

And yet it could be argued, and certainly will be down south, that the most important return to the League of Ireland involves not a player, but a manager: John Caulfield, who has taken over the reins at Cork City FC. Caulfield epitomised a generation of players in the 80s and 90s that put Cork City FC on the map.

He, along with the likes of Dave Barry, Declan Daly, Patsy Freyne and Caulfield's striking partner Pat Morley, was an inherent part of the City team that achieved so much for the club in famous matches against Bayern Munich in '91 and Galatasaray in '93. They were central to the club's first league win achieved at the RDS in '93 also.

Those men and their colleagues presented a standard of football in Cork that was recognised by the Cork community as worthy of praise and attention. It was simple, sometimes brutal fare. It was before the Premiership was created and before the arrival of the overseas contingent to English football.

It was before the tackle from behind was outlawed and one could still knock the ball back to the goalkeeper's hands. There were very few seats and little shelter at Turner's Cross. Footballers were tough, tackles were tackles, and you went down only when you were injured. Every once in a while you could expect that someone was about to be tackled around the neck.

This is not to overlook the skill that these players possessed. Every week arriving at the Cross, a City fan could expect all of the above together with immense leadership and bravery from Daly, moments of sublime skill from Freyne, a classy goal or two from Morley or Barry before the inevitably scrappy goal from Caulfield. For the thousands who came in the cold and the wet, they, and the other great players who played for City at the time, rarely disappointed.

When Caulfield finally retired in or about 2001 he had become the club's most capped player by a country mile and shared the top scoring record for the club with his striking partner Morley. A hell of a lot has happened to the club between then and now. A very successful period of full-time football occurred between 2004 and 2007 before a calamitous period of decline and ultimately demise in or about 2010. The rise of the club under the control of fans' organisation 'FORAS' resuscitated the club back into existence, and eventually Tommy Dunne and a younger team would bring the club back to stability in the Premier League of Ireland. Despite all of this, Caulfield's records remain.

Others are returning to Cork City this year too. Liam Kearney has returned from Australia, Darren Murphy from Britain, and Billy Dennehy from Shamrock Rovers. These along with some impressive new signings augur well for the season ahead. There is a buzz about the place not felt for some time. It all starts on Friday. It will probably be a cold, wet and windy night. Expect a certain type of order to resume on the return of Johnny C to Turner's Cross. If you're lucky there might even be a scrappy goal or two.

(From *The42* – www.the42.ie – 5th March 2014)

Friday 7th March 2014

League of Ireland Premier Division

Turner's Cross, Cork

Cork City FC 1–1 St Patrick's Athletic FC

Caulfield's first match. He's strengthened the team already in my opinion, choosing good physical players instead of any particular system. He's got Dan Murray and Darren Dennehy as centre-halves, Colin Healy supporting young Garry Buckley and Gearóid Morrissey in midfield, and Billy Dennehy and Liam Kearney on the wings. The big singing that was Anthony Elding is struggling to find fitness and was withdrawn after 65 minutes for Mark O'Sullivan, who Caulfield has brought in from Avondale. I wasn't on the bench, which is no surprise – in reality I'm as far away from the first 11 as I've ever been. But that's OK.

Sunday 25th May 2014

Caulfield and co have won their last three games while I haven't even attended a training session for three weeks. I turned up this morning with a pulled hamstring that I'd suffered in training with my GAA club. I'd asked JC about this arrangement in advance and he was cool about it as I'm unlikely to play a part at this stage – and anyway, UCC were finishing up and I needed a team to train with in the evenings. I had been hoping to play in tomorrow's League Cup game but that won't be happening now. Hopefully I'll make it back to full fitness after the mid-season break in June.

Brighter news is the arrival of John O'Flynn back at training. He's been playing over at Exeter (and Barnet) in the UK since he left in 2008/09. I bumped into him in the car park at Bishopstown and told him how great it was to see him back. It seems he might be signing and he looks happy to be home. Of all the lads I've played with at Cork City, I think he was the most exciting when in top form. His pace and instinctive finishing and play were excellent and our crowd just loved him. That he ended up getting the first goal in our league-winning match against Derry in 2005 was fitting, given the joy he'd brought to Turner's Cross. Our fans will get very excited when they hear he's back.

Monday 1ˢᵗ September 2014
'One for the future' Lenihan joins Hull in £200,000 deal
Ireland U-21 defender Brian Lenihan has chosen Hull City over Brighton as his preferred destination after a week of intense talks.

Lenihan was also in discussions with Crystal Palace but selected Hull after being impressed by Steve Bruce's sales-pitch. Cork City, his home-town club, will receive £200,000 in return for his services.

"The Lenihan deal is done and dusted. He's one for the future," said Bruce yesterday.

Cork chairman Pat Lyons, said: "As a club we never want to see our best players leave but we are pleased to have reached a reasonable agreement with Hull for this transfer and that Cork City stands to benefit should Brian progress further, as we expect him to do."

Meanwhile, Cork's manager John Caulfield remains confident his side can remain in contention for the league title in spite of Friday's meltdown in Athlone when they twice coughed up a lead against the Premier Division's bottom side.

Still second, but now six points behind leaders Dundalk, Cork have it all to do if they are to overcome the gap in the last seven games of the season. ...

(Garry Doyle, *Irish Independent*, 1ˢᵗ September 2014)

Brian – or Lenny as we call him – has been a sensation at full-back this season. I feel I contributed by paving the way as a slow right-full the last few years. His lightning pace and amazing energy must've been like a bolt from the blue for the long-suffering City supporters who've watched me traipse up and down the last few years! A great kid; we all wish him well.

Saturday 13ᵗʰ September 2014
Last Wednesday I played a friendly versus Cobh Ramblers at St Colman's Park. Caulfield had called me and said he needed to give a few guys a run. I wondered if he was checking for

cover now that Lenny's gone. He named me as centre-half in a relatively strong team. We won 2–1; I had a particularly dodgy first 10 minutes and was probably at fault for the Cobh goal but other than that managed to get through the 90 minutes, which was impressive enough considering I haven't trained with the lads for two months.

But the team are still going very well. You can see the confidence growing, even in the lads who played tonight. Ross Gaynor played very well next to me at left-back. He's in good shape, likes to get on the ball and gets up and down the pitch. That's the big problem for me these days. Oh, to be a few years younger…

Thursday 9th October 2014

The team are in with a chance of winning the league. Three games to go and they're level on points with Dundalk – although Dundalk have a better goal difference and have played one less game. Also, Brian Lenihan over in Hull has been included in the full Irish squad, which is fantastic news.

My own situation is that I've started a new job with JW O'Donovan Solicitors. On the day I found out that I'd got the job, I played a friendly on the old Mardyke pitch versus UCC and nearly scored a rocket from the halfway line. I played well enough in general too, half buzzing because of my new role. Caulfield was laughing on the line with the other lads after my shot nearly went in.

At this point I can tell I'm not going to be playing anymore, and I really don't mind. A few years ago maybe I would've been disappointed – especially as the team are going so well – but now the realisation comes as a relief.

Monday 13th October 2014

Why John Delaney has a fraught relationship with League of Ireland

The Football Association of Ireland's CEO might be an expert in celebrity but he describes the League as a 'difficult child' as interest dwindles and clubs struggle to stay afloat. ...

Delaney remains at the head of Irish football as a "labour of love". He has not given an interview to a football journalist since the aftermath of Euro 2012.

Delaney had been earning more than €430,000-a-year before taking pay cuts in 2010 and 2011, while many of the association's workers on the ground were made redundant. In July, he agreed a new contract to take him up to 2019. There are incessant murmurs of discontent within the domestic game when it comes to the CEO. He is an expert in dealing with the convoluted politics of grassroots football and retains plenty of support from smaller clubs who have benefited from FAI investment – but his relationship with the League of Ireland is fraught.

Recently, he described the league as a "difficult child". However this season's total prize pool of €241,500 is eclipsed by Delaney's annual income by more than the €100,000 the winners will receive when the season concludes in a fortnight. Little wonder there is a long history of financial problems, with the association often accused of neglecting its own clubs. ...

And for all its existential crises, the impact the league has on the international team is constantly understated. Five of the starting XI which faced Gibraltar honed their trade on home soil. The squad, which has travelled to Germany before Tuesday's meeting, contains nine former League of Ireland players.

Among that group is Shane Long, who joined Reading from Cork for around £30,000 as part of the deal for Kevin Doyle in 2005. His combined career transfer fees passed £30m with a move to Southampton this summer. The first choice goalkeeper, David Forde, disenchanted following a failed spell at West Ham, was about to quit the game before the League of Ireland gave him a second chance. And that's before Seamus Coleman at Sligo Rovers is mentioned. ...

Yet the Republic of Ireland's problems extend far beyond a lack of quality. Interest has dwindled alongside rugby union's surge in popularity over the past decade, and Gaelic football and hurling remain the true love for the majority of Irish sports fans. Euro 2012 provided a short boost but that soon evaporated following the mess which unfolded on the pitch.

The FAI said more than 35,000 were at the Aviva on Saturday despite swathes of empty seats around the ground. The stadium, which replaced the decrepit Lansdowne Road, remains a financial burden, even though Delaney insists the FAI will be debt free by 2020. But interest in the team is so low that it is desperately struggling to fill seats – to such an extent that Delaney gave a free ticket to everybody in the audience on the Saturday Night Show for next month's game against the USA. It's just a pity he's not as keen to promote the country's clubs.

(Alan Smith, *The Guardian* ('Sportblog'), 13th October 2014)

Friday 17th October 2014

League of Ireland Premier Division

Turner's Cross, Cork

Cork City FC 1–0 Bohemian FC

Caulfield is a magician. This result means they go two points clear with one game left – away to second-placed Dundalk with the title on the line. I cycled to the game and missed the goal but caught the second half. There was a huge crowd of between six and seven thousand, despite it being a terrible rainy night. Caulfield has done what he promised – and more – in one season.

Tickets for the game in Dundalk will be impossible to get hold of now. A small part of me is jealous that I'm not out there and involved in the excitement, but the more mature part of me knows that my body couldn't deal with the intensity.

Friday 24th October 2014

League of Ireland Premier Division

Oriel Park, Dundalk

Dundalk FC 2–0 Cork City FC

My brother managed to get tickets and we went to Oriel together. We had to run from his car to get there on time – the excitement was huge. While the game didn't go City's way, it was amazing that they came so close. Second place and back in Europe is a great start from Johnny C and co. It's good to be a supporter again.

Thursday 27th November 2014
There are more unsavoury headlines circulating about John Delaney. Apparently a video of him singing a republican song late at night in a Dublin bar has surfaced. Perhaps the most worrying aspect of this story is the use of legal threats against those writing factual pieces, seemingly just because they don't paint Delaney in a positive light.

The greatest threat to Delaney is John Delaney himself…
… Why did John Delaney's lawyers tell the Guardian: "My client's position is simply that it is not him singing in the video" only hours before Delaney went on several radio stations to admit that it was, in fact, him in the video? How did

Delaney's lawyers end up making legal threats on premises which Delaney must have known to be false? ...

Rather than try to give a serious answer to the question of why the spurious legal threats were made, Delaney has campaigned about the unrelated issue of cyber-bullying, and attacked this newspaper's soccer correspondent, Emmet Malone, claiming that he has been motivated by an "agenda". Delaney warned on Tuesday that the "backlash" against Malone was beginning. On Thursday, Delaney's partner Emma English retweeted several messages criticising Malone and The Irish Times.

The essential argument is that if, in Delaney's words, to be "an Irishman, singing an Irish song" is to attract controversy, the men of 1916 must be spinning in their graves. Whatever happened to an Irishman's right to free expression?

That misses the crucial point, which is that the only ones trying to suppress free expression of anything were Delaney or the FAI, with the risible threats of legal action against media outlets who tried to report the truth. ...

After years of Delaney's rule the board has acquired a more settled, senescent look. There's nobody that reminds you of the younger Delaney. It's difficult to imagine anyone within the association leading an internal heave against the chief executive.

It looks as though at some point in the past, John Delaney took note of Julius Caesar's aside to Mark Antony:

"Let me have men about me that are fat,
Sleek-headed men and such as sleep o'nights.
Yon Cassius has a lean and hungry look;
he thinks too much: such men are dangerous."

With no Cassius-types in the FAI mix, the greatest threat to Delaney's continued leadership of the FAI remains Delaney himself.

(Ken Early, *The Irish Times*, 27th November 2014)

Chapter Twelve – 3rd April to 29th July 2015

I may have finished playing for Cork City, but my desire to see the club and the LOI progress still burned brightly. At the end of 2014 I published my first book, *Death of A Football Club?*, with the aim of bringing some much-needed attention to the problems experienced by our clubs and players.

After 2014, the growing distance from the day-to-day concerns of being a player on the pitch meant I was better placed to take into account the surrounding issues effecting the game in Ireland – although I of course kept an eye on the main developments at Cork City FC at the same time.

Friday 3rd April 2015

Changes may be afoot. Hope came from Europe as it was announced during the week that UEFA have significantly improved the prize money for clubs that appear in the earlier qualification rounds of UEFA competitions. This could be a game-changer for the LOI and some of the other smaller leagues in Europe.

It seems European money will be the driver of positive change in our league, rather than any funding from the FAI, whose focus always seems to be elsewhere.

Saturday 6th June 2015
John Delaney claims playoff seeding change was basis of legal threat to FIFA

A joke by FIFA president Sepp Blatter about Ireland's failure to qualify for the 2010 World Cup sparked the "extraordinary" €5m payout to the FAI, the association claims.

The association last night answered a growing clamour for transparency on the deal with a detailed statement.

It reveals the negotiations behind the €5m payoff to Irish football following Thierry Henry's infamous handball in a crucial World Cup qualifier – and that the decision to allow

*the subsequent goal to stand had only been one of the factors
for what followed.*

*In the aftermath of the November 2009 game, FAI officials
met with FIFA "to raise the hurt caused to the Irish people by
what had happened, the damage done to football in Ireland
and worldwide".*

*The FAI said it was agreed the meeting would remain
confidential, but days later Blatter made a joke of Ireland's
bid to be the World Cup's 33rd team.*

*This was "in breach of confidentiality" and "brought
reputational damage to the FAI" which led to the €5m payout
being agreed at a meeting in Zurich. ...*

*The FAI at first looked for a "sporting solution" to the
issue – a replay or an extra place at World Cup 2010 – before
seeking compensation.*

*Mr Delaney revealed that the legal claims by the FAI were
based on FIFA's decision – in the weeks before the playoff
games in late 2009 – to seed the draw. This, the FAI CEO
claimed, was essentially a rule change, and one of the factors
that gave Ireland a potentially strong legal case. However,
there is no mention of the seedings in the documents released
by the FAI last night. ...*

(By Gareth Morgan, Adam Cullen and Daniel McDonnell,
Irish Independent, 6th June 2015)

The question this raises is whether the FAI should've
brought a legal claim on the basis of the re-seeding rather than
compromising for the €5 million. Surely the players and fans
have the right to a fair competition? FIFA changing the rules
to seed the play-offs at a very late stage stinks to high heaven,
in my opinion. It was patently unfair. You can't change the
rules of a marathon in the final 100 metres. So why did the
FAI accept a compromise from FIFA and take the cash?

Regardless, the efforts in seeking a 33rd place at the World
Cup because of a handball are an embarrassment to all football
people in this country, and Blatter was right to laugh.

Wednesday 29th July 2015

Despite my disgust at the way in which they dealt with the World Cup re-seeding, I have to acknowledge that there has been a particularly good development originating from the FAI – one which I was very happy to write about.

Net gains from U17 League

Credit where it's due. Might Irish football be finally set to plug the gap that has dogged our game for so long?

The new national U17 League was officially launched on Monday by Ireland assistant manager Roy Keane and FAI High Performance director Ruud Dokter. While it comes on the back of the success of the national U19 league that was introduced in 2011, this new league promises to have a more profound impact than its predecessor.

The reason? It finally involves the FAI engaging with one of the most counterproductive features of Irish football since at least the 1960s; the 'gap' or divide between Irish schoolboy teams and the League of Ireland. …

An agreement has been reached between the schoolboy clubs and National League teams in respect of compensation for players that move from the schoolboy clubs to the league clubs and then onward (for a transfer fee) to England. Of course, the potential transfer fee a British or other foreign professional team is likely to pay multiplies when the selling club is a National League club rather than a schoolboy club. More importantly, players who travel to England or elsewhere later will be more mature and experienced to deal with the change. Overall it should prove to be a 'win-win' situation for the player, the schoolboy club and the national league. And of course should an individual decide that he desperately needs to go to England at 16, nobody is standing in his way. However, the new U17 league can at least offer him, or his parents, a viable alternative, especially should the player wish to complete his Leaving Certificate. …

Clearly, this is a positive step in the right direction for Irish football, but it is still merely part 1 of a plan to provide a viable alternative career path for Irish footballers. Part 2 will involve a plan for the National League itself to progress towards supporting sustainable and professional clubs. In my opinion, this plan will involve the bridging of another divide that has existed in Irish football since the day of the FAI's creation – the divide between the FAI and the IFA. But that is another day's work. For now, let's be thankful for the new U17 league, which kicks off in August.

(Neal Horgan, *Irish Examiner*, 29th July 2015)

Chapter Thirteen – Interview with Damien Delaney, June 2016

I met with Damien for a coffee during his off-season in 2016. I'd played with him at Cork City at the start of his career, and while I'd spent the next decade and a half at City, he'd gone on to have a fabulous career in England. In October 2000 he moved to Leicester in the Premier League, initially signed by Peter Taylor on the recommendation of his assistant Colin Murphy who'd had a brief stint with Cork City earlier that year. After Leicester, Damien played with a number of sides in the lower leagues, including Hull, QPR and Ipswich, before enjoying an amazing Indian summer in his career with Crystal Palace in the Premier League from 2012 onwards. When I met up with him in Cork he'd just signed another one-year contract with Palace which would see him turn 37 in the Premiership.

NH: Do you remember back in 1999/2000, when you were at Cork City; I'd played two years in the reserves but you b****ds, yourself and Joe Gamble, were fast-tracked through to the first team?

DD: [Laughs] Ya, we came straight out of the youth team in 1999.

NH: We weren't happy about it in the reserves! We were saying, 'What the hell is going on?!' [Laughs] But to be fair, you guys were ready for training with Dave Barry's side.

DD: Ya, I remember it well.

NH: And do you remember when Dave Barry then stepped down and we had pre-season for the 2000 season? I was lucky enough to be invited into the pre-season training camp at the Farm, and Colin Murphy had just come in as the new manager.

DD: Yeah, I remember that too – there was lots of running.

NH: But then after a few weeks of running Colin Murphy was gone. Martin O'Neill had left Leicester to take the Celtic job, and Peter Taylor took over at Leicester and wanted Colin

Murphy as his assistant there – which was too good an opportunity for him to turn down.

DD: Yes, Colin was only here a few weeks before going to Leicester – then Derek Mountfield came in as manager.

NH: Derek gave me my league debut, and I think he gave you your debut too?

DD: He did, and one of my first games was the Intertoto Cup against Lausanne, out in Switzerland.

NH: Yes: I remember you played at left-back in Switzerland and I was on the bench out there. That day was a big move forward for both of us.

DD: It was, but we lost 1–0 in Switzerland and when we came back home the league started. I remember there was a bit of chaos as the club and Mountfield were trying to go full-time but we had all these classy older semi-pros who'd been part-time for 10 or 15 years. We only had a few full-time players: myself, Colin O'Brien and Ollie Cahill were the only ones at the time, I think. I was on €80 a week back then. So I remember Mountfield, who was trying to push us towards full-time, trying to organise training at lunchtime, from 1pm to 2pm at the Farm so the older lads could make it. It was chaos. Imagine trying to get Patsy Freyne in to train at lunchtime? Pissing in the wind there.

NH: [Laughing] Very true. But a few younger lads came in at that time too: the likes of Dave Moore, Tony Tynan and Alan Carey were in contention. I got into the team at right-back in the home game against Lausanne. And Greg [O'Halloran]…

DD: Greg was already playing in the first team by then. I'd joined Cork City from Avondale under-16s back in 1998 and played with Greg during my first year in City's youth team when I was only 16 or 17. We had a really good side but got beaten by Home Farm in the semi-final of the FAI Youth Cup. Then Greg went up to the first team while I was in my second year with the youths. Stuart Ashton and Paul Bowdren came in as managers and brought in the likes of Alan Bennett, Damien

O'Rourke, Gamble and the goalie Seamus O'Donnell. We ended up winning the FAI Youth Cup that year.

NH: That was a great achievement for the club. And you were playing for the Cork minors in the All-Ireland Championships in Gaelic football that year too, weren't you?

DD: Yeah, and I was also doing a FÁS course for soccer run by Mick Conroy and Paul Bannon. So I had a lot on, and inevitably there was some conflict because things overlapped a little bit. When the FÁS course started I had a tough period of training twice a day and then going to Cork minor training at night. Mad, looking back.

NH: Christ!

DD: Yeah, it was hard work – but I loved it. Eating my sandwiches on the number 8 bus from Bishopstown where I was doing the FÁS course or training with Cork City, on the way to Páirc Uí Chaoimh to train with the Cork minors. We won the Munster Championships at the end of July; I remember the Cork minor selectors had a big problem with the fact that I was missing some of the training for soccer. I remember there was a selector out there who f**king hated me. He was like, '*Soccer? We have an All-Ireland semi-final coming up!*' But the manager was cool about it and looked after me. I was also in school at Coláiste Chríost Rí and obviously the [Gaelic] football tradition at that school was huge. I was only 16 or 17 and played full forward with the school when we won the Munster title, the Corn Ui Mhuirí. We had a hell of a team; lots of Barrs lads that you would know, and a lot of Nemo lads too.

NH: 1998 in Flower Lodge? I played against you in the final. I'd forgotten about that. Spioraid Naoimh was my school. We got to the Munster final in both soccer and GAA that year but only won the soccer. Anyway, I always felt playing GAA gave me an advantage in soccer in terms of being fitter and maybe more physical.

DD: I agree. And I think GAA also brings you a good attitude, where complaining isn't accepted and you need to become harder, more resilient.

NH: That resilience probably helped in your long career afterwards…

DD: It definitely did.

NH: And at Cork City FC – how long did you play with the first team before moving on to England? It wasn't a full season, was it?

DD: I played with the first team from July to October 2000, I think, before Leicester came in.

NH: So you were moving from a mainly part-time set up with Cork City to a fully professional set up at Leicester. Would it have been better preparation for you if Cork City had been fully professional at the time?

DD: My honest opinion is that I couldn't have had a better preparation for England than playing with that Cork City side back in 2000. I mean, the team that you and I came into – you run through some of the names: [Pat] Morley, [John] Caulfield, Mark Herrick, Derek Coughlan, Decky Daly… The mentality of those lads. I was a 17 or 18-year-old kid coming into that environment. It was amazing. I saw who they were and what they were and that had a big effect on me. Training meant everything; the games in training were 110%.

NH: I remember the intensity and bite of the training: it was electric.

DD: Yes it was, and they were great players. The mentality of those players had a great effect on me. They were like, 'We leave it all on field' – even in training. But then on the other hand, I remember Patsy [Freyne] having a fag after training. So that's far away from what I know to be a professional attitude now. At the same time, Patsy was a hell of a player. I remember the lads going for pints after games, and coming back from Dublin on away games there were cans all over the bus. So it was different then. But they helped me in terms of forming my mentality. I needed to recognise and take the good points that those players had, and if I could add the rest on top then maybe I could have a chance – as opposed to going, 'Oh well, the lads are smoking fags and then having 10 cans on the way home from Dublin, so I'll do that too.' So instead I took what a Patsy, a Decky, a Stephen Napier or a Fergy O'Donoghue gave on the pitch and in training and I kept that with me.

NH: And it took you a long way. You're 36 and have just signed another year with Crystal Palace in the Premiership. That's unreal.

DD: The experience of playing alongside those lads really helped me. I didn't have any expectations; I was just growing up in a youth team. And when I was in my first year in the youth team in 1998, the first team won the FAI Cup with Derek Coughlan's goal. So for me, growing up, they were my heroes. I was just happy to be there amongst them.

NH: Looking back now, was the league itself a help? Was there anything it could have done better?

DD: Well, I suppose the facilities weren't great. And the travel – the preparation could've been better. And some of the training grounds were poor... That being said, it's not as if I was going out to the Farm and thinking, 'This isn't good enough.' I was just happy to be there. If someone had put seven miles of sh*t in front of me I wouldn't have cared less; I was going through it. If I was that age now, with all the TV and exposure and professionalism, maybe I'd be asking for it to be better than it was. But would I have gone up to Dave Barry as a young lad and said, 'Here Dave, what's the story with the training pitch?' [Laughing] No chance.

NH: So you'll be aware of all the trouble we've had in the league over the past few years? I still feel that the league can be a great pathway for players – especially with the underage leagues starting – and I think if we put real investment into it, it could be even better. So for me sitting here, after all these years, it's great to hear you say that playing with Cork City and in the LOI was so important for your career.

DD: It was everything, man. Everything. I would never have been the player I am now if I hadn't played in the League of Ireland. I mean, if you take it back even further – I've often thought about it – my father was in goal for Avondale, and when that Avondale team was coming through they played FAI Cup games. They played Derry up in the Brandywell and got stuck in. I remember they played Shels or Bohs in Dublin and it was the same thing. This Irish mentality – they f**king competed. I was an impressionable 12-year-old, travelling with them up to Dublin. They got beaten but they showed up. Liam Treacy was the manager and there were some great players. Damien O'Connell was there, Len Downey, Eric Smith, John O'Leary. That was an introduction for me and I wanted to be like them. They were heroes to me. So every Sunday I used to go to my Dad's games, home and away. And then you consider the League of Ireland side of it and the GAA side of it and I think all of it coming together has made me what I am. I'd be the first to say I'm not the most talented human being or player in the world. I've no problem saying that, when I look at some of the players I've trained with or played against over the years.

NH: So when Leicester called you must've been delighted?

DD: Well, yes and no. At that time Cork City was the pinnacle for me. I'd already been over to England on trials: I'd been to Manchester City, Preston… they told me they didn't want me, so when I came back I remember signing for City and thinking, 'This is it for me now. I want to be a LOI player.' And I remember when Derek Mountfield called me and asked if I wanted to go to Leicester on a trial – I had to go home and think about it. That's the truth. I remember thinking, 'I've done this [going on trials] for two years. I'm not going on trial again; this is f**king bullsh*t, man.' Going across there and training with the reserves and you're like, 'This is f**king crap.' So at the time I genuinely didn't want to go. Why would I, when I was playing here every week for Cork City? I was living at home. I had everything I wanted and I was getting paid €80 a week, which was great for me at the time. I went home and I said, 'Dad, I don't know will I bother. Is it worth it? I've already been over and been chucked out.' But he told me I should go over and take a look at least. So I went over with an attitude of, 'I'll train for a week and see how it goes.' Leicester were in the Premier League at the time. But this was different to the other trials.

NH: Was it different because you were under a guy who knew you? [Colin Murphy was Leicester's assistant manager at the time.]

DD: Well, yes... but I was going with a different mentality as well. I'd played LOI and come off the FÁS course, played Cork minors and played in Europe. My mindset was, 'I don't need this. If you guys don't want me, that's fine.'

NH: Like a job interview... They say you're more likely to get a job when you're already in one.

DD: Well, I was thinking, 'If they take me, they take me; and if not I'm happy with what I'm doing at home.' As I said, my Dad actually had to convince me to go. The difference was when I went over this time they put me with the first team. Not all the time, but on the Monday and the Tuesday I remember training with the first team with Neil Lennon, Matty Elliot, Emile Heskey... all these guys were there. And I remember thinking, 'This is different; I'm not training with the 18s.'

NH: You felt more wanted?

DD: Exactly, yeah. And I was older too and had played first team over here.

NH: So would you say ideally players should get blooded here in the League of Ireland before going across?

DD: It's the best way to go. For me, I wouldn't have had it any other way; and I'd never recommend a kid to go into a Premier League academy.

NH: You wouldn't?

DD: I wouldn't say they'd have no chance... but you have to be pretty f**king special. For a kid to come out of the youth team at Palace or the 21s now and come play with us in the first team? I see them try all the time. On a Tuesday the manager might bring over two under-21 players to train with us and they're nowhere near it. *Nowhere* near it, honestly. And that's the best two guys! They're the best two we have – they're England underage internationals. The level is just too high. When you're continuously buying the best foreign players, the gap is huge. So for kids coming from the youth team or 21s it's not going to happen unless you're f**king exceptional or the club's in a position where they have little choice. You have to have the amalgamation of those two things – where you're unbelievable and the club can't spend money because of a transfer embargo or some other issue. Look at Palace: when Wilfried Zaha came out of the youth team and Victor Moses came in, Palace were in administration. George Burley at the time was like, 'It's them or nothing.'

NH: And if you're exceptional it might be the case that if you stay in Ireland they'll take you when you're older anyway – especially if you have first-team football behind you. If you were a 17 or 18-year-old now coming through a Premiership academy, do you think you would still have had such a successful career in England?

DD: No, I don't think so. And that's because I wouldn't have had the mentality, the mentality that got me through – which I'd picked up because of the path that I took. I got my debut with Leicester from pure mentality. I played centre-midfield because there were a couple of injuries and the manager was looking to the reserves and the young lads. There was kind of an injury crisis and he needed some central midfield players. I was playing centre-back at the time, and the manager just went, 'You know what – he'll f**king run around.'

NH: I remember just before you left, I met you in the gym in Rochestown Park that we used at the time, and you said, 'You know what? I know what I'm doing.' You seemed so focused; it marked you apart from others. You obviously took that focus with you when you went across…

DD: When I went to England there was a big 'looking behind the curtain' kind of thing going on, because everybody wants to be there. And when I got over there my attitude was, 'Yeah, they're good – but I'm f**king better.' I said to myself, 'This is it? I can do this.' Maybe I'm wrong, but it seems to me that a lot of people go over and they're in awe because they're used to seeing these people on the telly and they're like, 'That's him there, f**king hell – I was watching him yesterday on *Super Sunday*! I can't train here!' With me it was more like, 'Yeah, they're good, but I can do this.'

NH: I remember talking to Gareth Farrelly about this, and he said that the guys who make it in the Premiership are not the guys with the best ability necessarily; they're the guys that feel they belong there.

DD: If you go to training and you have anything like an inferiority complex, you'll get ruined. If you're hesitant in anything… because the training levels now are a joke.

NH: In terms of levels, is it about physicality in League One and Two for guys going over today?

DD: Those leagues aren't as bad as they used to be in terms of long balls. The people that were playing in the Premier League have trickled down to the Championship, so there's been kind of a knock-on effect. You're getting a lot of kids coming out of Premier League academies and playing League One, League Two and keeping the ball on the deck. When I was in League Two it was a [physical] f**kfest, pretty much. That said, while a few clubs might play football, it's still lower-league football and very physical. Listen, if I wasn't playing football and I was going on a Saturday to watch a game, I wouldn't watch a Premier League game. I'd go watch League Two and Conference games. Just a load of guys giving everything they have and they're all angry and I just think that's brilliant.

NH: So if it's very difficult to get through from the academies in the Premiership – or even the Championship – and if the lower-level leagues are still playing good physical football without such an emphasis on keeping the ball, is that an argument for the LOI as a stepping-stone? Playing at home, getting to play a bit more at a younger age maybe, and having time to reach the physicality that's needed?

DD: I think it's the best way to go. Stay and get your education.

NH: How does our league need to improve in order to get more of our best players to stay for longer?

DD: Well, from what I'm seeing, it's the facilities. If you can improve the facilities, you'll encourage more people to stay. Some of the stadiums… I know Roddy Collins had a right moan there recently about toilets and showers and lighting. I kind of have to agree with him; but that's something that can be fixed. Turner's Cross now is immaculate, with the pitches and the stands and the changing rooms – but that standard is rare in the league from what I gather. If each club had their own place with a building, with a gym, showers, changing room, three pitches – so you can have 17s, 19s and the first team… That might not sound like much, but a lot of these clubs don't have a base like that. If you had that you'd encourage a lot more people to stay.

NH: They're apparently building a base in Glanmire; the FAI are involved, and the council. It's for Cork City.

DD: Yeah, well that's exactly what you need, and what the club needs. You get the facilities right and people will want to stay – especially if they're in school. Get your Leaving Cert, go to UCC, like you did. If you had a base where people could go it would make a huge difference.

NH: Anyway, I should let you go, Damien. I know you don't have much downtime back in Cork. But to sum up: the LOI was massively important for you, wasn't it?

DD: It was crucial for me. And I'm not the only one. [Kevin] Doyle came out of it; [Shane] Longy too. Wes [Hoolahan] was here – he went over late and did very well in the end. Keith Fahey was over and back. You look at some of the most successful players in the Ireland team at the moment:

they all played in the LOI, and that's no accident. James
McClean played at Derry; Séamus [Coleman] was at Sligo…
So the LOI is crucial. Crucial for Ireland.

NH: If you were CEO of the FAI, would you put more
emphasis on our league?

DD: I would, yeah – because a lot of the kids go over to the
academies in the UK at 15 or 16. And it's difficult because
they're going into a world that's pretty f**king competitive
and the chances of making it are low. So one minute you're the
best thing since anything, and then all of sudden you step into
the world of Premier League football and you're probably
going to be middle of the road. Because in those Premier
League academies now we have kids coming in from Spain,
Belgium, Asia, Africa… everywhere. You might lose interest
because you're not progressing or you've hit a brick wall. But
when Leicester told me they didn't want me anymore I just
said, 'Fine: there are 91 other clubs in the UK and one of them
will take me.' Because I'd gone over with a different maturity
level. That happened to me at 18 or 19, so I was able to
process it and deal with it mentally. If it had happened to me at
17, when I had no real-world or first-team experience, I don't
know how I would've reacted. Essentially, when the going
gets tough you need to have the skills to deal with it, and I got
some of those skills from Cork City and from the GAA.

NH: But a younger lad, who comes back at 18 after going
over at 16; he must find it very hard… it must feel like
rejection, rejection, rejection – possibly for the first time.

DD: Yeah, I think with the best kids growing up in Cork,
Dublin, Kerry or wherever, they're going to have people
falling over backwards for them as they're the best players in
their pool. And then they step out of that world into the
Premier League and they're literally just another cog. Dealing
with that is the most difficult part of it.

NH: Does that need to happen at 16?

DD: Well for me, the grounding I got over here was key. I
had a different mentality; I was coming out of the Cork City

team we just spoke about, where you already had the sh*t kicked out of you in training. When people lost games, they were fighting with you. So I'd learned to deal with that. When I went to England I'd had months of Kelvin Flanagan roaring at me and Decky absolutely tearing lumps out of me. When the going got tough in Leicester I was like, 'Yeah, this is fine; this is how it is.' I was more accepting. Maybe Wes, Meyler, Séamus, Jamesie… maybe they all have the same story – I don't know. But I think going over to England at 16 to a Premier League or Championship team might still be the only route people have, because if you're getting scouted at 16, what are you going to do – sign for Pat's? Sign for Bohs? When actually, the reality is that if you stayed and played with the 15s and 17s at Pat's or Bohs or Cork City, if you were getting the same coaching as you'd be getting in England – and if the standards and facilities were improved – then you'd stay focused and concentrated. At the moment, we're bringing better coaches into underage football, but we haven't moved on with the facilities, which is a real shame. If you were to come through that proper coaching system and play in the LOI, then if you do well, people are going to see you. Scouts will be at those LOI games. So we have it within our power to create a real pathway here using the LOI. Because when you're playing on a Friday or a Saturday in the LOI, it really matters whether you get three points or not. That's what you want – and you won't get that coming through the academy system. Whenever you lose a schoolboys' game now in England it's like, 'It's fine.' There's this 'we did great' attitude – you're mollycoddled. Also, in the LOI you might get used to the media reaction, which you don't get in English academy football. If you get battered or don't play well, the media won't really report it. If they do, it might just be, 'Oh, he's not playing well.' You wouldn't be long finding out playing with Cork City how you're doing. And that's the beauty of it: when you get the criticism later, you know how to deal with it. You dealt with it at home, so you're ready to deal with at a higher level in England or wherever.

NH: Well, you're a living testament to the pathway that the LOI can provide. It's really amazing that 15 years after learning those lessons at Cork City FC, here you are still playing at the top level in England, at the age of 36.

DD: As I said, I'm very grateful for the experience I got with Cork City in the LOI. I really hope that Cork City and other LOI clubs can grow and continue to provide that type of experience for even more up-and-coming players into the future.

Neal Horgan

Chapter Fourteen – 2nd August 2016 to 24th November 2018

Tuesday 2nd August 2016

Stephen Kenny's Dundalk have been setting new standards for the league recently. They've won the title for the last two years, managing to hold off a resurgent Cork City under John Caulfield, but it's in Europe that they've really delivered something special. Kenny's side play attractive football that suits European competition, trusting in all of their players to play out from the back and retain the ball under pressure. I watched the game tonight and they thoroughly deserved the win. Stevie O'Donnell's ability to come deep and look for the ball at all stages is a joy to see in Irish football. They're guaranteed qualification to the group stages of the Europa League now, even if they lose in the next round, and they deserve all the plaudits. Imagine what our league teams might achieve in Europe if the league was properly backed by the FAI…

Dundalk make Champions League history on unbelievable night in Tallaght

Dundalk 3-0 BATE Borisov (Dundalk win 3-1 on aggregate)
Dundalk sealed one of the finest results in the history of Irish football at a rain-soaked Tallaght Stadium tonight. Two goals from David McMillan and one more from substitute Robbie Benson saw the current Premier Division champions overturn their first leg 1-0 defeat to BATE Borisov and progress to the Champions League play-off – just one round off the group stage. What will have made the achievement even sweeter is that they did it against the club that knocked them out of the competition 12 months ago. …

What a night for the club and the league. Dundalk go into Friday's play-off draw and they are now guaranteed eight more European matches this season with the two-legged tie and either the Champions League or Europa League group stages.

Dundalk: Gary Rogers; Sean Gannon, Paddy Barrett, Andy Boyle, Dane Massey; Ronan Finn (Patrick McEleney 32), Stephen O'Donnell (c), John Mountney; Chris Shields, David McMillan (Robbie Benson 78), Daryl Horgan.
(Ben Blake, *The42* – www.the42.ie – 2nd August 2016)

Tuesday 29th November 2016
Further highlighting the scale of Dundalk's European achievements, today's sporting news contained details of a recent Fifpro study which confirmed the particular difficulties encountered by footballers in Ireland. Given the underdeveloped and underfunded state of our league, it's no surprise that our players are not paid well and suffer from having some of the shortest average contract lengths in world football.

Majority of Irish footballers rely on second job due to poor pay
Around 60 per cent of players in the Airtricity League have second jobs because earnings in Irish football remain so low and contracts so short, a major survey by the international footballers' trade union, Fifpro has found.

In a study organised in conjunction with the University of Manchester, the organisation surveyed around a fifth of its 65,000 members, some 13,870 players, with the PFAI gathering responses to 23 questions from 176 players in the two divisions of the league here as part of the project.

The results confirm that players in Ireland endure low rates of pay, some of the shortest contracts in any of the leagues surveyed and little or nothing by way of paid holidays.

Average take home pay in the League of Ireland remains low despite the economic recovery, the survey shows, although problems with getting paid have eased as clubs become more stable. Just the top one per cent of players surveyed by the PFAI had a monthly take home pay in the €3,775 to €7,550 range with more than half earning between €565 and €1,880 per month. Just over a fifth of players in the league earn less than €280 per month and three fifths have a second job with many obliged to work in sectors like taxi driving so as to be able to train and play games as required by their clubs.

The survey is not all bad news from an Irish perspective with players here having significantly above average education levels and, it seems, relatively few problems with their employers but just 4.6 per cent of Irish players get the paid holidays that workers in other sectors are entitled to – one of the lowest figures recorded – while the average contract length is, at 11.5 months, half the international average and the second shortest in any of the more than 50 countries surveyed – with only Brazil's players, at 10.7 months, faring worse. …

(Emmet Malone, *The Irish Times*, 29th November 2016)

~~~~~

Tuesday 4th April 2017

Today the Ireland women's team, with the assistance of the PFAI, stood up to the FAI. It seems they've been treated very badly to date.

Sharing tracksuits and changing in toilets – Irish women's team hit out at treatment as FAI respond with statement
The Ireland women's team have been treated like "fifth class citizens" by the FAI and have been forced to the point where an international at home to Slovakia next Monday is in danger of not going ahead, it was claimed today.

A long-burning resentment by members of the senior women's international side came to a head today when a group of 13 players, supported by players' union, the PFAI, spoke to the media in Dublin.

Players outlined their grievances, such as the lack of remuneration for players on international duty, the lack of proper kit, gym membership and other matters which have come to a head and left the danger of strike action.

A key issue is the FAI's refusal to allow the PFAI, which also acts for League of Ireland players and represents the senior men's international team, to act for the women's players in any negotiations with the FAI.

Players spoke of the humiliation of having to go into a public toilet in airports to change into, and then out of, tracksuits for international games as the tracksuits had to be handed back for use by other teams.

"We are looking for the basics. In the past we have been getting changed in public toilets on the way to matches, this just highlights the lack of respect, it's not a lot we are looking for, just the basics," said Aine O'Gorman, one of the key players in the side.

"We are fighting for the future of women's international football, this isn't just about us," said team captain Emma Byrne today. …

(Aidan Fitzmaurice, *Irish Independent*, 4th April 2017)

~~~~

Sunday 5th November 2017

John Caulfield and his players have reached a zenith. After three years in a row finishing second place to Stephen Kenny's Dundalk, they finally outpaced them, winning the double tonight – the first time a Cork side has done so since my grandfather Jackie Lennox's Cork Athletic back in 1951. It's a fantastic achievement for a club that was on its knees at the start of the decade. Champions League football back on Leeside next year means so much to the fans and also helps the club coffers. On top of that, the Cork women's team have won the FAI Cup on the same day at the Aviva. I'm not sure this moment for the club will be surpassed anytime soon.

Cork City claim the club's first double while international influence dominates final
For the first time since 1951, the city of Cork got to welcome home a double of league and cup as John Caulfield's side, thanks to a penalty shoot out, got the better of Dundalk at the Aviva Stadium. The two clubs have gone head to head for honours for four seasons and even 120 minutes of tense football in front of 24,120 fans yesterday could not separate them, forcing the tie to a penalty shoot out.

After seven perfect conversions, Dundalk man Michael Duffy saw his kick saved by Mark McNulty, then Kieran Sadlier stepped up and converted past Gary Rogers to seal the win, and that historic double for Cork, the first in the club's history. …

Dundalk: Rogers, Gannon, Gartland (Hoare, 90), Vemmelund, Massey, McGrath (Connolly, 71), O'Donnell, Benson, Duffy, McEleney (Mountney, 107), McMillan.

Cork: McNulty, Beattie, Bennett, Delaney, Griffin, Keohane (Sadlier, 58), McCormack, Buckley (Campion, 97), Dooley, Morrissey (Bolger, 97), Sheppard.

(Aidan Fitzmaurice, <u>*Irish Independent*</u>, 5th November 2017

Thousands gather to welcome victorious Cork City teams back to Leeside
You'd know if you spotted Cork City's double-winning squad while traveling the M50 earlier this evening, because their Kearneys bus had 'DOUBLE WINNERS 2017' plastered across the side of it.

City completed the first double in their history, and the county of Cork's first since 1951, as they captured the Irish Daily Mail FAI Cup at the Aviva Stadium on Sunday, edging rivals Dundalk on penalties.

The women's team ensured it became a double-double of sorts by completing their own personal treble, Clare Shine's goal enough to see off UCD waves before both Cups were hauled back to Cork. …

(From *The42* – www.the42.ie – 6th November 2017)

~~~~

Friday 27th April 2018

During the early part of Cork City's brilliant double campaign, one player stood out: a small but skilful centre-forward named Seanie Maguire. Here was a player who was ripping defences apart both in Ireland and in European competition. Back in 2004/05 I'd seen the same type of performances from players at Cork City such as Kevin Doyle, George O'Callaghan and John O'Flynn. I'd also witnessed the ability of the likes of Wesley Hoolahan and Keith Fahey who played in our league during that same period. Yet none of those players were capped while playing in the LOI during that spell. I'd be surprised if they were considered at all until they crossed the Irish Channel. And here again, some 13 or 14 years later, was another example. Seanie Maguire joined up with Preston at the end of July 2017 and was selected in a provisional Irish squad in August 2017. While he didn't make his full debut until October 2017 it's clear that the move coincided with his consideration for the squad. It's a problem that needs addressing and I decided to give my view.

Time to ground the magic plane

Last month Martin O'Neill discussed the League of Ireland on the podcast 'Greatest League in the World' with broadcaster Con Murphy and Conan Byrne of St Patrick's Athletic.
When asked about the pattern that has developed over the past 10 to 15 years of League of Ireland players being very swiftly selected for the Irish squad on the back of a transfer to the UK – a journey known in domestic football circles as 'the magic plane' – O'Neill raised the argument of the higher standard in the Championship in England as against that which prevails in the Premier Division of the League of Ireland.

Given the vastly superior wages and attendances, together with the proliferation of international players from around the world, in England's second tier, O'Neill certainly has grounds for assuming that, in general, a player from the Championship will be better prepared for international football than his equivalent playing in the League of Ireland. ...

This status quo takes no account of a very significant change in the landscape of Irish football since the Charlton era, and that is the hugely increased number of players who have graduated from the League of Ireland to make careers for themselves in the UK and further afield.

To give just one illustration, since the turn of the millennium, a total of 10 ex-Cork City players have been capped for the senior Irish team: Damien Delaney, Kevin Doyle, Shane Long, Alan Bennett, David Meyler, Kevin Long, Daryl Horgan, Seanie Maguire, Alan Browne, and Joe Gamble.

By contrast, when speaking with former City captain Declan Daly recently, he told me that from his time as a player – roughly spanning the years from 1985 to 2003 – he could count on the fingers of one hand the number of players who went on from the club to make careers for themselves in the UK.

Indeed, from my own time playing with City through to the present day, there have been many more former players who, though they never gained international caps, have gone on to play in England and elsewhere – the likes of Roy O'Donovan, Leon McSweeney, John O'Flynn, George O'Callaghan, Denis Behan, David Mooney, Graham Cummins, Danny Murphy, Gearóid Morrissey, Brian Lenihan, and Chiedozie Ogbene among others.

In short, there has been a near five-fold increase in the number of Cork City players going on to play outside the League of Ireland since Declan Daly's time, a trend which, of course, has not been confined to just this club. ...

The best available players, wherever they play their football, should at all times be selected for Ireland. What should change, in my opinion, is that when it comes to a 50/50 selection decision, the League of Ireland player should get the benefit of the doubt.

There can be no denying that outstanding individual talent was, and is, on display in our domestic game. So imagine the benefit for both the League and the national team, if the Irish manager would select the next Sean Maguire or Kevin Doyle while they were still destroying defences at Turner's Cross.

Or the next Wes Hoolahan while working his magic at Shelbourne. Or the next Keith Fahey while showing his class at Richmond Park. Associations all around Europe use their national side as a means to assist and improve their domestic leagues and clubs. The IRFU does so too.

Why can't the FAI follow suit and adapt the mandate of our national manager to take advantage of those occasions when an exceptional player like a Maguire, Doyle or Hoolahan comes along?

The benefits would not just be confined to the pitch. A player's status as a full international would doubtless greatly enhance any future transfer his Irish club might achieve and that too would help further improve the overall standard of our national league.

Instead, we're stuck with this strange transformation in an already talented player's ability and status which seems to take hold somewhere between take off and landing.
The magic plane doesn't just carry off our best players – it also takes away the reward and recognition which our league deserves.

(Neal Horgan, *Irish Examiner*, 27th April 2018)

Sunday 8th July 2018
More bad news on the league today: players' wages not being paid. Every year is the same, it seems.

Banks for Nothing
*Limerick and Bray Wanderers players have not been paid –
again. The Seagulls squad is now waiting over a week for its
June wages.*

*The Bray boys were told that money which was due on June
29 would come on July 2 and then July 4 – but they remain
unpaid. It means that Wanderers have not trained at all since
the June 29 loss away to Limerick. But they will face Sligo
Rovers at the Carlisle Grounds this afternoon.*

*Limerick's survival hopes were given a boost by last week's
win as it opened up a nine-point gap over basement side Bray.
But, like the Wicklow outfit, their own financial woes continue.
The club was late paying wages last month and, again on
Friday, the players were not paid on time. …*

*An FAI spokesperson said: "The Football Association of
Ireland are aware of financial difficulties at both Bray
Wanderers and Limerick.*

*"The FAI are working closely with both clubs to provide
assistance and ensure all staff and players get paid monies
owed."*

(Owen Cowzer, <u>*The Irish Sun*</u>, 8th July 2018)

Thursday 26th July 2018
There's more controversy involving the players' union (the
PFAI) and the FAI. The relationship seems to have hit an all-
time low.

PFAI launch scathing attack on FAI over fund proposal
*The PFAI have lashed out at the FAI, who they claim have
announced a new fund to assist players and clubs in financial
trouble without consulting them and for which the PFAI are
expected to contribute 50 per cent.*

*The FAI announced the fund on Wednesday afternoon,
which they claimed would be worth €300,000 and would help*

clubs who are experiencing difficulty in meeting contractual obligations to professional players.

The announcement comes after Bray Wanderers and Limerick FC both struggled to pay their players in recent weeks.

According to the FAI, the cost of the proposed fund would be split equally between both them and the PFAI.

However, while the PFAI broadly welcomed the creation of such a fund, they launched a scathing attack on the FAI and they claim that the organisation not only failed to consult them before the announcement, but that senior management within the FAI has refused to meet them. …

The PFAI also lashed out at the prospect of the cost of this new fund being split equally between the FAI and PFAI, insisting that the prospect of players being forced into paying into such a fund is 'deeply insulting'. …

(From RTÉ – www.rte.ie – 26th July 2018)

Tuesday 7th August 2018
A Dying League, In Need of Help

Before a ball was kicked this season, there [were] a lot more questions than answers. Some of the questions asked: [Were the contracts] offered by Bray Wanderers sustainable? Is the new 10-team league a good idea? Was the fixture pile up in the first half of the season needed? Will we have a title race that will have more than two teams? The answers came a lot quicker than expected. …

It is the same people in the same positions year on year that has seen no growth or change in the league. Changing the format of the league is not what we need. Playing each other 4 times is not what we need. We have excellent media coverage and we have [the] strong, passionate fans that a good league needs. We lack a good TV deal that can show the world the product we have here. We also lack fresh air right at the top, where it matters.

From the facilities to the TV coverage, the league is a shambles. We cannot seem to take the next step, whether that is a TV deal where clubs are compensated or whether we move with the times of social media and show live games on Facebook. We need something fresh, we need a new direction. We have to stop having clubs going through financial difficulties every season if we are to improve. A clear out is needed so a change can begin. Unfortunately, we are a dying league in need of help!

(Aaron Doherty, *League of Ireland* – http://leagueofireland.ie
– 7th August 2018)

Saturday 29th September 2018
Cork City FC aren't faring quite as well as they did last year and John Caulfield is starting to field some criticism. A resurgent Dundalk comfortably beat City last week at the Cross, and it felt like a coronation of sorts.

Caulfield has enough credit in the bank... and respect
… You hear a lot of talk now of [the FAI Cup semi-final at Bohs] being a last or, should they prevail tomorrow, second-last chance for City to 'salvage' something from a season of underachievement, with some of the more disenchanted elements in the City support even casting it as a potentially defining game in Caulfield's management of the club. Indeed, there are a few keyboard warriors out there who seem to have already decided that, regardless of what happens between now and season's end, it's time for a change at the top.

For the benefit of the proverbial visitor from Mars who, on the basis of access to Planet Twitter and a passing interest in League of Ireland football, is seeing this stuff and rubbing his huge cycloptic eye in disbelief, yes, my little green friend, this would be the manager of a club which did the double last season, won the cup the previous year and has never finished lower than second in the league in his first four seasons at the helm. And who, despite their recent slump, still look set to finish runners-up again in 2018 and are still in the running to make it three FAI Cups in a row.

Actually, never mind the Martian, I'll wager there are a few parties much closer to home – from Waterford to Tallaght and from Derry to Bray – who must be looking on and asking what they wouldn't give to be able to share in Cork City's current woes.

Interestingly, there was some supportive comment this week from what many might regard as an unlikely source. Over the course of their raging 'New Firm' battle across the last five years, there has been little love lost between City and Dundalk but, even allowing for the fact that it's easier to be gracious from a position of renewed strength, the Lilywhites' Robbie Benson did provide some much-needed context and perspective.

"Maybe [Cork] haven't had the credit they deserve for their achievements," he observed.

"It's taken what's developed into a bit of a dynasty situation at Dundalk to stop Cork winning more league titles. They could have won three or four but unfortunately for them they have come up against us. But I think it has been great for the league that there has been two teams that have been so strong at the same time."

Which is true. To have taken City from where they are were five years ago to where they are now – and, last season, to have actually eclipsed one of the best League of Ireland teams of all-time – is simply an outstanding achievement on Caulfield's part and one which simply can't be dismissed as irrelevant because City's standards dipped this season and the wheels came off in recent weeks.

Of course, Dundalk will be fully deserving of their title this year. Their impressive stats and the no less impressive quality of their football brook no argument, with the cool, commanding display they delivered in Turner's Cross last week living up to the stuff of champions in every respect. …

(Liam Mackey, *Irish Examiner*, 29th September 2018)

Monday 5th November 2018

In the end Dundalk sauntered to the 2018 league title, finishing some 10 points above City. But City, for their part, remained 15 points clear of third-placed Shamrock Rovers – which shows the divide between the top two and the rest. The fact that these two sides played each other again in the FAI Cup final yesterday – the fourth consecutive year they've met in the final – is further evidence of their dominance in Irish football for the last half-decade.

Dundalk's 2–1 triumph yesterday in front of 30,000 at the Aviva means it's honours even, with each club enjoying two FAI Cups and two runners-up places in the last four years. However, Dundalk have dominated in the league, winning it four times over the past five years, with Cork City finishing second in each of those years apart from their double-winning year in 2017. That's four second places and one league title for City since Caulfield took over, and two FAI Cup wins. That's an amazing tally and must've been beyond the expectations of even the most ambitious FORAS member when they were giving Caulfield the job back in 2014.

Despite JC's incredible results, the fact remains that Stephen Kenny's Dundalk have outperformed City in the league as well as in Europe, and with the backing of new American owners Peak6 they appear to be moving further ahead. The increased money from UEFA for European club competitions has definitely assisted both these clubs in staying ahead, and possibly helped attract those new investors for Dundalk. But Caulfield, Kenny and their players deserve massive plaudits.

Saturday 24th November 2018
Stephen Kenny to take over as Ireland under-21 boss and replace Mick McCarthy after Euro 2020
THE FAI have taken the unprecedented step of appointing two people to become Ireland manager in the space of one week

with Stephen Kenny agreeing a deal to take over from Mick McCarthy in 2020.

McCarthy will be unveiled as the replacement for Martin O'Neill tomorrow, but he will only be in charge for one campaign cycle with new U21 boss Kenny assuming control of the top job once the next Euros campaign draws to a close. ...

(Daniel McDonnell, *Irish Independent*, 24th November 2018)

Just before Kenny's new position was announced I happened to bump into John Caulfield at UCC. There had been rumours linking Kenny to the vacant manager's job at the national team and I laughingly suggested that Kenny getting the Ireland job might be a good thing for Cork City. John didn't feel the FAI would be interested in giving it to Kenny, and I thought he was probably right – so we were both proved wrong when it was announced that Kenny would have the under-21 job for two years and then take over the full national team from Mick McCarthy in 2020. On reflection, it seems a wise choice by the FAI. Allow Stephen Kenny two years to ingratiate himself at Abbotstown with the up-and-coming Irish players while the experienced McCarthy takes over the reins to try and get us to the 2020 Euros. Are the FAI finally seeing a link between our league and the national team? Is there hope of backing for the league from the FAI? Are things getting any better in the league? I decided to put some of these questions (and others) to JC, who knows more than most.

Chapter Fifteen – Interview with John Caulfield, March 2019

Neal Horgan: I remember meeting you for coffee, John, sometime in late 2013, just after you were announced as manager, during the off-season before the 2014 season. You were asking would I be interested in coming back for another season. And you might remember that while I was happy to try it out, I couldn't really commit to the full-time training that you were bringing back to the club, alongside my job as a solicitor. As for you, though, had you quit your previous job at that point?

John Caulfield: No, I hadn't. I got appointed as Cork City manager in early November I think, but I continued in my job as sales development manager with Diageo until the December, and continued managing the UCC soccer team too. Even though it was announced that I'd been appointed, my contract with Cork City didn't actually start until January 1st. So as there was no training with the Cork lads to deal with, I started out just trying to bring in players during the off-season. That was around the time that I met with you. I think the club had only six players registered when I took over – although some of those hadn't signed new contracts, as it was during the time that players had only 35-week contracts. So the club had the registration of a handful of players: Shane Duggan, John Dunleavy, Daryl Horgan, Mark McNulty and a few others. They were registered for the club but not being paid during off-season, as was the way at the time. I went around asking those players about a new contract with the club, and Shane Duggan and Daryl Horgan decided they weren't going to stay and left for Limerick and Dundalk respectively. I felt they were uncertain of me. Johnny Dunleavy and McNulty stayed, though.

NH: So by that point in 2013 you'd been a long time outside of the club. I remember playing with you in your last season in 2001, so it would've been 12 or 13 years. It must've been exciting coming back as manager?

JC: Oh yeah. To be honest, it was probably the dream day.

NH: That's brilliant to hear. So had you been hoping or aspiring to get the job during your time coaching with Avondale and UCC?

JC: I'd always thought there might be a day to do it... but to be blunt with you, I thought that day was gone, that it had passed me by. I'd had opportunities to do it before, but for whatever reason the timing hadn't been right – maybe my family hadn't grown up yet, or the club was a bit rocky, or I hadn't the experience for it. I'm not sure I would've been ready for it back then, when those approaches came, and from a family point of view and considering the job that I was leaving behind... the risk was too high. So when the opportunity came up again in 2013, I hadn't expected it but it was probably the ideal time, as my family had grown up by then. And despite the lack of players, it was one of those moments when I said to myself, 'This is it. This is what I want to do; this is where I'm at.' There might have been massive problems facing me and massive work to do, but I knew deep down that this was right for me. It was that kind of day, when I got appointed.

NH: You were taking on a lot – and going full-time too...

JC: Yes, it was my first full-time experience. I'd always worked in a day job when I was playing, and also while coaching UCC and Avondale, so this was a bit weird. And my job with Diageo was a good one... so I'd be on a lot less money [laughs] with CCFC, but it was never about the money. It was about going in and doing a job that I wanted to do. There were a lot of people close to me that were apprehensive; they were saying to me privately, 'I'm not sure about this,' but in my head I was clear. It was the right time.

NH: What were those first few weeks of January like? Was it a bit disconcerting, waking up to your first full-time day in football?

JC: To be honest, it was exciting. I suppose it makes you appreciate what being in professional sport is really about: it means dedicating your whole life to full-time training, instead of getting up to do your day job and then running into training or coaching three times a week at the end of the day. These days I try to explain to young players that it's the most privileged job they'll have. They might not realise it; they might miss out and let the opportunity that it presents pass them by. So sometimes my job is about helping young players to realise that this is a privilege and that it's also a massive opportunity for them.

NH: So I suppose the point is that you knew, you were well aware from playing part-time for Cork City for 16-plus years while trying to hold down a job, that this was a golden opportunity for you.

JC: Yes – I knew what a chance this was. I also… well, you know, Hoggie – it wasn't even about how long I'd been here. I was given the opportunity and I knew it would be hard work, but that didn't faze me. I had a plan, but where would I get to? I had no idea. Could I make it as a manager at this level? I didn't know. Yes, I'd been a player for so many years, and a supporter; I'd coached and had done reasonably well coaching in amateur football… but I always remember the nervousness at the start of the league that year [in 2014]. I was thinking, 'Am I near it in respect of where the players should be, or am I a mile off? Are we near it in terms of the coaching they should be getting?' We wouldn't really know until the season kicked off. So there was never a fear of putting in the hard work – the question was how did I know if I could do this?

NH: So it was a step into the unknown, despite everything you'd done?

JC: Yes, it was – particularly that first week.

NH: Do you remember the difficulties that you encountered early on, or what you brought in that worked?

JC: Well, straight away John Cotter came in as my assistant. He took a contract on much lower wages than what he'd been on in his day job. He had a young family and I was very conscious of that, but he was determined that he wanted to come in. Phil [Harrington] came in, Woodsy [Billy Woods] stayed and Lisa Fallon was scouting the opposition in a voluntary capacity. So all of a sudden I had what I considered loyal Cork City people around me who I knew would be trustworthy. I had a base to work from, and we could spread from there. After that it was about signing players. Although the club was in debt and there were a lot of problems, I was happy to deal with everything. My drive was: 'This is Cork City – my club – and I'll chip away at it no matter what.' Perhaps if it had been a different club I would've been more like: 'I'll just concentrate on the first team and not worry about the club,' as we had huge problems with training and other matters initially. We moved training in pre-season into UCC's Farm as Bishopstown wasn't in good condition. Then I decided to change to morning training – whereas Tommy had you guys doing evening training.

NH: Which I suppose brought its own challenges, as you're talking about full-time players and full-time hours?

JC: Yes, well I was looking to assemble players who would be passionate and would dedicate themselves to morning training and give it all on match day. I knew the crowd would always back that team. That was my plan, anyway – bring the crowds back and get a passionate team. However, at the time, wages were incredibly low; there was no payment for pre-season. And it was difficult to attract players who were better paid at other clubs. Maybe they were looking at me thinking I was a fan favourite or golden child coming back to manage the club but that I'd never managed before and wouldn't be any good. I think Daryl Horgan and Shane Duggan might've left because they were thinking that way at the time, as I was unproven. But funnily enough, despite losing out with players like that, a few things happened: my knowledge of the amateur game and the MSL [Munster Senior League] was very good, so I was able to recruit well from there – the likes of Mark O'Sullivan, Josh O'Shea and Michael McSweeney. Also, McNulty and a few of the other boys were re-signing for us, and then [Anthony] Elding signed for us and he was one of the biggest PR statements that we ever made. He and Liam Miller were probably the biggest names in the end, and while it might not have worked out on the pitch…

NH: You were making a statement?

JC: Yes, Elding was after getting the winner for Sligo in the cup final and taking his shirt off, which made the news. We signed him at the end of November and we were basically saying: 'We got the guy who got the winner in the cup final.' Like I said, it might not have worked out on the pitch for Elding, but his signing gave us huge profile and confidence. After that we got Billy Dennehy, which was a big signing for us too. So there was a bit of a buzz. Then the season started and Marky Sull [Mark O'Sullivan] was on fire. People thought he'd come out of nowhere…

NH: But he hadn't. I'd seen him come to the club on three occasion before that, under Damien Richardson, Paul Doolin and Tommy, but he'd never looked comfortable.

JC: Well, to be fair, I can see why other managers might not have taken to Marky if they didn't really know what he was about. But John Cotter had a very good relationship with him from Avondale – as did I – so we knew him inside-out and he was never a risk for us. Did we think he'd do OK if he signed? Yes. Did we think he'd do as well as he did? Probably not. He was sensational for us for three years, to be fair.

NH: And so you hit the ground running in that first season, with both Marky and Billy Dennehy scoring a lot of goals. And all of a sudden you were playing Bohs in the penultimate game of the season – which you won one-nil on a day of lashing rain at Turner's Cross – and you were ahead of Dundalk going into the last game against them at Oriel Park.

That was mad stuff for your first year. It must've beyond all expectations.

JC: I suppose it was, Hoggie. But it was… it was just a f**king rollercoaster of a season.

NH: [Laughs]

JC: It was. We drew our first match against Pat's in Cork. Then we went away to Derry and won, and we were off and running. We were going OK until we got battered by Dundalk away 4–0. We made a few mistakes; for example, we hadn't left early enough on the bus up, which effected the start of the game. That was my fault, not the players'. Then we had a few wins that lifted the fans. Healers scored an overhead kick in the last minute against Pat's to keep us in touch with Dundalk. Then, with eight games to go we played Athlone away, I think it was late August. At one stage that night we were beating Athlone and Dundalk were losing to Drogheda, but then Dundalk turned it around and won 3–2 while Athlone came back and equalised against us. That pushed Dundalk six points clear with seven games left. It seemed over. Everyone thought we were gone, but then in our next game Dan Murray scored in the last minute to beat Rovers and after that we won the next five in a row. And in our penultimate game against Bohs that you mentioned, Billy Dennehy scored from the sideline from a free kick – a fluky goal. Meanwhile Dundalk had drawn a few matches, including their second-last match. So going to Oriel in the last game we only needed a draw to win the league, while they needed a win – but we hadn't beaten Dundalk once that season. They'd beaten us three times, and of course they ended up winning that final game 2–0. It was a crazy season and a crazy final game. I can still see it. Gearóid [Morrissey] was injured. Johnny [Dunleavy] went to midfield, [Michael] McSweeney came in at left-back and did well. Marky had a chance from 12 yards and put it past the post, and Billy hit the post. Rob Lehane had a chance late on. But it wasn't to be. It was a crazy year alright.

NH: But looking back, that has to be one of the most important seasons the club has ever had. To come back and challenge for the Premier Division... it put to bed any doubts that we were going to survive, that this was the same Cork City we were involved in before. Those questions were answered affirmatively with the club back at the top of the Premier Division.

JC: Yes, I always say that our best achievement was that first season. The club was in debt; I was new to the club; but the crowds came back. We had four amateurs on the pitch at final whistle in Dundalk, but we could've won the league and on another night we might have won it. It was madness.

NH: I remember the excitement going to the game in Oriel...

JC: You didn't take much part in the season due to work and whatever, did you?

NH: Yeah, well with you going back full-time, and with me working behind a desk... I had a knee issue but my legs were gone really at that point. I remember running around the Farm in pre-season: we did this long run and myself and Elding were at the back. All the other lads were well finished and waiting as we came in slowly a few minutes later. That was a bit embarrassing as it wasn't me – I was always among the fittest in those types of runs. I know I was getting older, but still. I did OK in the doggy/sprints, etc., but my real fitness was gone.

JC: Yes, but you were around the dressing room.

NH: Well it was a nice way to go for me – quietly and gently. I played a few friendlies, was on the bench for a few league cup games, but that was it really. My abiding memory, though, is of when you came in on that first day of training in Bishopstown in pre-season and you were talking about the Dublin clubs coming down here and the proper Cork welcome we'd need to give them. That moment sticks with me; it was like I'd time-travelled back to when Liam Murphy was manager in 2001. That attitude towards the Dublin clubs... that

Cork welcome… none of the managers we'd had since then had really made reference to it, as most of them had been Dubs themselves – Rico, Mathews, Doolin and Tommy were, at least. So you came in and told us how we needed to approach the games against the Dublin teams, and I thought that was brilliant. That meant something to me. Not that we had to be reduced to 'Cork versus the evil Dublin clubs' – is was more like, 'Yeah this is familiar. This is the club I remember from when I was starting out.' And I knew then that the club was back in safe hands. In any event, that seemed to be your approach – you knew what had worked for the club in the past – and I was delighted to witness that. And what a year the first season turned into…

JC: Yeah, it went well. It was brilliant. I just remember the crowds coming back, and we needed it at the time. In fact when you really think about it, if we hadn't had a good first season the club might've been in trouble again. We were in huge debt, and at the same time I was trying to lay down standards for full-time football. Lads had to be in at 9am; food was to be provided after training; there needed to be enough gear given to the lads for training… I wanted the players to have as much as they could. I was hoping we could get away from the 35-week contracts too. I wanted the dream day where lads were paid for 52 weeks; I wanted these things for the players. I also did some small gobsh*te stuff, but still important. I got someone to build a panel in the hallway at Bishopstown that said this was the players' area and no one was to enter except players and playing staff, so that the players had their own space and atmosphere. We created a TV/relax room and brought in a dartboard: gobsh*te, seemingly trivial stuff as I say, but it was important. I was trying to change it as much as I could, within the financial limitations.

NH: It must've been satisfying, bringing in those full-time aspects for the players.

JC: Yeah it was – but the main aim was bringing in the 52 weeks, which we were able to do after a couple of seasons.

NH: Payment all year round?

JC: Yeah, well you know what it's like. People would often drive past in the morning and see us training, and later they'd ask me, 'Yee were out training? Do you not do anything else for the day?' And I might've responded, 'We were training – that's what we were doing for the day.' But did Munster do anything else? Was it OK for Munster to train and be fully professional and not for us to do the same? There was a perception out there that it was fine for Munster but not for Cork City; but when you think about it, in a city like Cork, how the hell can you not have a guaranteed professional soccer team every year?

NH: Yes, and the city's growing so that argument is growing also. One of the things you said to me when I was launching my second book – you were very good to help me with a video or two; I owe you a few lunches! – was that the Association is not interested in full-time football. While we've had the advances with the underage leagues, and the colleges getting closer ties to LOI clubs, that position from the FAI hasn't really changed. The decision you made to go full-time wasn't influenced by the FAI or by the Department of Sport; it came from you and you alone. I've read the FAI reports on the league: the Conroy Report, for example, effectively ignores full-time football. So the FAI still haven't broached the issue, despite everything that's gone on. Clubs are still consistently getting into financial difficulties. There are no guidelines for or against full-time football and I have to say that really galls me.

JC: Yeah, and the only reason CCFC pay 52 weeks is because I felt morally it was wrong to have part-time contracts. I told the Board we had an obligation. As in any other industry, we needed to treat the players with respect – they were entitled to be treated as professionals. And once we did that, then I could train them hard and we would get results. But morally, it was the right thing for the players.

NH: That has to be applicable across the league, where there are other players being treated unprofessionally or without due respect.

JC: Yes, but like you were saying, if I hadn't implemented it at Cork it would never have happened. I brought it to the Board and the chairman backed me, but I could still see people on the Board failing to realise that these players were employees and needed to be treated accordingly. And I think a lot of boards that run soccer around the country would take the same view: they don't really see the players as employees and they don't really view the set-up as professional, which of course it must be. And at the higher level, within the Association – and I hate to say this, as I have so much enthusiasm for the league – nobody is backing it from above. If you're asking me do the people at the top have a real interest in professional soccer, I'd say no f**king chance. In that organisation they might say they want professional football in Ireland, but they don't really. The votes are carried by the junior football leagues, who are really against us having professional soccer here. They won't admit it, of course, but they have no interest in our league. They want to follow Manchester United and Liverpool. I really hate to say it, but in all my experience and especially over last few years, I've found that I've wasted my time talking about it. No one from the FAI or those junior clubs that carry the votes in the FAI really want to back it.

NH: I would have the same view.

JC: The only way we could have a fully professional league is probably by having a breakaway league, run by businessmen rather than the club committees. You'd need business involvement. And it's the same with our club. It would be preferable to have the support of three or four businessmen – not like when Brian Lennox had to carry the full weight of the club on his own. He let his heart rule his head and was losing money to be fair to him. Ideally, going forward you might have a number of businessmen backing up FORAS, because ultimately we're in a professional business.

NH: FORAS was created to act as a support to the club but became more centrally involved as a result of the problems in 2008 and 2009, so there's probably a conservative nature to them which is totally understandable. That mindset of being scarred from before – but they'll need to get over the scars in order to advance. Plus it's a co-operative, which inevitably brings restrictions.

JC: If you think about it, the club was on its knees. FORAS did a brilliant job in saving it, but their whole philosophy was to save the club and be a backup with the assistance of others – not to run it themselves. Then, as things worked out, they ended up running the club on their own. The late Pat Shine gave a speech about this. CCFC is at a crossroads; it's a €3 million operation now – so the decision is whether to move on and keep moving, or stay put. The problem you have, if you aren't going to let outside money come in, is that you need to grow the membership and increase the membership fee. If you don't, you get left behind. So does the club change the constitution to bring in more money? FORAS need to be sure in that regard, of where they're going in the future. They could possibly sell up to 49% of the shares and keep control while raising investment; that's one option. The danger is if we have one or two bad years on the pitch then the club could quickly get into trouble again, as it's so reliant on first-team results.

NH: But what kind of change do we need for the league itself?

JC: Well, looking at the big picture, the FAI are no help at the moment and that will need to change.

NH: Niall Quinn's recent suggestion – to bring in government funding and a different entity to run the league instead of the FAI – would you be open to it?

JC: Anything would be better than the current situation. The thing about Niall Quinn is that he gets air time because he's a name and you want to see what he's thinking; but yes, anything at all would be better.

NH: You were in the game with Cork City from 1986 – maybe even before that. There's never been any real investment by the authorities into the league, has there?

JC: Never.

NH: So we're talking more than three decades... And at the local level, the minute the first team goes down we could be in trouble again?

JC: If we have a few bad years, then yes, we might need begging bowls in order to survive. That hasn't changed really.

NH: And in another 40 years' time it could still be the same...

JC: In another *100* years it could still be the same fragile league if the FAI don't decide to support it. Hoggie, you were there in 2005; you won the league and the FAI Cup. The crowds were there and you were going well... then three years later you were bankrupt. What's the difference between then and now? You were full-time then – have things progressed? No, they bloody haven't.

NH: So despite FORAS saving the club and doing a great job to get it back on its feet, and despite doing so well, winning the double, multiple cups, European runs... because of the lack of support and leadership from the FAI we're potentially still only a season or two away from all of that again. Is that the case?

JC: Absolutely – and I hate to sound so negative.

NH: Well these are negative questions...

JC: There's been so much good progress with Cork City, be it with the UCC connection, with the underage structures, the women's team... Lots of progress in some ways. But unfortunately, yes, it could all fall with one or two bad years on the pitch – despite what people might think. And that's primarily because we don't have the proper support and planning from the Association. Whether that will ever change, I can't say.

Chapter Sixteen – FAI on the Brink

As it happened, a few days before I interviewed John Caulfield back in March 2019 a story that would have huge implications for Irish football reached the papers. Football was in the High Court again – but this time the story didn't involve Cork City or Tom Coughlan; this time it was about the FAI and John Delaney.

Saturday 16th March 2019
@marktigheST – 3.05pm

Just spent the last three hours in the High Court after John Delaney tried to get an emergency injunction to prevent us reporting on FAI and Delaney payments. The judge ruled in our favour! Story in @SunTimesIreland tomorrow.
> (From journalist Mark Tighe's Twitter account)

Sunday 17th March 2019
Delaney's unexplained €100,000 cheque to FAI

John Delaney, chief executive of the Football Association of Ireland (FAI), wrote a personal cheque for €100,000 to his employer in 2017. Delaney has refused to explain the reason for the payment.

Last night the FAI boss failed in an emergency application before judge Anthony Barr of the High Court to prevent The Sunday Times revealing details of the payment. Following a three-hour hearing, the judge ruled in favour of the newspaper's right to report the existence of the payment.

A copy of the cheque has been seen by The Sunday Times and its authenticity verified by several sources. It is dated April 25, 2017.

The €100,000 payment was drawn from Delaney's account at Bank of Ireland in Waterford. The cheque was subsequently lodged at Bank of Ireland in Blanchardstown, near the FAI headquarters in Abbotstown.

Questions in relation to the €100,000 payment were first made to the FAI on March 1. In his ruling last night, Barr noted that it was significant that Delaney had 15 days to respond to queries from the newspaper and had instead launched a last-minute application to the court. ...

In the High Court last night, Delaney attempted to get an injunction based on the claim that documents seen by The Sunday Times could have emerged only from in camera family law proceedings involving his ex-wife.

The judge ruled that the rights of the in camera rule had to be balanced with the right of the media to report on matters of public interest. He added: "I am satisfied that the finances of the FAI and any payment and repayment to its chief executive are matters of significant public interest." ...

(Mark Tighe, *The Sunday Times*, 17th March 2019)

Saturday 23rd March 2019

That was only the beginning. Revelation after revelation has been emerging in the press of misgovernance in the FAI boardroom.

A few days after the failed injunction, it's been announced that a report by Jonathan Hall Associates had recommended the creation of a new position of Executive Vice-President at the FAI. And they had already recommended someone to fill the role: John Delaney.

FAI CEO John Delaney to step down from position and take new role within organisation

John Delaney has stepped down as the CEO of the FAI - to take up a new role as the Executive Vice President.

The FAI released a statement this evening to confirm the dramatic change after strong speculation throughout the day regarding Delaney's position.

The news comes one week after it emerged that he had paid €100,000 to the association in the form of a bridging loan back in 2017.

However, the FAI statement said that the changes were a consequence of a governance review that was commissioned in February and undertaken by sports governance expert Jonathan Hall Associates, and their principal Jonathan Hall, who is a former Director of Governance and Director of Football Services with the English FA. ...

It subsequently emerged that an FAI statement was being prepared. The lengthy missive outlined the recommendations made by Hall.

It said: "The report recommends that the FAI considers creating a new role of Executive Vice-President and starts the process of appointing a new Chief Executive Officer in order to put itself in the best position possible for the strategic period ahead.

"The new role of Executive Vice-President would be a specific defined role with responsibility for a range of international matters and special projects on behalf of the FAI. It is envisaged that the current CEO would step into this new role. This would allow Irish football to continue to benefit from his extensive football experience and contacts across Europe and the rest of the world." ...

The FAI say the review was adopted unanimously at a board meeting of the association held yesterday. ...

(Daniel McDonnell, *Irish Independent*, 23rd March 2019)

Tuesday 9th April 2019

So Delaney has stepped down as CEO but taken up the new position of Executive Vice-President – on the recommendation of a report that was apparently commissioned in February. As *The Sunday Times* had only contacted the FAI on 1st March about the €100,000 loan, it would seem their enquiries had no influence on Delaney's change of role. In any event, news of Delaney's new role hasn't prevented Sport Ireland reacting to the revelations.

Sport Ireland to 'suspend and withhold future funding' to FAI

Sport Ireland is to immediately suspend and withhold funding to the FAI.

The statutory authority said it has made the decision after the FAI said they "did not comply with Clause 4.3 of Sport Ireland's Terms & Conditions of Grant Approval."

The board of Sport Ireland met earlier to discuss the ongoing controversy over a €100,000 "bridging loan" given to the FAI in 2017 by former CEO and now Executive Vice President, John Delaney.

Sport Ireland said that in making its decision to suspend and withhold funding "the Board of Sport Ireland notes that the FAI has already been paid 50% of its 2019 funding to date and some positive steps taken by the FAI in recent days."

Sport Ireland said the decision will be reviewed by the board "as a standing item at each of its future meetings".

The board said it will consider reinstatement of funding "once all ongoing reports commissioned by the FAI have been completed and the recommendations adopted".

Sport Ireland said it would continue to provide non-financial assistance and guidance to the FAI.

(From <u>Irish Examiner</u>, 9th April 2019)

Delaney stepping down as CEO came as a shock. But the news that Sport Ireland has suspended funding is very disturbing and could have huge implications for Irish football – not least from a Cork perspective with regard to the promised delivery of a home for Cork football in Glanmire. It's hard to understand what exactly is going on. Fortunately, Delaney and the FAI are due to appear at the Oireachtas tomorrow to clarify matters. One wonders whether they'll get the same warm welcome and praise they received 10 years ago when Cork City FC were on the ropes…

Wednesday 10th April 2019

(Note: the following are selected extracts from an Oireachtas joint committee debate. The extracts are not intended as a summary of the discussion. A full account can be found at https://www.oireachtas.ie/en/debates/debate/joint_committee_on_transport_tourism_and_sport/2019-04-10/3/)

[Oireachtas] Joint Committee on Transport, Tourism and Sport debate – Wednesday, 10 Apr 2019
Engagement with the Football Association of Ireland

Mr. John Delaney: *'I thank the Chairman, Deputies and Senators. I want to address the committee on the issue of €100,000 I gave to the Football Association of Ireland, FAI, in April 2017, which was repaid to me in June 2017.*

'First of all I want to say how truly saddened I am that Sport Ireland, which provided annual State funding of €2.9 million to the Football Association of Ireland, has announced that it has temporarily withdrawn the funding to the association pending reports from the FAI, Grant Thornton and Mazars.

'I wish to make it clear that I have urged a speedy response to the queries received from Sport Ireland, and this week I have already met with Grant Thornton and with the FAI on these issues. I will respond to any request to a meeting as soon as I hear from Mazars.

'On Tuesday, 25 April 2017 we had an internal finance meeting at the FAI. This meeting was attended by our director of finance, Mr. Eamon Breen, our financial controller Ms Yvonne Tsang, and me as the CEO. At this meeting I was advised that if all cheques and FAI bank transfers issued to third parties at that time were presented for payment that the FAI would exceed its overdraft limit of €1.5 million on its bank accounts, which were held with Bank of Ireland. I expressed concern and surprise at the meeting as to how the FAI could have arrived at this position. I recall thinking at the time that if

I had been approached even a few days earlier I may have been able to better address the issue. I asked if any funds were due to the FAI that could resolve the matter and I was informed that there was nothing due imminently that could be confirmed at that stage.

'As the matter was pressing and we only had a few hours to resolve the potential issues that would arise if the bank overdraft limit was exceeded, as a precautionary measure and to assist the FAI I wrote a cheque for €100,000 from my personal account to the FAI. This cheque was made payable to the FAI and I gave it to our director of finance, Eamon Breen, telling him to only lodge the cheque if it became clear that the bank overdraft was going to be exceeded.

'Later that afternoon I travelled to London and the next day I travelled on to Geneva, Switzerland, where I was attending UEFA business on behalf of the FAI. I recall phoning our honorary secretary, Mr. Michael Cody informing him that I had made a precautionary payment to the FAI by way of a personal cheque for €100,000 to assist in the event that the bank overdraft was going to be exceeded. I informed him that I was very concerned and that I had to act quickly to assist the Football Association of Ireland. I recall also informing the then president Mr. Tony Fitzgerald who was chairman of the board at the time.

'The following day while I was in Geneva I received a call from our director of finance, Eamon Breen, informing me that there was a requirement to lodge the cheque for €100,000 and he subsequently confirmed that request to me by email. I agreed that the cheque should be lodged. I asked the director of finance when I would be paid back and he said it would be as soon as the funds came in.

'I subsequently received a cheque for €100,000 on 16 June 2017 from the Football Association of Ireland, repaying the amount in full and which I lodged to my personal account on 23 June 2017. I did not receive any interest payment and I

*would never have expected it. I was only acting to assist the
FAI and for the benefit of Irish football. ...*

'On legal advice I am precluded from making any further
comments at this hearing in relation to the finances of the
association or my former role as CEO, or on the €100,000
payment, either directly or indirectly. In the interests of fair
procedures and natural justice I have made this statement to
the committee and attended this meeting voluntarily, as I have
attended many Oireachtas committees in the past. I am not in a
position to answer any such questions here at this time. Given
that some members of this committee have made highly
prejudicial public pronouncements about me personally prior
to my attendance here today, and in light of the recent
Supreme Court ruling in the Kerins case, I ask that the
committee respects this position.*

'I am happy to answer any other questions in relation to my
current role as executive vice president responsible for UEFA
and FIFA matters. ...'*

Deputy Imelda Munster: *'Would Mr. Delaney like to state
whether he ever considered his position at any stage with all of
this happening? I do not have to go through it all again.'*

Mr. John Delaney: *'I have read my statement to the
committee already.'*

Deputy Imelda Munster: *'It is just a question.'*

Mr. John Delaney: *'I have read my statement.'*

Mr. Donal Conway: *'That offer of resignation would have to
have been made to me to the board and that did not happen.'*

Deputy Imelda Munster: *'I am asking Mr. Delaney,
personally, did he ever consider...'*

Mr. John Delaney: *'I have answered already.'*

Deputy Imelda Munster: *'Mr. Delaney is not answering but that is his answer.'*

Mr. John Delaney: *'I have made my statement.'*

Deputy Imelda Munster: *'I would have thought it was a question to which there was a "Yes" or "No" answer. As an observation, I think the former CEO of the FAI, Mr. John Delaney, has behaved disgracefully today. He came in with a last minute statement. He knows the procedures for this committee. He has furnished us with a statement but is refusing to answer any questions on that statement. He is also refusing to answer questions that are ongoing in respect of his time as CEO. What has been going on here has been an absolute disgrace and farcical. The only good thing is that the public have witnessed these events first-hand as well. I would have thought that anybody would have been glad to be handed the opportunity to put the record straight. Mr. Delaney, however, has not taken up that opportunity.'*

Mr. John Delaney: *'I note Deputy Munster's comments.'*

Deputy Imelda Munster: *'Is there a reason he has not taken up the opportunity?'*

Mr. John Delaney: *'I note Deputy Munster's comments.'*

Deputy Imelda Munster: *'Yes, but is there a reason he has not taken up the opportunity?'*

Mr. John Delaney: *'I have read my statement, as Deputy Munster knows.'*

In the context of what John Delaney said (and didn't say) at this meeting, it's startling to look back at some of the things he stated in the same setting back in 2009, during the height of Cork City FC's troubles:

***[Oireachtas] Joint Committee on Arts, Sport, Tourism, Community, Rural and Gaeltacht Affairs debate –
Wednesday, 16 Dec 2009
League of Ireland: Discussion with Football Association of Ireland***

Mr. John Delaney: *'Notwithstanding the progress made, there is no underestimating the damage that is done each time a club is a party to legal proceedings involving Revenue or any other creditor. Club mismanagement of finances, as exemplified by high profile cases such as this season's disappointing incidents in Cork City FC, undermines the integrity of the competitions, weakens the credibility of the regulatory processes and reflects poorly on the sport overall. Each participant club must appreciate the impact of mismanagement where it fails to meet its obligations not only on its own club's stakeholders but also on the overall image of the League of Ireland. ...*

'It was common practice here, and indeed still is across Europe, for directors, benefactors and investors to put money into clubs in the form of soft interest-free loans with recourse to cover losses. This practice is not allowed under the FAI's financial regulations. ...

'The improvement in the financial management practices in clubs must be acknowledged. A number of clubs have completely overhauled their financial controls and reporting has improved. This is to be welcomed. There are clear examples, such as Shamrock Rovers, Sporting Fingal and UCD, to name just a few. In recognition of the FAI's work in this area, UEFA has invited the FAI's internal compliance officer, Padraig Smith, who is with me, to join its club

licensing working group as it looks to improve the effectiveness of financial regulations and controls across European and domestic competitions. Indeed, UEFA's CEO at the time, David Taylor, is on public record as commending the FAI's work on good governance, especially in the area of financial regulations and commending its success in running licensing across each of the national league divisions. ...'

(See a full account of the debate from which the above extract is taken at https://www.oireachtas.ie/en/debates/debate/joint_committee_on_arts_sport_tourism_community_rural_and_gaeltacht_affairs/2009-12-16/2/)

~~~~

New FAI role for Delaney was created only after loan discovery

FAI president Dónal Conway ... disclosed a review of senior roles that led to the creation of a new position of senior vice president was only commenced after The Sunday Times made enquiries about the loan in March this year. It was completed within a matter of weeks, with Mr Delaney being appointed without interview.

[When questioned by the Committee for Transport, Tourism and Sport] the former chief executive did not answer any questions relating to the loan, or on his previous role. Members of the committee repeatedly asked questions surrounding the terms of the review of senior roles, and about who sanctioned an erroneous statement in March, but officials were not able to supply complete answers. ...

Committee members repeatedly questioned the FAI delegation about the report into senior roles in the organisation that led to the creation of Mr Delaney's new position of executive vice president.

The committee heard that Jonathan Hall and Associates was commissioned in early March and Mr Delaney was appointed to the position recommended by the report on March 23rd, immediately after its conclusion. ...
(Harry McGee, *The Irish Times*, 10th April 2019)

It turns out the Jonathan Hall and Associates report was only commissioned after *The Sunday Times* had made enquiries to the FAI about the loan. So why did the FAI say it had been commissioned in February, before those enquiries were made?

Tuesday 16th April 2019
[Oireachtas] Joint Committee on Transport, Tourism and Sport debate – Tuesday, 16 Apr 2019
Governance and Funding of Football Association of Ireland

Minister for Transport, Tourism and Sport (Deputy Shane Ross): *'I am joined today by the Minister of State, Deputy Brendan Griffin, who will also make an opening statement. I thank the committee for its tireless work on this matter and for the light it has shone on serious issues within the FAI. Investigative journalists have also played a commendable role, particularly Mark Tighe, whom I wish to thank. I apologise to the committee for failing to provide my opening statement in advance as requested. As I am sure members will appreciate, this has been a very fluid situation, including significant developments as late as this morning, which would have overtaken any script provided earlier.*
'I regret that there has been a cloud over Irish sport, especially Irish soccer, since 17 March, St. Patrick's Day, when news broke about the loan of €100,000 to the FAI by its then chief executive, John Delaney. On 19 March, we wrote to Sport Ireland, directing it to engage with the FAI to clarify matters of concern. Since then, there has been intensive activity between the FAI, Sport Ireland and my Department. The decision of the board of Sport Ireland to withhold and

suspend funding to the FAI was an extraordinary moment for Irish sport. I do not have to remind the committee of the scale and reach of the FAI. This is an organisation with more than 200 employees, and an annual turnover of close to €60 million. It is also an organisation with several thousand clubs, the national governing body, NGB, for the most popular team sport in Ireland by participation rate. While it may not be among our native sports, soccer is a sport which is at the heart of Irish life and culture. …

'While it is the case that due process is hugely important, the committee will not be surprised that I have become increasingly concerned with these developments. Here we have a clear case of the FAI admitting it failed to abide by the conditions for receipt of State funding. We had a shambolic appearance by the FAI at this committee last week at which even the most basic questions, for whatever reasons, went unanswered. Concerns remain around a financial transaction, basic levels of corporate governance, the creation of the new executive vice president role, issues of a substantial nature being considered by the Office of the Director of Corporate Enforcement and other developments which would suggest that all is far from well. …'

(See a full account of the Oireachtas debate from which the above extract is taken at https://www.oireachtas.ie/en/debates/debate/joint_committee_on_transport_tourism_and_sport/2019-04-16/3/)

Friday 19th April 2019
Further bad news has come the way of Delaney's home team, Waterford FC:

Waterford will appeal Uefa decision not to grant Europa League licence

Waterford chairman and owner Lee Power has said that the club will appeal the decision made by Uefa not to grant a licence for them to play in the Europa League this season.

Uefa confirmed on Thursday that Waterford do not meet the criteria required as the current entity of Waterford FC has technically been in existence for less than three years.

St Patrick's Athletic, who finished one place below Waterford last season and who wrote to the FAI earlier in the week about the issue, are in line to take their place and, in doing so, earn the estimated €240,000 from the competition which Waterford say they had already budgeted for.

Power claims the club received "assurances" from the FAI that they would be granted a licence having finished fourth in the Premier Division last season. Power has also said that they were visited by Uefa delegates over the last five months and no issues were raised.

"Everyone at Waterford FC are deeply shocked and saddened at the news that we have been expelled from playing in the Europa League this season," a statement released on Friday by Power read.

"We feel we have been totally misled by the FAI and were given assurances throughout this five-month process by them that the licence would be granted. We also had club visits by UEFA Delegates during this period of which no issues were raised.

"As a club, we entered into substantial commercial agreements and invested heavily again into the team and also budgeted for the qualification money due in November. This will now have a serious financial impact on the club going forward."

In his statement, Power has also called for a full investigation into the FAI handling of the matter.

"The circumstances to which this decision has been made and the events over the last week are unclear and dubious, bearing in mind representations made to us and assurances given," he said.

"We will be asking for a full investigation into the FAI handling of this matter.

"I have instructed my UK Lawyers to lodge an immediate appeal with Uefa and will pursue any legal avenue we have with regards to compensation and/or any wrong doing against a number of parties. ..."

(From *The Irish Times*, 19th April 2019)

Saturday 11th May 2019

I've met John Delaney on two occasions. The first was in the conference room at the Aviva Stadium in 2017 when I received a Hall of Fame award before the men's FAI Cup final between Dundalk and Cork City. Delaney came over for the photographs as the awards were being handed out; he told me that he remembered my late father (whom I had mentioned in my acceptance speech) and the good work that he'd done for football in Munster. It was a nice thing for him to say.

The second occasion was during my friend Mark Herrick's 'Headrite Sports' exhibition at Carrigtwohill FC. Mark was demonstrating his heading apparatus to the FAI delegates who were visiting the club as part of their 'summer of football' programme. Everyone was in great form as the heading apparatus was shown in front of Delaney, the other FAI delegates and the players and members of Carrigtwohill FC. Once the demonstration was over, on behalf of Mark, I asked Delaney whether Mark could do another demonstration at FAI headquarters in Abbotstown later that year. Delaney was very genial and accommodating and did indeed arrange for Mark to conduct a meeting with the FAI's medical team later that year. Maybe I was naïve, but Delaney seemed to me during those two encounters to be an approachable guy and clearly had a good knowledge of and interest in the LOI, which I found encouraging.

Also, there is no doubt that the recent reforms that have come about with regard to the underage national leagues will be hugely positive for Irish football in the long term. While

Ruud Dokter was the one behind this development, Delaney must have signed it off. A further encouraging move from the FAI was the appointment of former Dundalk coach Stephen Kenny as Irish under-21 manager, with the plan for him to take over the senior position from Mick McCarthy in 2020. These developments seemed to me to be the first real signs of an appreciation at the FAI headquarters of the role of our domestic league.

As such, I had begun to hope that Delaney might even sign off on more positive changes to the LOI over the coming years – even if his real interests lay elsewhere with the national team. For a time, even after the loan issue was revealed, I still felt that Delaney was someone with a genuine interest in promoting the domestic game, and that this could've been encouraged in due course had he remained in the CEO position.

However, the following article is difficult to reconcile with a CEO that was truly interested in growing our under-resourced and fragile league.

Sport Ireland was unaware of former FAI chief executive John Delaney's €2million 'golden handcuffs' deal

Sport Ireland was unaware of John Delaney's €2million 'golden handcuffs' deal, the Irish Sun can reveal.

The sports governing body is currently conducting a review of the FAI – but had no idea the pay deal existed until we broke the story on Thursday. When asked whether it was aware either historically or more recently of the deferred payment, a spokesman for the body said: "No, Sport Ireland was not aware."

Sport Ireland and the FAI set up a Governance Review Group to develop reform proposals for the embattled Association ahead of the AGM in July. That Sport Ireland was not aware of Delaney's loyalty payment raises even more questions over FAI governance.

Former FAI finance director Tony Dignam, who has been nominated for a new role in the Association, said he too was unaware of the 2014 deal. Dignam is one of two nominees to succeed Michael Cody as honorary secretary of the FAI.

He was finance director when the then CEO Delaney signed a monster loyalty deal with the FAI in 2014 — a payment that has never appeared in annual accounts since. However, Dignam told the Irish Sun: "I wasn't aware of it. The first I ever heard of it was in the paper. I may have been gone at that stage.

"I wouldn't have heard about something like that anyway, that information would be kept between the board.

"John Delaney's contract was out, it was kept very close."

…

(Neil Cotter and Gary Meneely, *The Irish Sun*, 11th May 2019)

€2 million! At this point it's worth remembering some more of Delaney's words at the joint committee meeting when Cork City players were losing their jobs in 2009:

> 'One of the problems has been player salaries. One player in the League of Ireland was on €4,000 per week up to recently, which is unsustainable. One club had eight or nine players on over €100,000 a year, which is also unsustainable. Full-time football is sustainable in this country but with a proper wage structure rather than the crazy figures I have just outlined. Five clubs work on a full-time basis. It is affordable but only when the correct wages are paid.
>
> …
>
> 'We cannot have people running clubs who are not fit to run them or who run them in a cavalier way that ultimately affects the community. …'

(From www.oireachtas.ie, 16th December 2009)

In any event, with John Delaney having stepped aside there appears to be a vacuum of power in Irish football. Unsurprisingly, some old factions have started to reveal themselves. Despite the revelations since March of this year, anyone who thinks Irish football's woes began when John Delaney took over as CEO is misguided. Its problems run much deeper.

Thursday 16th May 2019
FAI backs down on schoolboy summer scheduling
The Football Association of Ireland (FAI) has said that that schoolboy leagues can return to a traditional September to May schedule.

Following consultation with the Schoolboys Football Association of Ireland and the FAI board, the FAI has backed down on plans for the seasons to run over the summer months after it was met with resistance.

The March-October season, favoured by FAI High Performance Director Ruud Dokter, has not proven successful and just last month the Dublin and District Schoolboys' League confirmed it would revert to a traditional calendar.

In a statement this evening, the FAI has acknowledged the issues raised due to summer scheduling. ...
(From RTÉ – www.rte.ie – 16th May 2019)

Monday 24th June 2019
FAI plan runs into schoolboys trouble
The numbers are not adding up for the FAI in their bid to push through governance reforms next month to restore state funding.

Causing the uncertainty is the failure of the review report, published last Friday, to safeguard a position on the new board for a representative from schoolboy football.

John Earley, who sat on the board for four years as the chair of the underage committee, quit on Wednesday after he refused to endorse the proposals.

The report only recommends that the Schoolboy Football Association of Ireland (SFAI), of which Earley is chairman, share the place on the new board with the women's football committee (WFC).

As gender balance is foremost in the charter for change, it could mean the SFAI waiting eight years to have a voice at the top table, despite them being the largest affiliate, overseeing 120,000 players.

As a result, they won't be backing the review and that spells bad news for the FAI.

(John Fallon, *Irish Examiner*, 24th June 2019)

Monday 29th July 2019

In the end, the FAI managed to win over the schoolboy element and get the recommendations approved at their AGM. But they're not winning everyone over.

Ross 'disappointed' as Donal Conway re-elected as FAI President

Minister for Sport Shane Ross has accused the newly re-elected president of the Football Association of Ireland of reneging on an agreement that he would step down from the association's board.

Donal Conway was re-elected unopposed, with 134 votes in favour, five against, with one delegate abstaining at the FAI's AGM in Trim, Co Meath today.

Mr Conway reiterated his intention to step down after a year and said he wished to help the new board in its task of restoring confidence in the association.

However, Minister Ross said Mr Conway's re-election was 'disappointing'.

He said Mr Conway had promised back in April to step down from the board.

It comes after Minister Ross invited officials from FIFA and UEFA to a meeting in his department last night to reassure them that the Government has no desire to interfere with the independence of the FAI.

The officials were in Ireland to act as observers at today's FAI AGM.

Mr Ross said he briefed them on the various allegations of malpractice in the FAI and the inquiries that are underway.

He said that he told them that while the Government does not want to interfere, it does have a duty to make sure there is good governance where public money is spent.

Asked about how Mr Conway's election might affect public funding to the FAI, Minister Ross said that funding had been suspended, and while the Government wants to restore it, there must be a new reformed association with good governance established.

Meanwhile, speaking at the FAI AGM, Mr Conway said the organisation wanted to honour the Governance Review Group Report, which found the association must change its culture and behaviour.

The report was carried out in conjunction with Sport Ireland and was approved by UEFA and FIFA.

Mr Conway said that the organisation wants to honour that report and it is a road map for the future of the association.

The Governance Review Group Report will be calibrated over time, he said, but it is the first key milestone on the road to change. …

(Tony O'Donoghue, RTÉ – www.rte.ie – updated 29th July 2019)

Readers of *Second City* might recall the reluctance of some members of the Soccer Australia board to step away following the recommendations of their government-commissioned Crawford Report ('Report of the Independent Soccer Review Committee into the Structure, Governance and Management of Soccer in Australia', April 2003):

The Fathers of Australian soccer's success

… The so-called "rump board" of Soccer Australia (those who had not resigned or left following the Crawford findings) held firm and forced elections. To the horror of all those desperate for change, it became clear there was no certainty that Lowy [Frank Lowy: chairman of the new entity, Football Federation Australia] and his colleagues were going to win the day.

Meetings were held in private rooms, deals were done in the corridors and cafes of hotels near Sydney airport as the horse trading intensified while the election dates loomed.

Eventually, common sense prevailed, the old guard stood down and Lowy and his group assumed control.

Within months, the old debt-laden Soccer Australia had been killed off and wound up, with a new body, the Australian Soccer Association (which later morphed into Football Federation Australia), being formed. …

(From *The Age* – theage.com.au – 19th November 2005)

While most of the FAI's old guard have now stepped down, Deputy Ross wants them all to go. And while Noel Mooney hopes that the FAI will reach 'calm waters', one wonders if the current storm will gather more strength with the publication of the various investigative reports and FAI accounts in autumn 2019. The question is, will the FAI survive?

Chapter Seventeen – Interview with Pat Lyons, April 2019

Cork-born town planner Pat took an active role in the development of FORAS and in particular in the Infrastructure Working Group set up in 2009 by the first board of FORAS and CCFC. He was co-opted onto that board in 2010 and has been deeply involved with FORAS and CCFC ever since.

Pat was elected to the board in 2013 and was Chairman from 2014 to January of 2019, when his six-year tenure ended at the AGM. He is still involved in the Infrastructure Working Group, which has, together with the FAI and Cork County Council, acquired a site for a Munster football centre of excellence at Glanmire.

Neal Horgan: Pat, how did you get involved with the board of FORAS?

Pat Lyons: Trina Boyle – the lady who wrote the letter to the judge responsible for us staying alive back at the examinership stage – she left the Board to go teaching abroad and so I was co-opted in. Pat Shine, who has now sadly passed on, approached me and asked would I come onto the Board in her place. When you're co-opted onto the Board you can only stay for a year and then you need to step down, which I did. But before this I'd been asked by the Board to run an Infrastructure Working Group, and I said yes. Myself and a few others met with Cork City Council, NAMA, the HSE – anyone who had land. I had over 30 years' background in engineering and planning, having worked as a town planner with Cork County Council and also having worked with An Bórd Pleanála. So I was happy to get onboard with the Infrastructure Working Group to see if I could assist. I'm still helping in this role today.

NH: You were looking to find a home for the club?

PL: Yes, and the City Council offered us land – out by the Lee Road, near the Angler's Rest. It was zoned for sport use, but it was very much prone to flooding so it wouldn't have suited. If we'd taken it, we couldn't have risked putting money into it. So we declined that offer and moved onto looking at other areas.

NH: So this search for a home, was it for training facilities?

PL: Yes. As you know, the club never had anything; it never had a home or training facilities. It had Bishopstown at one point but that fell through. Turner's Cross is a fine stadium to play our games out of – one of the best in the league, if not the best. But as you also know, we rent that from the Munster Football Association [MFA – Munster branch of the FAI] so we needed, and still need, a home. A training facility could become that home.

NH: In my opinion this is a massive and ongoing problem for Cork soccer; we have no real home. It's clearly not an easy fix if you consider that in all these years since Fordsons FC back in the 1920s, we haven't managed to find a permanent home. We've had places like Flower Lodge, but unfortunately that was lost. The FORAS model seems like the best way forward, in that once a home is found it can be protected as it's kept separate from the running of the club. I think the continued existence of Turner's Cross as a soccer facility owes a lot to the fact that it's owned by the MFA. If Turner's Cross had been in the hands of a League of Ireland club then it might not have survived as a soccer facility. So the lack of a permanent home is a big problem, but one that FORAS seems almost designed to fix. But it can't be an easy task. It's revealing that when you first started the infrastructure group back then, that was your aim... and here you are today with the same task ahead of you.

PL: Yes, that's true – but we are getting closer with Glanmire.

NH: Well, fingers crossed for that; I see the FAI have promised it'll happen...

PL: Yes, they have; and it needs to happen for Cork soccer.

NH: It would offer so much to the club and soccer in Cork, and indeed Munster. We desperately need it so that the underage teams can all play near each other and get the feeling they're linked with the first team. In the Republic's second biggest city you'd think it would've happened before now. But hopefully you can drive it on, as the FAI have committed to it. So anyway, while we'll keep our fingers crossed for that, tell me how you got on during your time on the Board.

PL: Well, after being elected to the Board in 2013 we had to decide to let Tommy go. It wasn't easy. Mick Ring was chairman and he handled it very well. It wasn't easy for anyone, but we felt we had to do what was right for the club at the time and we ended up getting John [Caulfield], which was a masterstroke, looking back. We'd had over 50 applicants for the job, including a few big names from overseas – who spoke more about themselves than the club, to be honest.

NH: But were you involved in the early days before that, when FORAS first got involved?

PL: I was to an extent, but I wasn't on the first board. I was co-opted onto that board in 2010. There were early meetings at the Telecom Club and Presentation College. I was just a member of the audience, but I remember one night stating that the development of FORAS was the most important thing that had happened in Cork football since the 1920s. Trying to get the facility in Glanmire was probably the next most important thing. But also crucial, in my opinion, is the partnership with UCC.

NH: They've come on as team sponsor…

PL: Yes, but it's more than that; they're not just a sponsor. It's a partnership arrangement. I was involved initially with the first partnership agreement in 2017 and I'm delighted to say we've just agreed a new three-year extension until 2023.

NH: That's fabulous. How did that partnership transpire in the first place?

PL: Myself and Éanna [Buckley] were sitting outside in Bishopstown one day, going through various things – probably looking at bills coming in – and we said we really needed to get more sponsorship. We had an arrangement with UCC

Mardyke Arena; they were looking after us, and we'd had a good relationship for years in respect of getting pitches from them and things like that. So Éanna and I decided we'd take a leap and contact UCC to ask would they be interested in forming a partnership with us. It was a bit of a shot in the dark, but it transpired that the people we were dealing with in UCC were receptive to the idea and it just went from there. The president of UCC at the time, Michael Murphy, was incredibly supportive too.

NH: Yes, in fact Michael Murphy came in and did a speech at my workplace at JW O'Donovan on South Mall, and during his speech he said the most complimentary things about Cork City FC. I'm not sure if our club was ever spoken about in such a way on the South Mall – you know, in the business district of the city. So there was a move – a huge step, in my opinion – with UCC, and it gave a certain credibility to the club.

PL: Yes, it did – and to football in Cork. As well as Michael Murphy, Professor Patrick O'Shea – the current President of UCC – is also hugely supportive of the partnership. Even though he brings with him his incredible experience of three decades in top institutes in the US, he's actually only from across the road: next to the stadium at Turner's Cross. When he told me that, I was a bit uncertain as he has a strong US accent, but then he told me he 'used to go to the Box'. I knew then that he was a true supporter – he might even have been a Cork Celtic supporter – if he calls it 'the Box'. Very few people call it that anymore. So I was convinced of his real interest, knowledge and support at that point.

NH: So the partnership has been renewed...

PL: Yes, and all of UCC is behind it. We had a meeting up there at UCC the day we signed the three-year extension. The president was there, the vice-president, their sporting director Morgan Buckley... they all spoke so highly of Cork City FC that it was almost embarrassing. It was really fantastic.

NH: That's brilliant. But why are they so happy to be with Cork City FC? To be blunt, what do they get out of the partnership?

PL: Well, there's the usual exposure from being front and back on the shirt, on TV once a week, in every newspaper in the country, European nights... As you know, they're the only sponsor on the jersey for European nights, as UEFA regulations state that you can only have one – and we've been in Europe every year since we signed the first deal. Also, they have a page in the programme, adverts in the ground... But what they were delighted about at the last meeting was that the women's team now have full membership of the club and the percentage of women students is growing exponentially. They're delighted that we're moving in this direction, supporting women's football.

NH: Which is only right and long overdue...

PL: I agree with you, and it's a strong and growing part of our club now, which is fantastic.

NH: And so going back to the agreement, what does Cork City FC get, apart from the usual financial backing of a sponsor?

PL: Well, we have agreements in relation to scholarships for our players, both men and women, and in relation to the use of the Mardyke Arena – which is an amazing facility – and we have Seán Ó'Conaill who runs the Sports Law Clinic at UCC, providing support. And there are far more advantages in addition to these.

NH: It all seems so good it's almost unbelievable!

PL: I know. And besides these benefits, UCC is not a drink or gambling sponsor. The partnership with UCC is fantastic and we have that extension for the next three years. It's growing and has potential to grow even stronger into the future.

NH: I'm not sure something like this could ever have happened in my day. We wouldn't have dreamed of this type of sponsor. We had good sponsors, but not with the same level of benefits. We would've felt we weren't good enough for that; that was the way I felt when I was playing, anyway. We weren't really a club that would attract this type of sponsor. We weren't mainstream enough.

PL: Well, to stop you there Neal – we have to get over that type of thinking, don't we? We have to tell ourselves we're good enough to be at the top table. Do you know what I mean?

NH: Yes, you're right. I completely agree.

PL: And the FORAS model has worked; it's brilliant. There are people out there who say we should stop talking about FORAS – but that part of the club's history is so important and should never be forgotten.

Chapter Eighteen– The Dream

I've been drafted into an extended Irish squad for a series of
friendlies. I feel a little awkward around the place – as if
everyone knows it's just a token gesture. But even if that is the
case, it's still a chance…

We're in the dressing room on the day of the game. I'm
glad Colin Healy's here; he'll have my back. By hanging near
me he seems to infer that I'm a good player – although
whether I'm up to this level is down to me. Dan Murray has
been called up too from Shamrock Rovers and like me he
seems unsure of his status amongst the group.

Kevin Kilbane and a few others in the dressing room seem
to be wondering who we are. They're discussing things
privately in their own little corner.

Then Martin O'Neill comes in. He makes a speech and
names the team. I'm not in it. He says he'll decide the subs
after the warm-up. As the first 11 lads are getting their kit on,
Crazy Daz (another name that hasn't been called out) whispers
to me somewhat aggressively, 'He should've waited until later
to name the players and the squad, for f**k's sake.'

In the meantime my gear seems to have become mixed up
with Kilbane's and that of another first-teamer, who were
sitting near me. My Copa Mundial boots are missing. The
kitman notices and says sympathetically, 'Son, I think Kilbane
or one of the other lads has taken your boots out to warm up as
they forgot theirs.'

As the dressing room clears I'm left waiting without boots,
alongside the kitman and Martin O'Neill. The gaffer offers his
help. A pair of AstroTurf runners are found from somewhere –
but they're a size or two too big for me. 'That's OK son,'
O'Neill says. I gather from his unconcerned demeanour that
I'm not in his plans for the bench, no matter how well I do in
the warm-up. 'Go warm up and see how it goes anyway,' he
says.

The warm-up is very competitive. We have a full-blooded game. Those in the starting 11 are involved but take it easy; the rest of us are at it 100% to get a spot on the bench. I win a ball in a tackle with Wes Hoolahan (who's in the starting 11) and he hurts his leg and walks away pissed off. A physio or coach goes over to him and I can see Wes giving out to him but I can't hear the words. I reckon he's giving out about me – the annoying novice. I go over and offer an apology but I'm not sure if he accepts it.

The game goes on. I'm trying hard to get more involved. I know what's at stake: a full international cap... even if it is only for a friendly. I run my legs off, win the ball back a few times – which I'm good at – and leave it off easily to others. Will this be enough? I'm thinking it won't. I need to really impress. There's about 10 minutes left before we go back in. F**k it; just get on the ball and try something.

I'm in midfield now for some reason (maybe they're not aware of my position as a full-back with Cork City?). I take on a few players after winning the ball. With the Astro-runners on I can drag the ball this way and that – which is easier to do when you're not wearing studded boots. I drag it nicely past a few of them and I'm ghosting through the middle of the park with the ball.

I'm heading towards goal now, and without looking I take a strike. I hit it well, but the wind catches it and it goes well to the right, well wide of the goal... to where Martin O'Neill is standing, arms folded, watching. He seems to turn his head away as if to pretend he's not watching, just as the ball arrives near him. Then he walks away. *Damn it*. That's it, then. I'm going around injuring his players and taking crazy shots. I'd be too much of a risk to bring into the game. They must be regretting putting me into the squad at all now. Kevin Kilbane is in midfield too and after the shot he says to me, 'Aren't you a full-back or something?' I'm not sure if he's trying to be nice or not.

I make one more difficult pass forward but the opposing centre-half reads it before the centre-forward and makes it look like a bad pass. I get involved once or twice more before the whistle blows. As it blows I'm retrieving the ball from the end line and a fan has wandered onto the pitch with his son who's in a wheelchair. We chat briefly before I notice that all the other lads have disappeared into the dressing room.

I run in but arrive late, missing the gaffer's announcement of who's on the bench. I get to my seat, which still has some of my gear on top of it mixed in with other players' gear. My used boots have been returned, at least. Then Crazy Daz whispers to me, 'Are you gonna take a shirt?' He means as a memento. 'Be good to have one,' he suggests. He's going to get one but I'm still hoping I'm on the bench.

I hear 'Neal' called out from behind me. I turn but can't see if it was O'Neill that had called it. Séamus Coleman is in the way of my view but looks supportive. We enter into a conversation about his time at Sligo and his exposure to Bergkamp while playing for Everton. 'Class player, Bergkamp,' I offer, hesitantly. It's a good sign that Coleman is openly talking to me in the dressing room.

I just need to know now – am I in the squad or not?

When I turn there's an official waiting by my gearbag. There's a clipboard on my bag with 16 names on it. The official looks like he wants me to sign the board. It doesn't appear to be signed by everyone; just the 11 players and the subs. *Christ, I might be in.* Then Darren enters into my line of sight at the worst possible moment, just as I'm about to confirm. He's literally interrupting my gaze at the clipboard with his lit-up face. 'Nice one – they're giving out the jerseys! You can keep them!' he tells me, clearly thinking he's giving me good news.

'One second, Murph…' I try to get him out of the way. 'I just need to check the list.'

I pick up the clipboard.

Then I wake up.

~~~~

That dream – which I had in 2018 – is what it's about. All the money issues, all the hustling for positions of power in the FAI, the outlandish payments, City's falling and rising – they all get in the way of the dream. It was never meant to be for me. But for another player – a better player than me – perhaps the difference between living out that dream and not doing so was their club going under, or the lack of development of the LOI, or the lack of faith from the FAI or their representatives in our own talent.

Could some of that money have been put towards making the dream more of a reality for boys and girls from our own clubs? From our own league? Of course it could – and it really should have. Maybe in the future. That's the dream: for a player or players from our own league to feel comfortable and to seriously contribute to the Irish national side without having to leave the country. Imagine what it could do for football in Ireland if we had three or four current Irish internationals plying their trade at our clubs every year. Imagine crowds of five to ten thousand every second week at all of the top clubs on the island. That's not as far a jump as one might think. But we need to seriously invest in our league and focus on developing it to a higher level to make it happen. It's about time we did just that.

Oh, and get out of my dream, Crazy Daz – you ruined everything!

Afterword – A Time to Be Brave

The recent crisis at the FAI is not a triumph for anyone involved in Irish football; it's an embarrassment. However, if it has an upside, it's the revealing of a culture of misgovernance and misguided largesse in the upper echelons of the FAI which, left unchecked, would have continued to hamper the development of Irish football into the foreseeable future.

How long has this culture existed at the FAI? That's a difficult question to answer. What is clear, though, is that at some stage since its formation in 1921 the FAI has moved in a direction that is at odds with the role of guardians of the game of football in this country. At some point they began to see themselves, together with the national team, as the highest branch of Irish football. And up there at the top of the tree, the FAI were happy to soak up the sun while the LOI and other stakeholders were left in the shade below.

From this lofty position they might even have had the ability to direct the sun onto a particular spot or a particular club, if they saw fit. But if any person or club down below raised an objection about the performance of the FAI, they could very quickly find themselves in a darkened corner, cut off from all light.

John Delaney's now infamous quote that the League of Ireland was 'a difficult child for the organisation' perfectly demonstrates the position in the hierarchy – the elevated status – that the FAI assumed. The implication in his statement is that the FAI were the upstanding parents, doing their best to control their 'difficult child'. Given the revelations of recent months, that analogy has not aged well – but more importantly it clearly demonstrates that the FAI were looking down on the rest of us.

This has been the main problem with Irish football for as long as I can remember. The FAI should not have positioned themselves above the rest of us, celebrating at the national team's games in the European Championship Finals and the like, removed from the LOI and other stakeholders as we struggled along below.

They should have remained at ground level, preparing the soil. They should have been spreading the seeds for the growth of the game and supporting the ambitions of our players and clubs. Instead, it would seem they were more interested in being fat cats basking up there in the sunshine. And in the end they got too fat and came crashing down to earth.

We must not allow them or anyone else to climb back up and block the light and thus the progress for Irish football again.

At the FAI AGM in July 2019 there was much talk of rebuilding trust with the stakeholders and of bringing a new culture to the Association. This new culture must involve the FAI accepting their true role as administrators and a governing body of the game, with their goal being to provide a wide and healthy base for Irish football. Players of all levels and sexes must always be considered the future of the game and the governing body must do what it can to nurture them.

To what extent has the FAI's unwieldy and irresponsible position blocked the growth of the domestic game to date? Again, it's a difficult question to answer – and a somewhat moot point now anyway. The crucial thing is that it should never be allowed to happen again.

This could be a new dawn for Irish football. An opportunity has been presented. It's time to be brave; a truly reformed FAI or separate body could focus on what needs to occur within the game in order to provide an environment for excellence for our players. It could invest in our own clubs and players, and engage with government in a fully transparent way to ensure that we have facilities around the country that we can be proud to call our own.

Remember all those 'unique' challenges we faced as per Declan Conroy's 2015 report on the LOI? We'll be back there again if we don't demand change and priority for the LOI and our own game in Ireland. And if we were to end up back there: that's all, folks. It'll be over. The bell will have chimed without any real progress having been made. That's the real danger. We can't let the chance pass.

The League of Ireland can't hang on for 'fixing down the road'. That's how it's always been, and that road has never been reached… yet. Personally, I don't care if it's driven by Niall Quinn, Kieran Lucid or 'Richard Bleeding Branson' – we just need to move towards a modern and progressive league. And the women's national league should form an equal part of those plans; they should not be an afterthought.

The goal should be to provide the best environment to nurture all players; an environment for excellence. These books testify to the sad fact that while there are many good things and good people and players in the game here, as things stand we're light years away from providing that environment. We need to strive for excellence rather than being satisfied with mere survival. This approach would lift the Rebel Army and the rest of Irish football to higher planes. As Damien Delaney made clear, the League of Ireland can be the ideal place for our young adults to prosper. You'll always have people saying domestic Irish football doesn't belong at the top table, but as Pat Lyons said, it's time we got over that type of thinking. We need to strive to be the best that we can be. We're far away from that at this point but I believe we can get there if we try.

~~~~~

Finally, a thank you. Retirement can be a difficult time for any player. I know players who, rightly or wrongly, feel their club and the fans have dropped them and moved on. There can be bitterness. However, these books have helped support my continued involvement as a supporter of the club and of the LOI, in bringing about my writing with the *Irish Examiner*, punditry with Eir Sport and various podcasts on the League of

Ireland. So in buying these books (and hopefully reading them!), you're playing a part in keeping me connected to Cork City FC and Irish football. I appreciate that more than anything, still being connected. Life in the post-football wilderness can be a beautiful place, but it's good to come in from the cold now and then, to experience that particular warmth, shared with others who love the game. My love and ambition for the game in Ireland remain strong despite any criticism of the status quo here. While I hope my readers have also felt the warmth in these pages, it would be nice to think these books might contribute in some small way to the growing call for reform.

We can get there. We just need to keep going, to be brave and to keep fighting for progress.

Acknowledgements

Thanks to Sonya O'Neill, Graham Cummins, Cathal Lordan, John Caulfield, Damien Delaney and Pat Lyons. Thanks to *City Edition*, the *Irish Examiner*, the *Irish Independent*, *The Irish Times*, *The Irish Sun*, *The Guardian*, the *Evening Echo*, the *Herald*, PeoplesRepublicOfCork.com, rte.ie, Extratime.ie, the42.ie, leagueofireland.ie, BreakingNews.ie, corkcityfc.ie and *The Sunday Times* in Ireland for kindly consenting to the reproduction of sections of your respective articles.

A particular thanks to Liam Mackey of the *Irish Examiner* and Daniel McDonnell of the *Irish Independent* for taking the time to read the book and for reviewing it.

Thanks to Kostis Pavlou (https://kostispavlou.com) and Barry Masterson (www.barrymasterson.com) for the design of the cover. Thanks to Paul Murray of wallwebdesign.ie for the technical support. Thanks again to Georgia Laval of www.lavalediting.co.uk for all your help and guidance (you always believed in the trilogy George!).

Thanks to Patrick O'Riordan B.L. for your support. A big thanks to Gerry Desmond and Michael Russell for your assistance with the proof. Thanks to Mary, Trish, Eoin and Tara Horgan (who was always a better footballer than me), Caroline Kilty, John O'Riordan, Aoibheann Ní Mhearáin and Paul O'Connell for your continued support and input. Thanks to John Breen from Waterstones on Patrick Street for your kind assistance. Thank you to Éanna Buckley for all of your assistance with finding the league tables and other help. Thanks to Paul Deasy and Declan Carey of Cork City for your assistance and backing.

Thanks to Ruth Fuller of Fuller Marketing (http://fullermarketing.co) for your expertise and skill in marketing the book.

Who's Who: CCFC Playing Staff and Board, Seasons 2010–13*

**2014 not included due to my limited
playing time during that season*

Name	Position	Nickname/Used name
Tommy Dunne	Team Manager	Gaffer/Tommy
Billy Woods	Asst. Manager	Woodsy
Stuart Ashton	Int. Manager (2013)	Stewie
Mark McNulty	Goalkeeper	Nults
James McCarthy	Goalkeeper	Bilko
Kevin Burns	Goalkeeper	Burnsy
Dan Murray	Captain/Defender	Muzza/Muz
Kevin Murray	Captain/Defender	Kev
John Dunleavy	Captain/Defender	Johnny
Darren Dennehy	Defender	Daz
Neal Horgan	Defender	Hoggie
John Kavanagh	Defender	Kav
Jason Forde	Defender	Fordy
Danny Murphy	Defender	Murph
Stephen Mulcahy	Defender	Mul
Kalen Spillane	Defender	Kalen
Brian Lenihan	Defender/Midfielder	Lenny
Greg O'Halloran	Defender/Midfielder	Greg
Cillian Lordan	Defender/Midfielder	Lordy
Colin Healy	Midfielder	Healers
Shane Duggan	Midfielder	Duggie
Gearóid Morrissey	Midfielder	Chops
Garry Buckley	Midfielder	Bucks
Keith Quinn	Midfielder	Keith
Adam Rundle	Winger	Runds

Ian Turner	Winger/Full Back	Turner
Shane O'Connor	Winger/Full Back	Shane
Daryl Horgan	Winger	Daryl
Stephen Kenny	Winger/Forward	Steve
Billy Dennehy	Midfielder/Forward	Billy
Davin O'Neill	Midfielder/Forward	Davin
Cathal Lordan	Midfielder	Cathal
Ciarán Kilduff	Forward	Killer
Danny Morrissey	Forward	Danny
Paul Deasy	Forward	Deas
Tadhg Purcell	Forward	Tadhg
Jamie Murphy	Forward	Jamie
Denis Behan	Forward	Denny/Beehive
Tim Kiely	Forward	Timmy
Graham Cummins	Forward	Cummins
Vinny Sullivan	Forward	Vinny
Danny Furlong	Forward	Danny
Daryl Kavanagh	Forward	Daryl
Jerry Harris	Secretary	Jerry
Rafa	Kitman	Rafa
Mick Ring	Kitman	Mick
Paudie Horgan	Fitness Coach	Paudie
Anthony Fennelly	Goalkeeping Coach	Fenners
Dr. Gerard Murphy	Club Doctor	The Doc
Rob Savage	Physio	Rob
John Flynn	Physio	John
Éanna Buckley	Club Administrator	Éanna

FORAS board members 2010–13

Jonathan O'Sullivan (Chairman 2010/11)

Jonathan O'Brien (Chairman 2011/12)

Mick Ring   (Chairman 2012/13)
CCFC board of management 2010–13
Pat Shine
Paul Hartnett
Niamh O'Mahony
Laura Barry
Patrick Healy
Sonya O'Neill
Kevin McCarthy
Stephen O'Callaghan
Cathal O' Driscoll
Mick Ring
Erika Ní Thuama
Collin Power
John Kennedy
Alan Mooney
Wyon Stansfeld
Pat Lyons

Praise for *Second City*:

'The most entertaining and insightful account of the life of a
League of Ireland footballer that you will ever read'
Daniel McDonnell, *Irish Independent*

'An essential antidote to the caricature of the pampered
professional footballer, this remarkably candid player's
account of a season in hell for Cork City also succeeds as a
love letter to the enduring power of dressing room solidarity –
not to mention the benefits of gallows humour – in the face of
almost daily adversity'
Liam Mackey, *Irish Examiner*

'Horgan captures one of the most turbulent seasons endured by
an Irish football club with an account that will have you
bubbling with anger and laughing on the same page. Some of
the off-the-field tricks pulled on the players – from a lack of
payment to the infamous story of the bus driver that refused to
travel to an away game – will leave you startled, but the
obvious camaraderie within the team during such difficult
times is vividly brought to life. This book is not just a must-
read for League of Ireland supporters but an account that any
football fan should read'
Alan Smith, *The Guardian*

'Once again Horgan succeeds in bringing us inside the
dressing room, the team bus and the mind of a League of
Ireland player in a way I don't think anybody else has. Second
City is a thoughtful, astute and brutally honest account of life
at one the country's biggest and best football clubs during
what were particularly challenging times for it and an already
troubled league. It is a wonderful account of the often bizarre
world Horgan and his team mates inhabited, one told with
affection and, sometimes, justifiable anger. I laughed a lot only
for it dawn on me more than once that I should have been

crying, but I have a better understanding now of the league I've been covering for 25 years and the people who play in it than I had before picking this up. Anyone, regardless of their club loyalties, who wants to know what is really going on in the game they love should read it too. That they'll enjoy the read immensely might be considered a bonus'
Emmet Malone, *The Irish Times*

Praise for *Death of a Football Club?*:

'A fantastic account of Cork City FC's turbulent 2008 season … that brings you into the trenches of modern football'
Brian Sciaretta, *American Soccer Now*

'A fascinating and unique insight into the behind the scenes action as the club fights for survival … An excellent read and a must-have for all fans of football'
www.the42.ie

'This gripping insider's account of how a club which could go toe to toe with Bayern Munich on the pitch was brought to its knees by forces entirely beyond its players' control, is essential reading for anyone who cares about football in Ireland'
Liam Mackey, *Irish Examiner*

Death of a Football Club? and *Second City* are available to buy on Amazon in both eBook and paperback format.

Lightning Source UK Ltd.
Milton Keynes UK
UKHW041616220222
399070UK00003B/746